*Visions of Charity*

# Visions of Charity

*Volunteer Workers and Moral Community*

Rebecca Anne Allahyari

UNIVERSITY OF CALIFORNIA PRESS

*Berkeley    Los Angeles    London*

University of California Press
Berkeley and Los Angeles, California

University of California Press, Ltd.
London, England

© 2000 by the Regents of the University of California

Library of Congress Cataloging-in-Publication Data

Allahyari, Rebecca Anne, 1963–.
    Visions of charity : volunteer workers and moral com-
munity / Rebecca Anne Allahyari.
        p.    cm.
    Includes bibliographical references and index.
    ISBN 0-520-22144-3 (alk. paper).—ISBN 0-520-
22145-1 (pbk. : alk paper)
        1. Church work with the homeless—California—Sacra-
mento—Case studies.    2. Voluntarism—Religious aspects—Christianity—Case studies.    3. Helping behavior—Religious aspects—Christianity—Case studies.    4.
Social movements—California—Sacramento—Case studies.    5. Salvation Army—California—Sacramento—History—20th century.    6. Loaves & Fishes (Organization :
Sacramento, Calif.)—History.    I. Title.
BV4456 .A55  2000
261.8'325'0979454—dc21                        99-048705

Manufactured in the United States of America

09  08  07  06  05  04  03  02  01  00

10  9  8  7  6  5  4  3  2  1

*For James F. Brooks, Jeremy Hinton Brooks,
and Lila Anne Brooks*

# CONTENTS

# PREFACE

American public talk about caring for poor people—in government and in the media—tends to be highly moralistic. Who deserves caring for? How ought care to be provided? Should the welfare state or private charity provide care for society's poor? What does the manner in which we provide care for the poor tell us about our society? This study does not pursue these moral debates at the philosophical level but rather explicates, through two case studies, how the competing moral visions in two Christian social service agencies take on meaning for volunteers doing the work of feeding the poor.

I began this research in 1990 intending to analyze how homeless people experience social control in their day-to-day interactions with shelter personnel, social workers, and police officers. My participant-observation in the two largest feeding programs for the homeless in Sacramento, California, drew my attention to the significance of volunteers in this endeavor. My interest in relating the politics of welfare to the sociology of morality emerged from an awareness of my own moral struggles with the volunteer work of feeding the homeless. Many field-workers stress how their cognitive perspective filters what they record and analyze; fewer consider how they came to realizations based on their understandings of how they themselves struggled with violations of their own emotional and moral assumptions in their participation in the lives of those they study.

I entered into volunteer work deeply suspicious of the workers at The Salvation Army. I assumed that I would find the Salvationist approach to feeding the poor condescending and highly controlling. Academic literature on The Salvation Army supported this perspective. I was not prepared for how the civilian workers (as distinct from the religiously trained Salvationists concentrated in the management ranks) entered into their work with already established friendships and connections in the homeless world. While I remained ambivalent about Salvationist welfare policy, I met homeless and court-ordered volunteers who found inspiration and tools for forging an increasingly stable life. In the other setting, a Catholic Worker–inspired organization, Loaves & Fishes, I expected that homeless people would be treated with dignity and humanity, an attitude and practice that I respected. My liberal intellectual background and sporadic attendance at Quaker meetings formed the background of these assumptions. Instead I found myself unsettled by how distant the homeless remained for many of the volunteers. At Loaves & Fishes I could spend half a day preparing and serving meals and barely communicate with those who came to eat. Over time my focus gravitated from a comparative mapping of social control in these two agencies to exploring moral community and what it meant to be a caring person in both settings.

This study does not provide an evaluation of either organization and its effectiveness in helping the homeless. Rather *Visions of Charity* contributes to a sociology of morality wherein moral community, action, and personhood are available for empirical examination. I explore two different plans for feeding poor people and their moral consequences for volunteers who assist in this work. This study illuminates how the intersecting politics of volunteerism, faith-based charities and social movements, and the welfare state shape the day-to-day work of feeding the poor. The forms that interactions with the homeless take in each setting illuminate the moral meaning of volunteering, the construction of a caring self, and the welfare sensibility within a particular vision of charity.

# ACKNOWLEDGMENTS

I want to acknowledge first the volunteers and staff at Loaves & Fishes and The Salvation Army who work so hard to help others in their community. Not only do they invite newcomers to take on a membership role as volunteers in their community, they also warmly share their beliefs and convictions and good food. I appreciate the time they spent telling me about their lives and convictions and hope they feel I have honored these stories.

The intellectual path to completion of this book has been well guided. Lyn H. Lofland, as chair of my dissertation committee and then as a generous mentor, offered plentiful advice while profoundly shaping my sociological vision. John R. Hall introduced me to a sociology of culture with concern for moral discourse. Suad Joseph drew my attention to connections among selving, morality, social location, and the state. Her skill at crafting these connections inspired me. Nicole Woolsey Biggart supported me through this project since its beginnings in a fieldwork course. She challenged me to think further about linking structure, moral rhetorics, and the welfare state. Conversations with all of them gave me renewed energy for my work and a notebook full of useful advice about method, theory, and writing. I am grateful too that all offered me written comments that guided revisions on completion of the dissertation.

Many others at the University of California at Davis have helped me along the way. I thank Diane L. Wolf for opening the door to an inspiring world of sociology, fieldwork, and feminist scholars. The Gender and Global Issues Group and the Women's Studies Department shaped my thinking. Judith Stacey provided mentoring even from afar. Jan Gouldner and fellow editorial associates at *Theory and Society* provided yet another intellectual community. Julie Bettie, Pamela J. Forman, David Hall, Laurinda Herrick Hulce, Victoria Johnson, Cecilia Menjívar, Melinda J. Milligan, Debora Paterniti, Mridula Udayagiri, and many other graduate school scholar-friends helped me to think about my work. Jeni Cross, Lyn H. Lofland, and Rosemary F. Powers mailed me newspaper clippings after I left Davis. Rosemary F. Powers and Ellen K. Scott continued to inspire me in the years following with the possibilities for establishing intellectual community and discussion among peers and good friends with the creation of our writing group; I thank them especially for their sharp intellects, editors' pens, and unfailing support. These pages bear their imprint in ways both big and small.

Colleagues and students in the Women's Studies Department and Program and the American Studies Department at the University of Maryland provided me with community, work space, and support as I worked on revisions for this book. Students in my Volunteerism course and in the Women's Studies Internship course helped to clarify my ideas about the politics of volunteering. In Women's Studies, I am especially grateful to Claire G. Moses, Laura Nichols, and Cyndi Gaye for departmental support, as well as to Katie King and Seung-Kyung Kim for office space. Evelyn T. Beck, Elsa Barkely Brown, and Bonnie Thornton Dill provided inspiration. Katie King, Claire Moses, and Deborah Rosenfelt have been able mentors and have been especially generous with their time. I am grateful to John Caughey and Mary Corbin Sies in American Studies for their support. Friends and colleagues in the Department of History also lent support for my teaching and my book. In particular, I am grateful to William Bravman, James Harris, James Henretta, Hayim Lapin, Wendy Lynch, Robyn Muncy,

B. Marie Perinbam, and Daryle Williams. I would like also to thank Linda Sargent for help with a historical reference.

I appreciate the intellectual community extended to me at the Princeton University Center for the Study of American Religion's weekly Religion and Culture workshops during the 1998–99 academic year. Robert Wuthnow granted me affiliate status with the center, and Anita Kline facilitated the membership. Members of the School of Social Science at the Institute for Advanced Study, as well as at the center, helped me to think further about religion and politics while providing encouragement as I finished the book. In particular, I thank Joan W. Scott for the invitation to give a talk before the School of Social Science and Clifford Geertz for asking a simple question with a complicated answer. I also want to thank Patricia Bernard and Karen D. Lee at the Institute for Advanced Study for the many books and articles they located for me.

I am grateful to the organizers, discussants, and audiences at the meetings of the American Sociological Association, the Pacific Sociological Association, the Eastern Sociological Association, the 1992 Stanford Conference on Organizations at Asilomar, the American Studies Association, and the Society for the Study of Symbolic Interaction who have commented on my work. Participation in an American Sociological Association/National Science Foundation conference, Social Movements and Emotions, furthered my analysis of the politics of charity. I am particularly grateful to the conference organizers, Jeff Goodwin, James M. Jasper, and Francesca Polletta, and to my session discussant, Edwin Amenta, for reading my work. I also want to thank the following people for their feedback, points of clarification, and words of encouragement along the way: Kathryn Allahyari, Penny Edgell Becker, Joel Best, Margaret Brooks, Daniel H. Calhoun, Nancy Forsyth, Marshall Ganz, Helen Golde, Douglas Harper, Phillip M. Runkel, Rosalie Riegle Troester, Heidi Rolland Unruh, Brett Williams, and Alan Wolfe. LeRoy Chatfield, executive director of Loaves & Fishes in 1999, provided me with a very helpful detailed response to my

Social Movements and Emotions conference paper at short notice. They have all influenced this work, although perhaps not precisely as they wished. I appreciate the care each took in reading and critiquing this book.

Working on *Visions of Charity*, I have gained great appreciation for the art of writing a thoughtful, critical, and yet inspiring reader's report. Arlene Kaplan Daniels, Daniel M. Cress, and an anonymous reader for the University of California Press all possessed this skill. Arlene Daniels and Daniel Cress continued to provide assistance through e-mail exchanges. I am grateful to my editor, Naomi Schneider, for her guidance and to Ellie Hickerson for her assistance. I also very much appreciate the work of Rose Anne White and Sheila Berg.

Finally, and with all my heart, I want to thank those who helped me in the transition to being a mother and an academic. The Women's Studies Department and Program at Maryland has been a wonderfully joyous work setting in which to be a mother. I appreciate the support of my students over these last few years and hope that my experience has helped them to imagine how they might organize work and parenthood. I give my heartfelt thanks to Carola Valdes and her helpers and the teachers at the Lawrence Day School for their loving teaching and care of children.

I dedicated my dissertation to the memory of my grandparents, Lila Adelaide Hinton and John P. Hounsell, and to my parents, Nora H. Hinton and Richard L. Hinton. They supported my years of education in ways both emotional and material. Most important, they always encouraged me in my work. This book is dedicated to James F. Brooks, Jeremy Hinton Brooks, and Lila Anne Brooks. Jeremy and Lila bring me joy and wonder. James helps to weave together a life of the heart and the intellect from which I draw inspiration, stability, and hope. These pages have benefited from the grace of his thought and pen.

# Introduction

*Studying Visions of Charity*

Thousands of Americans pour time and money into urban "soup kitchens" during the winter holidays, but the day-to-day work of feeding the urban poor is undertaken by relatively small groups of volunteers. In Sacramento, California, Loaves & Fishes and The Salvation Army are the major providers of food and shelter for the urban poor and serve as the theaters of action and organization for these everyday, often morally inspired, groups and individuals. But these two organizations are different, and in their differences lies the larger meaning of this book.

Social commentators have long noted the prevalence in American society of altruistic and voluntaristic ideals. In 1838 Alexis de Tocqueville reflected on Americans' democratic participation in government and voluntary associations and concluded that participation in social institutions, especially voluntary societies, balanced the potentially excessive individualism of the American character. American social scientists continued this interest, particularly with regard to the social shaping of the American character through voluntaristic caring for others. In a few cases social scientists asked what role morality played in situating the self in social action. Yet a century after Tocqueville wrote, David Riesman ([1950] 1961) offered his dark view of the lonely crowd, an American people morally alienated from their voluntaristic past by changing institutional arrangements. Much social science research in the last forty years carries forward Riesman's grim perspective. *Visions of Charity* does not. In the people who dedicate days, weeks, and years of their lives to feeding the urban poor, I found a different story, and one that deserves a careful sociological telling.

The intellectual support for popular arguments that American culture has suffered a decline in moral community is formidable. In 1989 Alan Wolfe decried the moral eclipse of community by individualistic economic and political frameworks. Robert N. Bellah and his colleagues ([1985] 1996) argued that moral culture had swung in favor of individualism, at the expense of commitment to the social good. Christopher Lasch (1978) documented a culture of narcissism, Richard Stivers (1994) maintained that we inhabit a culture of cynicism, and Robert Putnam (1995a, 1995b, 1996) chronicled declining membership in civic groups.[1] These studies, primarily focusing on white, middle-class Americans, have laid the groundwork for an exploration of the social nature of the American character within the context of caring for others. *Visions of Charity* argues against these more pessimistic accounts of American character and, as ethnography, moves beyond the interview and survey research of Robert Wuthnow (1991, 1995) to suggest that in volunteer work Americans attempt to reconcile compassion with individualism, as they learn to practice, in Wuthnow's words, "institutional kindness." These volunteers provide insights that lead to an understanding of how volunteers learn institutional kindness, but also support for Bellah and colleagues' (1991) more optimistic argument that moral community may be established by individuals who take control of their institutions.

The preceding studies contribute to a sociological understanding of morality as determined by social-historical context. Yet, in attempts to understand American character, they have paid less attention to how particular contexts may construct moral personhood and social relationships quite differently within organizations dedicated to similar ends. Wuthnow's *Acts of Compassion* (1991) is particularly instructive. Wuthnow used interview data from 2,210 volunteers to construct a model that explains how volunteers take on compassion as a role. Borrowing C. Wright Mills's (1963) "vocabularies of motive" framework, Wuthnow mapped three dominant discourses used by volunteers to talk about their motivations for volunteering. The economistic rational-choice "exchange model" and the psychologically grounded "therapeutic motif" capture two socially available forms of motive-talk available to volunteers. The third model emphasizes "growth" and acknowledges that "sacrifice" may be important to "fulfillment." In his exploration of these three vocabularies of motive, Wuthnow favored the third as containing the most potential to resolve tensions between the individual and the community.

Yet the mostly white, middle-class volunteers working within Loaves & Fishes Catholic Worker–inspired moral rhetoric do not fit easily into one of Wuthnow's motifs, any more than do the predominantly male and nonwhite, working-class and lower-middle-class volunteers at The Salvation Army. Strains of the exchange, therapeutic, and growth discourse can be heard, however, in the moral rhetorics and the volunteers' stories at both organizations. Although Wuthnow's methodology provided him with the data to delineate large-scale cultural patterns structuring the language of compassion, his approach overlooked the nuances of how volunteers learn and refine moral rhetorics, as well as questions of why volunteers find particular moral rhetorics appealing. Of Wuthnow's respondents we may wonder: How much were they influenced by the moral rhetoric of charitable action available to them through their volunteer activities? How did the volunteer's biographical frame and social location influence the adoption of a particular vocabulary of motives? How did the relationships between their volunteer organization and the state influence the resonance of particular vocabularies of motive? These concerns turn our interest toward the importance of *context* in understanding how volunteers organize the meaning of their work.

This study asks questions about the American character, moral personhood, and moral community within the "institutional context of homelessness" (Wolch 1994) at two Christian social service agencies. Homelessness and volunteer work in service of the homeless emerged in the 1980s as dominant social issues, and researchers have examined shelters and kitchens from the perspective of the homeless,[2] but few have considered, as I do, the linkages among volunteerism, caring for the poor, and issues of moral personhood from the perspective of volunteers.[3] The comparison of two social service agencies, Loaves & Fishes and The Salvation Army, reveals variations in moral personhood among volunteers notable for their racial, class, and gender diversity. It also illustrates how social service agencies may structure very different relations to the state, with significant moral consequences for both volunteers and recipients within the charitable relationship.

The trend toward nonprofit, often religiously based, care for the poor surged in the early 1980s and has gained momentum in the two decades since. Loaves & Fishes and The Salvation Army exemplify how strikingly different a radical Christian and a fundamentalist Christian organization may conceive of the poor, the work of the volunteers, and their organizational relationship to the government (Robertson 1996). Loaves & Fishes offers its "guests" dignity and choice, whereas The Salvation Army focuses on honor among and rehabilitation of its "clients." The morality implicit in each of these charitable relationships imposes its own distinctive emotional and behavioral expectations on the volunteers, not only in their relationship with the urban poor, but also in terms of their own sense of virtue.

I explore volunteers' pursuit of self-betterment through an examination of what I call *moral selving:* the work of creating oneself as a more virtuous, and often more spiritual, person. Moral selving may be understood as one type of deeply emotional self work. It involves a concern for transforming the experience of an underlying moral self, in contrast to a situated identity.[4] By moral self, I mean the cognitive, and emotive, self-related elements of the social self that Michael Schwalbe designates as underlying moral action. In Schwalbe's (1991: 288) words, "As a disposition, it is the part of the self that might be described as the will to moral responsibility." That is, the volunteers at Loaves & Fishes and The Salvation Army expressed a desire to change their moral selves, not their identity as it inhered in social status or structural position within society. Although the moral self may be experienced as core, or in social scientific terms as essential, it is actually malleable and changeable as the individual encounters new resources for fashioning a more virtuous self. The moral self may, however, be more or less stable at different moments and in different contexts. This work focuses on the phenomenology of crafting a moral self.

Moral selving as a type of self work draws our attention to what John Dewey ([1908] 1960) called the "moral situation," wherein self and action converge in worthy ideas. In the claim that the moral self is best understood within its empirical context, this perspective argued against an abstract philosophical understanding of morality. In my study, the shaping of the self in accordance with virtuous ideals brings the actor into particular working relationships with social service staff and homeless recipients of charity, as well as local politics. The doing of charity structures moral selving and social relations at both Loaves & Fishes and The Salvation Army.

Because we do not have a concept that captures this type of important self-fashioning work, I offer moral selving. As Arlie Russell Hochschild's (1979, 1983) "emotion work" has drawn us to analyses of emotion management, I intend moral selving to help us consider the complexities of creating oneself as a more virtuous person. To employ *moral self-betterment* and *moral self work* as alternate concepts would not grasp the distinctive character of this activity. Moral self-betterment harkens to the legacy of a middle-class reform movement that I do not want to invoke. Moral self work seems less cumbersome but still falls short conceptually. Work on the moral self implies a narrower and more instrumental conceptualization of self-betterment than I wish to suggest. Because I analyze the work of creating oneself as a more virtuous person among the very different groups of people at a Catholic Worker and a Salvation Army kitchen, the concept must be more inclusive and flexible, capable of capturing a range of experience. Moral selving is more dynamic and encompasses a wide range of experiences and outcomes. In chapters 3 and 4, I develop moral selving in relation to a symbolic interactionist perspective, with its dynamic understanding of self and society and its attention to the centrality of role taking and the generalized other. Moral selving—as shaping, striving, creating, building, and sculpting—resonates with a symbolic interactionist understanding of how individuals experience themselves in relation to a dynamic moral orientation to the social world.

In doing this self work, the volunteers draw on the available moral rhetorics at Loaves & Fishes and The Salvation Army, as well as moral rhetorics and experiences arising within their biographies, to construct a moral self through the practice of feeding the urban poor. These two contrasting visions of charity induct volunteers into differing approaches to serving food, with very different relations to homeless people, local politics, and the national welfare state. In short, by exploring variation in what it means to construct a virtuous self and to take political action, we can see how differently *where* people volunteer and *what* that volunteering means to them can affect their construction of a "virtuous" self. *Visions of Charity*, therefore, moves between the "microfoundations of macrosociology" (Collins 1981) and the "macrofoundations of microsociology" (Fine 1991) to render visible the coconstructions of morality, charity, and politics in the moral selving of the committed volunteers at both Loaves & Fishes and The Salvation Army.

This approach to the American character has its precedents. Most notably, to compare moral communities, Kim Hays's *Practicing Virtues* (1994) grounds liberal and conservative orientations to individualism firmly within context through fieldwork and interviews gathered at six boarding schools. She explores how Quaker and military boarding school students exercise virtues most dramatically, not in harmony, but in conflict. Hays focuses less on self processes and more on the construction of community within these two contrasting moral traditions. Her work provides one answer to the religious studies scholar Elizabeth Bounds's (1997) call for studies of moral community that attend simultaneously to conflict, religion, and power.

In *Visions of Charity* we see how creating oneself as a more moral, and often spiritual, person through charitable action in the service of others is deeply emotional. Emotions not only enter as an outcome of the site-specific moral rhetorics but also texture the experience of moral selving. In a similar vein, using ethnographic work in a graduate seminary and Little League baseball, Sherryl Kleinman and Gary Alan Fine (1979) argue that moral organizations use rhetorics to demand changes in the "core self" of recruits. According to them, from the perspective of the site-specific moral educators the situationally available rhetorics (or meanings) ideally become tools for recruits in the work of moral selving beyond the parameters of the organization. Their respective subsequent ethnographies do not address emotions at a conceptual level. However, they reveal the deeply emotional experience of recruits as organizational personnel attempt to engage them in the moral reconstruction of the self using the situationally available rhetoric (Kleinman 1984; Fine 1987). In a more recent work, Kleinman (1996) shows us how even members of a progressive organization committed to an alternative moral identity may end up reenacting social hierarchies of gender, race, and class in the workplace.

In research on volunteers at the Gay Men's Health Crisis, Philip M. Kayal (1993) uses an "emotive language" to reflect the pain and hope of healing he heard among volunteers caring for persons with AIDS. He argues that volunteerism "heals" by conferring the dignity of all involved in the "carepartnering" relationship. Kayal's account of this volunteer community, although based on participant-observation, does not move beyond generalizations about the volunteers' self-transformation in character to rich, analytically organized description of the volunteers' experiences within accounts of their carepartnering work. Consequently, his work provides few clues to how situationally available moral rhetorics and emotions intertwine with volunteer work in the moral construction of the self. In my use of the concept of moral selving, I attempt to capture the emotionally laden desire of the volunteers to better their moral selves.

By asking questions about moral personhood and caring, I engage also with feminist critiques and extensions of Carol Gilligan's influential study, *In a Different Voice* (1982). Gilligan's work spurred wide-ranging debate among social theorists about the influence of gender, race, and class on moral reasoning and caring.[5] Her work suggests that women's morality overlaps with an ethic of care and responsibility while men's morality more frequently overlaps with a more individuated ethic of rights and justice. In *Moral Boundaries* (1993), the philosopher Joan C. Tronto's review of the feminist literature leads her to conclude that we should move beyond talking about women's morality to formulating an ethic of care, carefully contextualized within institutional arrangements. Furthermore, Tronto argues that morality should not be understood as a world beyond emotions.

Prominent studies of volunteers have examined gender and caring behavior within the context of particular voluntaristic settings,[6] but none have considered it within the institutional context of homelessness. Wuthnow's *Learning to Care* (1995) found that boys and girls mixed the language of responsibility and rights in their talk of caring for others. Wuthnow suggests that gender differences arise in talking about selves and roles and argues that this talk expresses differences in experiences; girls are more likely to identify caring as an expression of the self, whereas boys are more likely to associate caring with specific roles (173). His finding raises the provocative suggestion that while girls' and boys' volunteer activities may appear to be similar, the implications of this work for the construction of the moral self may differ significantly across gender.

*Visions of Charity* contributes to these debates by using a social psychological approach, which, with its attention to roles and selves, allows us to explore how structural arrangements influence the construction of the caring self. My goal here is not to provide an evaluation of social service agencies caring for the poor and hungry but to describe two distinct traditions of doing charity from the perspective of a diverse population of volunteers. Loaves & Fishes and The Salvation Army reflect progressive and conservative understandings of charity: Loaves & Fishes attends to the dignity of the poor by steadfastly meeting the poor's entitlement to food and shelter, while The Salvation Army works with local government to reward the honor of those individuals who demonstrate their willingness to work. By using a comparative ethnography approach (Cress n.d.), I attempt to test already developed theories of caring selves and to explore analytically both similarities and differences in moral selving within these two settings.

## THE SETTINGS

This study focuses not on the many people who donate time and money to the poor during the winter holidays but on those I call the *committed volunteers*, the smaller group of individuals who do the year-round day-to-day work of feeding the urban poor. Without the "charitable" labor of the committed volunteers neither Loaves & Fishes nor The Salvation Army could begin to meet the demands of the hungry and homeless in Sacramento. At Loaves & Fishes, white, middle-class volunteers serve the homeless guests, whereas at The Salvation Army, potentially coerced court-ordered volunteers and residents at the Shelter Services Center, mostly lower-class men, many of color, serve the meals. Within these two settings, volunteers receive lessons in two contrasting visions of how best to care for the urban poor. These visions entail moral ideals for charitable action.

Loaves & Fishes, founded by Catholic Workers, relies solely on private donations and volunteers to serve daily from 600 to 1,400 "guests," the city's largest free meal. The Loaves & Fishes complex is strikingly noninstitutional in appearance—green-trimmed signage, a flowering courtyard, the cheerfully appointed Friendship Park and Mustard Seed

School—all off a street closed to most traffic. "Street monitors" guide visitors to parking. The "volunteer coordinator" provides twice-monthly tours of the complex to interested community members. Each day of the month a different group, usually religiously affiliated and white and often predominantly female, takes responsibility for providing Loaves & Fishes with meat and a pool of volunteers to prepare the meal from approximately 8:00 in the morning to 11:00 and then to serve it from 11:30 to 1:30.

At Loaves & Fishes, the guests, understood within the moral rhetoric to be the "Ambassadors of God," receive food from the volunteers in a setting decorated with flowers and wooden chairs. Few rules govern the behavior of the guests, beyond the prohibition of violence enforced by the Loaves & Fishes staff and street monitors. Women and children may choose to eat separately from men. The guests can choose to take with them the bread and fruit provided with each meal, or to eat it at Loaves & Fishes. This setting highlights dignity, respect, and choice. The entitlement of the homeless to food arises out of the Catholic Workers' belief in personalism and hospitality. The homeless are not asked to give anything back, not even gratitude.

Just across the intersection, about one and a half blocks down a major thoroughfare, The Salvation Army Shelter Services Center presents a more modest facade. At the Salvation Army, enclosed in chain-link fence, homeless people may live on site for thirty days as the "In-house." Some of these In-house residents, most of whom are working-class men, and many of whom are men of color, volunteer in the industrially spare kitchen. Others, who are excused from looking for work during the day, may eat lunch at noon, following the feeding of the staff. During the winter months, the kitchen also prepares a late-afternoon meal for the "overflow," those homeless who cannot find shelter at The Salvation Army or other shelters in the city. The City of Sacramento pays The Salvation Army to feed and bus the overflow nightly to emergency shelter permanently set up in an old 4H barn at Cal Expo, Sacramento's sports and exhibition center. Volunteers at The Salvation Army include the In-house, some of the overflow, a few previously In-house, and people court ordered to do community service hours through the California State Alternative Sentencing Program (ASP). At The Salvation Army there are few church volunteers, and Burns Security Guards patrol the grounds.

The Salvation Army's practice of charitable action offers physical salvation to make way for spiritual and moral salvation. The military model of The Salvation Army structures a hierarchy wherein Salvationists and civilian staff extend, in the words of their motto, "Heart to God and Hand to Man" to rescue those trapped in "the sinking classes." The Salvationists understand charitable work as significant to their own spiritual salvation. New recruits who join the staff are disciplined into a work ethic that values sobriety and productivity. In contrast to Loaves & Fishes volunteers, many of the volunteers battle alcohol and drug problems, or the stigma of ASP court-ordered volunteer hours. The principles of Alcoholics Anonymous and The Salvation Army structure a moral rhetoric of charitable action wherein volunteers and staff endeavor to help others out of poverty and despair through hard work and self-discipline.

The words of the organizational founders of Catholic Workers philosophy and Salvationism lend insight into the contrasting visions of benevolence practiced in these two charitable organizations. At Loaves & Fishes, the mostly white, middle-class adherents learn that "the act and spirit of giving are the best counter to the evil forces in the world today" (Day 1963:82). This morality in the 1940 words of Dorothy Day encourages action in the service of the unfortunate:

> The vision is this. We are working for "a new heaven and a new
> *earth*, wherein justice dwelleth." We are trying to say with action,
> "The will be done on *earth* as it is in heaven." We are working for a
> Christian social order. (1983: 91)

The Salvationist vision calls on the unfortunate—predominantly working-class, many nonwhite and male—to lift themselves from "the sinking classes":

Our success will depend upon the extent to which we are able to establish and maintain in the minds of the workers sound moral sentiments and to cultivate a spirit of hopefulness and aspiration. We shall continually seek to impress upon them the fact that while we desire to feed the hungry, and clothe the naked, and provide shelter for the shelterless, we are still more anxious to bring about that regeneration of heart and life which is essential to their future happiness and well-being. (Booth 1890: 110)

These moral visions guide, although not perfectly, the relationships of the committed volunteers with the urban poor at Loaves & Fishes and The Salvation Army.

The volunteers working within these visions of charity can be understood in relation to three role situations: *holiday volunteers* (found at both The Salvation Army and Loaves & Fishes), *routine volunteers* (Loaves & Fishes only), and *drafted volunteers* (In-house homeless and court-ordered volunteers, found only at The Salvation Army). The differentiation of volunteer types allows for an exploration of how different volunteers understand, practice, and stretch the visions of charity embedded in each organization.

I trace these volunteer experiences through my participant-observation as a volunteer in both kitchens and through interviews (conducted with all but the holiday volunteers). In the broadest sense, the holiday volunteers show a sentimentalization of caring. The committed volunteers, composed of both routine and drafted volunteers, demonstrate steadfastness in their sensibility of caring. Both routine and drafted volunteers work to better themselves through volunteering.

These two settings provide case studies of how people use institutional ideologies in constructing moral identities. Put another way, this study allows for an examination of the role of morality in everyday life. Recent philosophers and religious studies scholars have reflected on morality as situationally particular and emotionally infused (Addelson 1994; Bounds 1997; MacIntyre 1984; Tronto 1993). Loaves & Fishes and The Salvation Army serve, in the imagery of George Miller, Eugene Galanter, and Karl Pribram (1960), as two plans guiding behavior toward moral fulfillment. This quest assumes different significance within the two organizations: The Salvation Army volunteers struggle to salvage stability, while Loaves & Fishes volunteers seek to infuse their lives with greater meaning and purpose. At The Salvation Army, the structure guiding behavior is largely external, whereas at Loaves & Fishes the structure is largely internal, fulfilled and given impetus by the experience of appropriate emotions.

In an era of increasing institutional pressures to volunteer, the Loaves & Fishes routine volunteers and The Salvation Army drafted volunteers fall on different ends of a spectrum of volunteerism/coercion. The routine volunteers at Loaves & Fishes do so freely. Loaves & Fishes embodies a radical vision wherein the mainly liberal volunteers in this organization struggle with the moral challenge to uncritically accept the homeless guests as the Ambassadors of God. The court-ordered and even more numerous In-house residents at The Salvation Army, who work in the kitchen, call themselves "volunteers." However, I use the term "drafted volunteers" to emphasize the ambiguity and irony of their status in the setting. While this term may appear contradictory at first glance, it seems less so in the context of contemporary "community service requirements" attached to legal sentencing and even public schooling. For example, the United States Supreme Court has recently upheld community service "volunteer" work as a high school graduation "requirement" (Biskupic 1996: A3).[7] This is just the complex, contradictory, and ambiguous condition that The Salvation Army drafted volunteer illuminates. In both cases, volunteers at Loaves & Fishes and The Salvation Army participate in organizations that stake out moral ground within the welfare state.

## STUDYING MORAL SELF-BETTERMENT

Visions of charity provide blueprints for how food is served, for understandings of the poor as guests or clients, and for organizational relations to the state. Also embedded within these visions are moral sensibilities for self-betterment. While the volunteer role provided for easy entry into these research settings and consequent observation of their food provision, my emergent interest in the ethnographic study of the moral self proved most challenging. I drew on my own experience in the settings and more formal training in the sociological study of emotions to attend to the moral dimensions of caring for the poor. Finally, writing this ethnography challenged me to consider issues of confidentiality in light of the deeply personal and value-laden direction I took in studying moral self-betterment.

## The Researcher-Volunteer Role

I began volunteering at Loaves & Fishes and The Salvation Army in early 1991 for a fieldwork seminar. My research consisted primarily of fieldnotes and a few interviews, gathered over four months. I volunteered periodically over the next two years and in 1993 volunteered in earnest for nearly a year as I gathered data for my dissertation (Allahyari 1995).[8] In short, I became a committed volunteer. I attempted to take an "active-membership-researcher" role (Adler and Adler 1987) and struggled with the rhetorics of charitable action in my own moral selving. However, I fit more easily into the membership category of committed volunteer at Loaves & Fishes than at The Salvation Army. Although I did not initially conceive of my study as an exploration of the organizational implications of volunteering as moral work, the site-specific moral rhetorics and their power in shaping selves inexorably drew my attention. My own experience in the settings provided me with "sympathetic introspection" (Cooley 1909: 7) as I listened and observed.

I found the volunteer role ideal for a participant-observer. At The Salvation Army, the resident manager told me that I could volunteer in the twenty-four-hour kitchen whenever it was convenient for me. He asked that I make a commitment to be there for two to three hours minimum and explained that I would be accountable to that shift's head cook. I worked primarily from early morning to afternoon and usually ate lunch with the staff and other volunteers. The volunteer coordinator at Loaves & Fishes asked that I join groups in need of committed volunteers, and so I joined the Metropolitan Church Community (a gay and lesbian church), the Jewish community, the Unitarians/Charismatics, and Our Lady of Assumption Catholic church. I chose these groups to explore the meaning of volunteering among diverse religious organizations that participated in the Loaves & Fishes feeding program to enact their visions of community involvement. Although I volunteered on other days as well, I entered most often into the workings of these four groups.

In both settings I made my own schedule for volunteer work and joined in the physical labor of cooking and serving large quantities of food. I usually ate lunch during my shift and became recognized by the staff as a committed volunteer. I attempted to be open with other volunteers about my role as researcher.

At Loaves & Fishes I stepped easily into the role of committed volunteer. The moral rhetoric of charitable action was readily available to me through the monthly newsletter, the visitor orientation, and special events such as the Thank You Dinner for Loaves & Fishes supporters and one-day spiritual retreats. The staff worked to make the moral rhetoric accessible to those interested in Loaves & Fishes. Either the kitchen manager or founding member Chris Delany explained often to the volunteers the Loaves & Fishes' philosophy of serving the guests. I also became part of Loaves & Fishes Bank of Faith, as I mailed in donations in envelopes provided with the monthly newsletter.

Volunteering at The Salvation Army did not provide me with an already established membership role. That moral rhetoric emerged in a less organizationally structured fashion, but not without coherence. For example, I was not an In-house resident, an ASP court-ordered volunteer, or homeless. And the fact that I was female, white, well educated, and of solid middle-class origins further underscored the dissimilarities between me and many of the other volunteers. Furthermore, the Shelter Services Center did not publish their own newsletter or conduct formal events to teach the moral rhetoric of charitable action to interested community members. Rather than donate money, I donated clothes and household items for sale in their thrift shops. I remained outside the In-house experience with its workshops and dorm life. I watched the incorporation of the ASP workers into the kitchen culture but was not subject to their strict regulation. In spite of the relative inaccessibility of The Salvation Army moral rhetoric and the on-site experience as lived by the In-house, I found myself incorporated into the disciplined work ethic, albeit with the special privileges accorded a nondrafted, female volunteer.[9]

Although my experience as a participant-observer at Loaves & Fishes and The Salvation Army gave me access to the volunteer experience, I did not penetrate the world of those who live among the Salvationists or the Catholic Workers; only at The Salvation Army did I enter the everyday life of some homeless people, mostly men, who spent their days at the organization.[10] My portrait of the moral rhetoric of The Salvation Army relies mostly on my experience as a participant-observer in the kitchen. In both cases, however, I interviewed staff to understand how they framed the vision of charity within which they worked.

At the height of my volunteer commitment, I was relied on in both settings to help organize the holiday volunteers at Thanksgiving and Easter. These moments revealed to me how deeply I had entered into the working arrangements of each organization. For example, at Loaves & Fishes the volunteer coordinator told me that I was like "a fixture" and a "super volunteer." At The Salvation Army one Thanksgiving day, one of the kitchen staff told me that he could more easily relax with me on the job, because I knew my way around the kitchen.

As I moved between settings, the two moral rhetorics, lodged as they were in quite different structural arrangements, led to feelings of disorientation. At The Salvation Army, I worked with formerly homeless men, many of color, and people sentenced to alternative sentencing program hours. My research role was often painfully funny, as when a cook told me to include another cook in the "chapter on psychos." This role marked me as someone from a different world. Nonetheless, the camaraderie and joking was great fun. At Loaves & Fishes, I felt troubled by how the guests remained the distant homeless, in a social world where racial and class segregation between the mostly white, middle-class volunteers and these guests appeared so transparent yet unacknowledged. Unlike The Salvation Army, where I frequently swept the floor after lunch, at Loaves & Fishes the volunteers left this task to paid workers. I found, however, that my limited interaction with the guests at Loaves & Fishes was comforting on days where I felt burdened with other concerns.

At The Salvation Army, I struggled to maintain my identity as a non-married woman with an academic interest in the volunteer experience. This became more difficult over time. My unmarried and childless status seemed more understandable to the men when I explained that I was divorced. To ward off the advances I experienced in my earlier fieldwork, when I reentered the setting in 1993 I presented my long-term committed relationship as an engagement. Sometimes my partner was referred to as "your hubby," but other times men asked me when the wedding would be. I came to suspect over time that the staff felt I was being strung along, since the wedding did not take place.

I was often greeted with terms of endearment by the men in the kitchen at The Salvation Army: Gorgeous, Sweet Becky, Fair Rebecca, Angel (after a label on a banana one of the men stuck on my shirt), and Meanness. The use of these nicknames fluctuated with my participation in the setting. When I volunteered consistently, I was greeted by them; as I came to the setting less frequently, the use of these endearments faded. Familiarity was not without its difficulties.

Toward the end of my fieldwork experience at The Salvation Army, I found myself struggling to maintain my boundaries. I received increasing numbers of invitations to go out and had to fend off advances. Although the kitchen workers still asked about my "report," I seemed unable to reverse this process. I was reminded of Ruth Horowitz's (1986,

1989) experience as she attempted to hold on to her identity as "lady reporter" among Chicano gang members. Familiarity threatened her ability to maintain her identity as an apparently single, friendly young woman unavailable for dating. In my case also, increased camaraderie threatened my comfort in the setting. This struggle heightened but not, thankfully, until the time drew near to leave the field and begin writing.

## EXPERIENCING MORAL SELVING

As I moved between these two settings, I experienced the everyday nature of what Lyn H. Lofland (1994) calls "social locational shock" in response to my geographic, temporal, and social movement through the structural arrangements of these places. As with culture shock, my social locational shock involved disruption as familiar cues changed. This emotional disorientation led me to consider how fieldworkers studying morality might learn from qualitative researchers of emotions. Sociologists and anthropologists (Hochschild 1979; Lutz 1988) who study emotions have made clear that emotion norms are moral ideals and that emotional maturity involves a moral imperative. My approach to studying morality concurred with the symbolic interactionist Donileen R. Loseke's (1993) argument that the social construction of good and bad people involves the simultaneous construction of both moral and emotional orientations. In short, this study provides for an ethnographic examination of the emotionality of moral self work.

I adapted an "ethnopsychological" approach to understanding the volunteers' experience. Ethnopsychology, as defined by the anthropologist Catherine A. Lutz (1988: 83), "is concerned with the way people conceptualize, monitor, and discuss own and others' mental processes, behavior, and social relationships." This perspective focused my attention on how two organizations, both concerned with feeding the urban poor, actually manifested quite different emotion cultures and assumed the volunteers to be "sentient actors," that is, individuals who are conscious and rational, as well as feeling (Hochschild 1975: 283).

Attending to ethnopsychology and sentient actors draws our attention to how culture shapes emotional experience. Morality and the emotional experience of the caregiver intertwine in the provision of hospitality. Virginia Olesen (1994) submits that hospitality, as a "social form," allows us to examine the dynamics of structure and interaction across contexts and varied productions of selves. The use of a social psychological approach helps to illuminate the complexity of the social construction of the caring self in a charitable relationship. This approach helps us to see *how* social inequality, as manifested in class and material inequality, gets enacted. We are able to see *what* demands are put on *who* by *whom*, *whose* emotions are taken care of, and *how* selves are shaped. In short, a social psychological perspective on the social construction of the volunteer role enriches our understanding of how caring for others is structured and experienced in the everyday life-world of the welfare state.

In the kitchens, I chopped celery, broccoli, carrots, and lettuce, baked cookies, and stirred vats of spaghetti sauce, sloppy joes, or soups, which left ample time for what Carolyn Ellis (1991: 300) has called "interactive introspection" wherein "the object of study is the emergent experiences of both parties." Following the fieldwork suggestions of Sherryl Kleinman and Martha A. Copp (1993), I combed through my own emotional experience of the moral rhetoric for insights into the experience of the other volunteers. Because I explained to other volunteers that I was interested in the experiences of volunteers at Loaves & Fishes and The Salvation Army, they often reflected with me on the meaning this work had in their lives. We shared our own experiences within, and our reaction to, the site-specific moral rhetoric.

Thus moral selving as a felt experience arose out of my data collection on the emotion experience of volunteering. As I began to interview volunteers from Loaves & Fishes,[11] I was particularly struck by their work to achieve moral self-betterment. This effort entailed emotion work. These interviews led me to think about moral selving as one type of self work. At The Salvation Army, my interviews with staff provided useful organization material and insights into the transformation from drafted volunteer to kitchen staff to manager.[12] Yet interviews with the drafted volunteers were awkward and revealed seemingly little new data.[13] Although I managed only two formal interviews with drafted volunteers, while volunteering I was easily able to engage in "interviewing by comment" (Snow, Zurcher, and Sjoberg 1982) wherein I used primarily puzzlement, replays, motivational comments, and evaluative comments to probe the experience of the drafted volunteers. Thus I relied primarily on my fieldnotes to analyze The Salvation Army. I spent more days at The Salvation Army than at Loaves & Fishes and recorded encounters among the Salvationists, civilian staff, In-house, and ASP volunteers. Because I usually worked on consecutive days at The Salvation Army, I maintained greater contact with the volunteers than at Loaves & Fishes, where most volunteers worked only once a month. As I reviewed my voluminous fieldnotes from The Salvation Army, I saw indications of how the committed drafted volunteers embraced a disciplined work ethic and attempted to tie their moral identity to a work role.

In retrospect, I believe that interviewing yielded insights into Loaves & Fishes routine volunteers' experience because of their highly contemplative and self-reflective approach to volunteer work.[14] The Salvation Army drafted volunteers, however, especially those involved in Alcoholics Anonymous or Narcotics Anonymous, did not shy from self-reflection. They focused on the attainment of the institutionally provided definition of the good worker. I found fieldwork most useful in considering their experience. Although Sherryl Kleinman, Barbara Stenross, and Martha McMahon argue against methodological determinism, they suggest that interviews and fieldwork may yield "different kinds of accounts":

> Fieldworkers write social-organizational accounts—they put behavior and organizational constraints in the foreground and keep meanings and feelings in the background. Interviewers write social-psychological accounts—they highlight meanings and feelings and put behavior and organizational constraints in the background. (1994: 45)

This work illustrates, however, that in different contexts participant-observation and interviews may provide different types of information.[15]

*Visions of Charity* contrasts two constructions of the charitable relationship and also provides a social psychological account of self-processes lodged within these ideological contexts. I found that interviews may yield greater data among individuals who are concerned with matching emotions with moral rhetorics, whereas participant-observation may be more useful among subjects concerned with role attainment and the accompanying concerns for the interplay of deference and demeanor.[16] Yet in my own fieldwork, which relied on both participant-observation and interviewing, I also found that participant-observation provided critical insights into the institutional context from which to draw interview questions.

Finally, the relative usefulness of participant-observation and interviewing may have been influenced by the different rhythms of time in these two organizations. In his aptly titled work *The Dance of Life* (1983), the anthropologist Edward T. Hall argues that "individuals are dominated in their behavior by complex hierarchies of interlocking rhythms" (149) and that synchronization of rhythm makes possible two events (154). At Loaves & Fishes, many volunteers arranged their schedules around a commitment to volunteer once a month. Although it was a relatively infrequent event in many of the volunteers' lives, this work seemed to be of great emotional, often religious, importance to them and a cause of moral reflection. Interviewing elicited reflections about this work and its importance for their self-betterment.

Many of the volunteers at The Salvation Army had experienced a dramatic shift in the rhythm of their lives either by becoming In-house or by being sentenced to community service hours. These events seemed to work in a manner similar to chronic illness as described by Kathy Charmaz in *Good Days, Bad Days* (1991), as they interrupted the taken-for-granted experiences of time and threw into sharp relief the co-construction of time and the self. My strategy of visiting The Salvation Army several days in a row allowed me to be present as people struggled to gain control over their lives in a setting that constructed virtue as adherence to behavioral principles.

## WRITING AND ISSUES OF NAMING

In writing this ethnography, I was troubled about whether to identify my settings as "soup kitchens," about the objectification implicit within the category "the homeless," about the politics of naming the work that Loaves & Fishes and The Salvation Army do "charity," about whether and how to identify the race of those in the setting, about how to indicate emotionality and conviction to the reader, and finally about how much to fictionalize my settings and those in them. I attempt to convey how the participants in the study saw these issues and to convey an explanation for my sometimes contrary writing decisions as an ethnographer.

In describing my work, I initially found myself explaining that I did fieldwork in two "soup kitchens." Because committed participants in neither setting used this term, this seemed a misnomer that conjured up images of tattered men waiting for watered-down soup during the depression. After a local newspaper reported that The Salvation Army had pretty good food for a "soup kitchen," one of the cooks complained to me and others that the organization ran a dining room, not a soup kitchen. The same cook tried unsuccessfully to enlist his superiors to change The Salvation Army's "overflow meal" to the more dignified "patio meal." At Loaves & Fishes, the staff resolutely referred to their "dining room" and talked about the importance of hospitality. I decided to avoid the denigration implicit in "soup kitchen," especially because only new volunteers in either setting described themselves as working in such a place.

At both Loaves & Fishes and The Salvation Army, staff and volunteers, some homeless, some not, talked about "the homeless." Yet experience in both settings substantiated what social scientists argue: the homeless are a fluid, ever-changing, difficult to define and measure population of poor people.[17] Loaves & Fishes served not only homeless people their daily meals but also poor people trying to stretch their monthly incomes. In this setting, however, the use of "*the* homeless" often signaled difference from the domiciled more than sameness. Compared to The Salvation Army, at Loaves & Fishes deeper class divisions often existed between the volunteers and the guests. At The Salvation Army, when In-house volunteers in particular spoke of "the homeless" it was with the familiarity of a shared plight. Because of the universality of this term in both settings, I use it, but cautiously. I try to impart the class and emotional divides it frequently conveyed at Loaves & Fishes, especially among some volunteers and the poor, and contrast this to the greater familiarity of experience evoked by it at The Salvation Army.

By calling this study visions of *charity*, I move into dominant frame the word's connotation of a stratified relationship of caring across unequal power and status. While the charitable nature of Americans' propensity to volunteerism receives great valorization, it is not without its dark underside. Although a gift, it may be received with great reluctance and shame (Poppendieck 1998: 230–32). As Mary Douglas (1990: vii) wrote in her formulation of its central paradox, "Though we laud charity as a Christian virtue we know that it wounds." Different visions of charity may wound differently. Chapters 1 and 2 show that Protestants and Catholics brought different formulations of charity into play in the politics of welfare (Katz 1986).

Both The Salvation Army and Loaves & Fishes resisted being labeled charities. Yet this label, with its paradoxical connotations of caring and wounding, hints at the moral complexity of caring for others in the ambiguous location of organizations neither entirely in the state nor beyond it. The political sociologist Theda Skocpol (1996: 295) notes in her summation of the "close symbiosis" between voluntary associations and the welfare state, "Voluntary civic federations have both pressured for the creation of public social programs, and worked in partnership with government to administer and expand such programs after they were established." Loaves & Fishes and the Shelter Services Center have positioned themselves very differently in relation to local politics and national welfare policy, yet the two are central to the politics of charity in Sacramento. In this book I interweave individual and organizational visions of caring, visions of welfare, visions of rehabilitation, and visions of social change. One writing strategy would be to invent new metaphors, for "complex phenomena need complex metaphors" (Czarniawska 1997), but instead I have chosen to use "charity." I intend to "work in its shadow but also outside of it, with the grain but also against it" (Jasper 1997: 40). The Charitable Choice provision of the 1996 Welfare Reform Act (discussed in chapter 5), with its support for public funding of faith-based charity work, underscores the deep resonance charity maintains with American culture and the politics of welfare.

The politics of labeling places, groups, and practices—soup kitchens, the homeless, charities, charitable work—surfaced at the level of the individual as I considered whether and how to identify race, class, patterns of speech and emotionality, and true identity. For example, at Loaves & Fishes the predominantly white, middle-class population made few references to either their race or their class. The class standing of the volunteers became apparent from their talk of gratitude for security in their lives. In contrast, the workers at The Salvation Army made much more frequent references to their race and class standing. I used participants' own racial identifications to acknowledge that these labels reflect important aspects of personal identity. For example, I chose between "Chicano" or "Mexican-American" based on how the participant identified himself or herself. I also attempted to provide ethnic or religious identification, for example, "Jewish" or "Irish," for the white kitchen workers at Loaves & Fishes, who framed their identity around such labels.[18]

I also attempted to impart through the use of italics words spoken to me with unusually great emotion or stress. My use of italics when quoting people from either fieldnotes or interviews thus indicates, not points that I wish to underscore as a writer, but rather words that were spoken with emphasis in an attempt, I believe, to convey to me as a participant-observer emotional or moral conviction. Although I have altered spoken language to some extent to improve readability, I have retained some of the repetition and used punctuation to convey the rhythmic feel of the original.

I decided not to attempt to fictionalize either the organizations or the city. The Salvation Army is an internationally familiar organization. Many large cities contain Catholic Worker–originated hospitality houses. Because I use Loaves & Fishes newsletters and publications, as well as newspaper accounts of local politics, fictionalization of either the organization or the city seemed unnecessary and a violation of the public record. All of my interviewees readily agreed to the use of their real names in this study. I decided to give them pseudonyms, however. Although I explained my interest in the volunteer *experience*, my focus on moral selving places great attention on values and identity, two aspects of the self many consider personal. Their biographies, however, are not fictionalized.

A few very public figures in each setting remain readily identifiable. The founders of Loaves & Fishes and some members of the executive board frequently appear on television and in the local papers; the Sacramento Catholic bishop is a well-known figure at Loaves & Fishes. They, as well as the Salvationist staff, but not the civilian staff, at The Salvation Army, retain their real names. Public relations is a part of these individuals' work, and they appear to be well aware of this.

## THE STUDY

The chapters that follow describe the social nature of moral community and moral selving in two organizations that rely on volunteers to care for the urban poor. At Loaves & Fishes, the routine volunteers (mostly middle-class, white committed volunteers), almost equally women and men, offer charity with the intent to maintain the dignity of the guests and to engage in their own virtuous self-betterment. At The Salvation Army, the drafted volunteers (working-class and lower-middle-class volunteers, many of whom are men of color) strive to help others and to battle their own homelessness or the stigma of court-ordered volunteer hours. A comparative view on the shaping of American character within two charitable organizations devoted to producing moral selves casts in high relief the salience of class, race, and gender in American life.

Part 1, "Working Arrangements of Charitable Action," lays out the moral rhetorics of charitable action and structural arrangements within both organizations. The chapters therein open with the historical roots of Catholic Worker personalist hospitality and Salvationism. They then trace how these rhetorics emerged at Loaves & Fishes and the Shelter Services Center within the rhetoric and working arrangements of each organization. These rhetorics structure and reflect two quite different visions of charity, which corresponded to a diluted radical Catholic Worker vision of charity at Loaves & Fishes and an unabashedly conservative and Protestant-inspired vision of welfare at The Salvation Army. Furthermore, I show in this section how the moral rhetorics and working arrangements of Loaves & Fishes and The Salvation Army provide ideals for moral selves.

Although Catholic Worker and Salvationist ideals permeated the practice of volunteerism, the everyday working arrangements of these organizations revealed complications and ambivalence. Tensions between these moral ideals and organizational practices peaked at the holidays, when each organization juggled crowds of inexperienced volunteers. The staff had to organize these inexperienced holiday volunteers to expand the moral community and support each organization's fundraising drives; for both Loaves & Fishes and The Salvation Army raised most of their resources for the year during the Thanksgiving and Christmas holidays. In my analysis, the holiday volunteers provide a comparative foil to the committed volunteers, for although they expressed a concern with self-betterment, most did not lodge their moral selving within the mundanity of committed volunteer work.

Part 2, "Constructing Moral Selves," explores the self work of moral self-betterment among the routine and drafted volunteers. The two chapters in this part explore how the working arrangements of Loaves & Fishes and The Salvation Army guide, although not perfectly, the moral selving of these committed volunteers. The volunteers used the organizational rhetorics, as they settled into the working arrangements of the organizations, as ideological guides in their moral selving. I trace their different experiences in a comparative examination of how concerns about authenticity, self-esteem, and agency shaped character in these charitable settings.

Part 3 elucidates how, in shaping moral selving, these two visions of charity also shape charity and political action within the welfare state. By volunteering to do the work of caring for homeless people, participants enter into particular political traditions with unique relations to the state. Social psychological interpretations of the self reflect political orientations to social inequality. The consideration of morality as a terrain of decision making and action allows us to grasp how people deeply committed to moral betterment experience the world and take political action to support that commitment. The chapter comprising part 3 concludes with a consideration of how local and national politics may hinder or enable organizational visions of charity. Loaves & Fishes suffered a fall from grace in the local media after fieldwork for this study concluded, while the 1996 Welfare Reform Act encouraged faith-based participation in the work of the welfare state. The epilogue revisits a few Loaves & Fishes routine volunteers several years after fieldwork concluded. We find them still committed to doing the work of feeding the urban poor.

## PART ONE

# Working Arrangements of Charitable Action

Loaves & Fishes and The Salvation Army exemplify contrasting philosophies of doing Christian charity. Catholics introduced to the United States a form of charity far less demanding and judgmental of the poor than that brought by Evangelical Protestants (Katz 1986: 61). The Catholic Workers espouse a loving hospitality, free of ties to the state. This radical vision of charity asks nothing of the poor. The Salvationists promote disciplined self-help, practiced in conjunction with the local government. A conservative vision of charity, Salvationism emphasizes social control and behavior modification. The working arrangements at Loaves & Fishes and The Salvation Army reflected and reinforced, although not perfectly, the guiding images and metaphors of the Catholic Workers and Salvationists.

Chapters 1 and 2 trace the working arrangements of visions of charity through organizational publications, interviews with staff, and participant-observation. The national Catholic Workers' organization publishes a newspaper, and the Loaves & Fishes staff writes a monthly newsletter. The international Salvation Army organization produces a bimonthly magazine, the *War Cry*. While these publications provide insights into the Catholic Workers' and Salvationists' visions of charity more broadly, fieldwork illuminates the complicated and sometimes contradictory articulation and practice of these moral rhetorics as presented to volunteers at Loaves & Fishes and The Salvation Army.

Staff served, in Howard S. Becker's terms, as "moral entrepreneurs" who crusaded for the creation and enforcement of organizational rules consistent with their vision of how to best help the poor:

> Moral crusaders typically want to help those beneath them to achieve a better status. That those beneath them do not always like the means proposed for their salvation is another matter. But this fact—that moral crusades are typically dominated by those in the upper levels of the social structure—means that they add to the

power they derive from the legitimacy of their moral position, the power they derive from their superior position in society. ([1963] 1973: 149)

The working arrangements of the organizations provided guidelines, or moral rhetorics, for recruiting volunteers into the everyday practice of feeding the urban poor. The staff used these moral rhetorics to map interactional guidelines among themselves, the volunteers, and homeless people. And the committed volunteers used them to guide their moral selving.

My theoretical approach to these moral rhetorics follows in Becker's symbolic interactionist footsteps as I trace how the staff "do culture" in each setting, with the assumption that culture "explains how people act in concert when they *do* share understandings" (Becker 1986: 13). This approach, which treats moral rhetorics as "ideology in action" (Fine and Sandstrom 1993), assumes that just as individuals and groups *do* culture, they *do* ideology through the creation, and re-creation, of moral rhetorics of charitable action. This examination of the moral rhetorics reveals how the framing images and metaphors of each organization have become "sedimented into structure" (Busch, cited in Fine 1992: 96). In practical terms, the morality implicit in each of these charitable relationships imposed its own distinctive aesthetic on the built environment.

Clients or guests and volunteer kitchen workers learned ideologies of welfare service provision from their inscription in the built environment. A reading of these constructed environments reveals how their aesthetics and boundary drawing conveyed social messages about the moral worth of charity recipients. I hope to show that, while symbolic, moral rhetorics and the environments they constructed had very real impact in their establishment of boundaries. As Chandra Mukerji explains,

This constructed environment includes both what sociologists usually think of as the realm of social construction (a symbolic world of

meanings embedded in language) and a meaningful *physical* setting
for more or less coordinated action. Importantly and surprisingly,
the distinction between the physical and symbolic in the socially
constructed environment often breaks down. (1994: 145; emphasis
in original)

Physical boundaries and their monitoring prescribed different patterns of
movement through The Salvation Army and Loaves & Fishes. In a study
examining how workers draw boundaries between home and work,
Christena Nippert-Eng (1996: 569) describes how boundaries mark "territories of the self": "the idea of a 'territory' is important because it implies that a self does not equate with a mentality, alone. Rather, we por-
tray and reinforce a self through our bodies and our physical, tangible
surroundings." The Salvation Army and Loaves & Fishes territories offered charity recipients very different constructions of the self. The institutionally spare built environment at The Salvation Army reflected a
conservative vision of redemption through hard work, self-discipline, and
sacrifice. The welcoming facade of the Loaves & Fishes complex reflected a progressive vision of social change in which poor people merited
love and dignity, without the obligation to give back. These environmental contexts, while at moments negotiated and contested, became part of
the taken-for-granted understandings of each setting (Fine 1992: 96).

Religious ideals permeated the environment—both built and
moral—at Loaves & Fishes and The Salvation Army. Taking my cue
from Peter L. Berger (1967) and Robert Wuthnow (1992), who address
religious communities as social groups, I analyze religious discourses as
moral rhetorics of which I ask sociological questions about the construction of virtuous selves. What is the relation between the sacred and
the everyday? How do individuals practice charity? What sorts of social
services agencies do they design to help the poor? What types of moral
selves do these religious discourses construct? This part therefore addresses these organizations as communities for the construction of

moral selves. As George Herbert Mead ([1934] 1962: 385) wrote, "The conception of the religious life is itself a social conception; it gathers about the idea of the community." As we shall see, the framing images of Catholic Workers and Salvationists, sedimented into the working arrangements of each organization, contained blueprints for ideal typical moral selves.

The sociologist Harriet Martineau argued in 1838 that the spiritual workings of a society could be discerned in its morals and manners:

> The rules by which men live are chiefly drawn from the universal convictions about right and wrong which I have mentioned as being formed every where, under strong general influences. When sentiment is connected with these rules, they become religion; and this religion is the animating spirit of all that is said and done. ([1838] 1989: 55)

At Loaves & Fishes and The Salvation Army religion may be understood as an animating spirit guiding the bettering of moral selves.

These two portraits of the working arrangements of charitable action suggest preliminary answers to the following questions: How do the moral rhetorics help frame the situated vocabularies of motives (Mills 1963) that are constructed for the volunteer role? How do the feeling rules at each organization resonate with the social locational background of the volunteers, and how do they reflect on the volunteer self? Finally, what is the interplay of emotions, ideology, and morality within each organizational culture of caring?

# CHAPTER I

# Performing Personalist Hospitality

## *Works of Mercy and Social Justice at Loaves & Fishes*

The moral rhetoric of Catholic Worker "personalist hospitality" (Murray 1990) undergirds the practice of works of mercy, both physical and spiritual, at Loaves & Fishes. The founding members and staff of Loaves & Fishes played important roles in distilling these rhetorics into working arrangements in the kitchen and dining room. The Loaves & Fishes newsletter, volunteer orientation sessions, volunteer appreciation dinners, and organization of the volunteers in the dining room were significant contexts within which the staff incorporated the committed volunteers into the doing of this moral rhetoric.

## THE ROOTS OF PERSONALIST HOSPITALITY AT LOAVES & FISHES

In 1933, in New York, Dorothy Day, a journalist and recent convert to Roman Catholicism, inspired by her interactions with Peter Maurin, organized the publication of the *Catholic Worker*. This paper carried the "Easy Essays" of the prolific Maurin, a French peasant and Christian agitator, and spread the four tenets of the Catholic Worker philosophy:

works of mercy, personalism, hospitality, and social justice. Within just a few months the circulation jumped from 2,500 to 25,000 copies per month (Day [1952] 1981). Day encouraged Maurin to join her in the establishment of "houses of hospitality" in which Catholic Workers practiced these tenets in caring for the homeless and hungry. Catholic Workers remain committed to the practice of these tenets and not mere philosophizing. Houses of hospitality, such as Loaves & Fishes, are central to this vision of charity. "The houses of hospitality have remained from the start one of the cornerstones of The Catholic Worker movement, as they were a cornerstone of Peter Maurin's original program" (Day 1963: 192).

Maurin advocated the practice of both physical and spiritual works of mercy.[1] Day understood works of mercy to be critical to the "direct action" of the Catholic Workers:

> Works of mercy are feeding the hungry, giving drink to the thirsty, clothing the naked, sheltering the homeless, visiting the sick, ransoming the prisoner, and burying the dead. The spiritual works of mercy are instructing the ignorant, counseling the doubtful, rebuking the sinner, bearing wrongs patiently, forgiving all injuries, and praying for the living and the dead. (1963: vii)

Catholic Worker houses of hospitality organized with the intent to practice these works of mercy.

Personalism, a belief that Maurin brought to the Catholic Workers, propounds the spiritual worth of each person. In a more purely Christian interpretation, guests at houses of hospitality are seen as messengers from Christ, or bearers of the divine. In the words of Maurin, "Although you may be called bums and panhandlers you are in fact the Ambassadors of God" (Ellis 1988: 29). For some, however, the commitment to personalism may mean more simply that each individual has the responsibility to care for his or her poor neighbors. The "Aims and Means of the Catholic Worker Movement" advocate personalism, defined as "a philosophy which regards the freedom and dignity of each person as the basis, focus and goal of all metaphysics and morals."

> In following such wisdom, we move away from a self-centered individualism toward the good of the other. This is to be done by taking personal responsibility for changing conditions, rather than looking to the state or other institutions to provide impersonal "charity." We pray for a Church renewed by this philosophy and for a time when all those who feel excluded from participation are welcomed with love, drawn by the gentle persuasion Peter Maurin taught. (*Catholic Worker* 1994: 3)

Catholic Workers strive to construct charitable working arrangements imbued with intimate caring and respect for their guests.[2]

The doctrine of personalism thus channeled the Catholic Workers away from bureaucratic, judgmental treatment of their guests toward the renunciation of capitalism (as well as communism) and into the practice of hospitality. Maurin's "Open Letter to the Bishops of the United States," first published in the *Catholic Worker* in 1933, advocated houses of hospitality:

> We need Houses of Hospitality
> to give to the rich
> the opportunity to serve the poor.
> We need Houses of Hospitality
> to bring the Bishops to the people
> and the people to the Bishops.
> We need Houses of Hospitality
> to bring back to institutions
> the technique of institutions.
> We need Houses of Hospitality
> to show what idealism looks like
> when it is practiced.
> We need Houses of Hospitality
> to bring social justice

through Catholic Action
exercised in Catholic institutions.
(*Maurin, cited in Ellis 1988: 30*)

Day ([1952] 1981) explained in her autobiography, "Voluntary poverty means a good deal of discomfort in these houses of ours," yet she also acknowledged diversity among the houses:

> No two houses of hospitality have ever been alike. The house directors have differed widely in personality and in their approach to their work; though poverty's problems may seem the same everywhere, poverty's conditions within each community have varied, as have the response and support of benefactors and diocesan leaders. (1963: 40)

In 1992 the nearly ten-year-old Sacramento Loaves & Fishes was one of approximately one hundred thirty houses of hospitality that associated themselves with the Catholic Worker movement (Delany and Delany 1987). Loaves & Fishes embodied greater bureaucracy, regimentation, and material comfort than were present in houses of hospitality historically. In the older houses of hospitality, soup more often served as a mainstay meal, and volunteers "took the door," managing the line of guests and quelling violent interactions.[3] In contrast, today's houses may evidence a relative wealth of amenities and staff and are even sometimes quite fancy. For example, the Syracuse Unity Kitchen Committee's "lavish hospitality" (Elie 1998), with meals served on china amid fresh flowers, seems to be close to Loaves & Fishes' concern with a pleasing setting in which to feed the poor.

Rosalie Riegle Troester's 1987 interview with Loaves & Fishes founders Chris and Dan Delany for her work, *Voices from the Catholic Worker* (1993), helps us to understand how these moral entrepreneurs initially conceived of the working arrangements of Loaves & Fishes and its relation to Catholic Worker houses of hospitality. In keeping with the anarchist bent of the Catholic Workers, Loaves & Fishes did not apply to be part of the movement. Dan Delany discussed the beginning of Loaves & Fishes: "And so we met [with another Catholic Worker], and I said, 'How do you start a Catholic Worker [house of hospitality]?' He said, 'You just start it.' I said, 'Just start it?' He said, 'Yes, just start it' " (Delany and Delany 1987: 11).[4]

Dan Delany acknowledged to Troester that Loaves & Fishes provided far greater organization than other Catholic Worker hospitality houses. He explained that many Catholic Worker houses are "hurly-burly wild" (Delany and Delany 1987: 7) but that model did not fit his and Chris's ideal for Loaves & Fishes.

> But it was better organized than a lot of . . . other Catholic Workers [houses]. . . . But we weren't young when we started in this. We had been through a Catholic Worker experience before, and both of us were very familiar with burnout and knew if we wanted to do this at all, we'd have to be organized. (Troester 1993: 7)

Chris and Dan Delany expressed cautious hope that Loaves & Fishes would remain true to its Catholic Worker ideals. Chris said of Loaves & Fishes, "It's got the Catholic Worker philosophy behind it. We push that, and we're trying to keep that in there. We're the only non-paid personnel at Loaves & Fishes, though" (Delany and Delany 1987: 32). Dan added, "A lot of people work full time. It will probably end up being something capitalist, I'm afraid. So what? I have no illusions" (32).[5]

The Delanys' commitment to living as Catholic Workers revealed institutional flexibility. When asked explicitly about the dangers of Catholic Worker communities becoming "institutionalized" and thereby losing their anarchist roots, Dan replied, "The Worker is a great thing. The Worker was founded by Dorothy and its history was the story of her life. They were synonymous. The same is true of us who run Worker Houses. Our history and the history of our houses are intertwined. We are the Worker" (Delany and Delany 1987: 34). Chris added, "If the Worker becomes institutionalized, it won't be the Catholic Worker anymore. It will be something else.

We will still be here. So will lots of other radical Christians" (34). Yet Chris saw the future in the Catholic Worker model of charitable action:

> I think it's part of God's plan. Small communities are going to sup-
> plant [the older religious communities]. Not necessarily the Catholic
> Worker, but that type of community, one that lives the Gospel and
> resists the forces of evil and cares for the poor. Or maybe caring for
> the poor and then going out to do something about the root causes
> of poverty. (34)

Although the Delanys explained to visitors that Loaves & Fishes arose from Christian-Judaic roots and was not officially affiliated with other Catholic Worker houses, the philosophy of personalist hospitality clearly permeated the Delanys' vision of charity. Although Catholic Worker philosophy shaped the moral rhetoric of charitable action at Loaves & Fishes (as demonstrated most dramatically in the newsletters), the staff moderated its personalist hospitality to facilitate the inclusion of volunteers less comfortable with one-on-one contact with the homeless in the mundane work of feeding the poor.

## PRACTICING PERSONALIST HOSPITALITY

The history and beliefs of personalist hospitality structured the working arrangements of Loaves & Fishes. While the newsletter provided the clearest documentation of the Catholic Worker vision of charity at Loaves & Fishes, fieldwork data on holiday meals, the monthly volunteer orientation sessions, the annual appreciation dinners, and the everyday working arrangements of the kitchen revealed how the staff incorporated community members into personalist hospitality devoid of its anarchist roots. Within these varied contexts, the staff served as moral entrepreneurs who encouraged volunteers to participate in a modified Catholic Worker vision of charity.

WRITING PERSONALIST HOSPITALITY

The Loaves & Fishes newsletter followed in the tradition of the *Catholic Worker* newspaper. In Day's words, reprinted in the *Worker*, "Since the Catholic Worker is also a movement, our editors and writers cook, clean and wash dishes" (Belisle 1994: 2). In addition to providing information about upcoming events, such as special holiday meals and building projects, the two-sided typed newsletter also discussed such topics as the impact of the economy on the urban poor and taught Catholic Worker philosophy. Not only did the staff provide stories about the practice of charity at Loaves & Fishes, they frequently requested readers to make donations, call local governmental officials, or volunteer.

Each month the newsletter and the enclosed, small envelope addressed to Loaves & Fishes appeared in a different color. For example, the Easter letter and envelope were yellow, and the Christmas letter and envelope were red. At the bottom of the many of the letters appeared a proverb: " 'As often as you did for one of my least brothers and sisters, you did for me,' Matthew 25:40," or "If you shut your ears to the cry of the poor, you yourself will call and not be heard,' Prov. 21:13." The letters open with "Dear Friend," or "Dear Friend and Supporter," and close with "Your Friends, Members of the Staff & the Board of Directors."

The importance to the organization of volunteers is expressed in the February 1991 newsletter, which refers to them as "the life blood of Loaves & Fishes, literally." The 1990 Loaves & Fishes statistics sheet revealed that on average monthly volunteers numbered 901, with 696 of those in the dining room. The Easter 1992 newsletter read: "You [volunteers and supporters] are the ones who free us, who are on the scene, to do this work on your behalf. We are grateful for your support. Thank you a thousand times for your generosity."

Not only did the staff thank the volunteers, but they also marveled in their diversity. Speaking of this "miracle," the Fall 1992 newsletter reflected on the serving of one million meals:

We have folks from churches of all faiths, from clubs and service groups, members of different political parties, youth groups, senior citizens, etc. And we have folks that come on their own, who are not attached to any group.

They all put aside whatever differences they might have, and pitch in and work side by side, month after month, year after year, to help feed and to lend a helping hand to hungry and homeless folks in Sacramento who are in such desperate straits. We feel pretty fortunate to be witnesses to such a miracle. It certainly does lift one's spirit.

This celebration of the volunteers resonated with the Catholic Worker philosophy that caring for the poor did not require specialized training.

### Hospitality: Guests as "Ambassadors of God"

The newsletter imparted to volunteers the Catholic Worker vision of the poor as God's Ambassadors. The February 1992 issue reprinted Maurin's "The Duty of Hospitality"on the spiritual importance of the poor.

Modern society calls the beggar
bum and panhandler
and gives him the bum's rush.
But the Greeks used to say
that people in need
are the ambassadors of the gods.
Although you may be called
bums and panhandlers
you are in fact the Ambassadors of God.
As God's Ambassadors
you should be given food,
clothing and shelter
by those who are able to give it.

The Christmas and Easter letters traditionally underscored this vision of the poor. For example, the Christmas 1990 letter opened with the birth of Jesus: "It is a beautiful account of God's preference for the poor: poor shepherds without a roof over their heads get to hear the

Good news of Christ's birth first." At Christmas 1993, the letter implored, "Our hope both for you and for us is that we may recognize the penniless and no doubt illiterate Mary and Joseph and their baby in the growing army of beleaguered folks we all see begging . . . and eating at Loaves & Fishes." This vision not only taught that the poor come as God's Ambassadors but also that they are our brothers and sisters. The February 1994 newsletter beseeched, "We at Loaves & Fishes must recommit ourselves to see that each guest is a child of God, our long lost brother or sister and a member of the human family."

Within this vision of the poor as God's children, our brothers and sisters, Loaves & Fishes recognized "guests," not "clients":

> We have found in our ten years of welcoming society's outcasts that we do not have "clients," we have guests. Yes, guests. And the use of that word by our 1,000 monthly volunteers and our anchor staff makes all the difference in our attitude. It reminds us that these folks who find themselves at the door of our modest facility belong to someone. They are someone's brother, someone's daughter. We at Loaves & Fishes are not here with them primarily to rehabilitate or save them or to retrain them. Others are doing that work. We are here to be nice to them, to love them, and to make them feel welcome as our brother or sister. By calling our daily visitors "guests," we constantly remind ourselves why we ourselves have committed ourselves to this work. (October 1993)

The May–June 1992 newsletter suggested that when they are addressed as "guests," the poor retain greater dignity.

The Christmas, Easter, and Thanksgiving newsletters often included a picture of recent guests at Loaves & Fishes, thereby underscoring the intimacy of personalist hospitality. This vision of personalist hospitality entailed self-monitoring on the part of those serving the meal; it was their duty to cast off judgment of the poor so as to honor each guest's dignity.

> For our many volunteers, our staff and Board of Directors [the mission of feeding the hungry and sheltering the homeless] means a lot

more than putting food on a plate or a roof over one's head. First and foremost, we must learn again, each day if necessary, to welcome the homeless, the downtrodden, the rejected and society's outcast with the hospitality and respect they deserve, and not to slacken off in that area. We must learn again to be nonjudgemental as we try to ease the daily suffering of our guests by providing them our simple survival services. (Newsletter, February 1994)

It was the volunteers, not the poor, who received encouragement to change their attitudes through self-guided moral work. Personalist hospitality asked little of the guests. Unlike volunteers, they were not required to give anything back or to engage in self-monitoring. As the Easter–Spring 1992 newsletter spelled out, "We do not expect to be repaid nor do we necessarily expect gratitude. (Indeed, it is far easier to write these words than to put them into practice. But, despite all our failings and backsliding, we are clear about our purpose and intention.)" The newsletters did, however, occasionally relay the guests' gratitude: "We constantly hear a lot of gratitude from a lot of our guests, especially the words, 'Please thank whoever is making all of this possible.' So we all, guests and staff, thank you once again for keeping Loaves & Fishes and its myriad programs alive" (October 1993).

Personalist hospitality asked that those who are not poor shed their selfishness: "Homelessness and hunger . . . are clearly caused by a want of caring enough" (Christmas 1993). This emphasis on renouncing selfishness peaked at the holidays.

So we recall Christ's words, "I was hungry and you fed me, I was a stranger and you took me in." Thanks to your involvement, we are able to receive the stranger with open arms, whether she or he or their children are citizens or not, and to serve them a good hot meal to fill their stomachs. With your help we at Loaves & Fishes will continue to struggle to lift the mantle of shame of all who come to us in need, by giving them love and yet more love in your name. (Christmas 1994)

The Easter–Spring 1993 issue closed with the hope that the good Lord help us all to achieve self-betterment by "putting off our selfish 'old person' and putting on the forgiving 'new person' in its place."

Not only did the Loaves & Fishes enactment of personalist hospitality entail selfless providing for guests (not clients), it also included providing a pleasant and hospitable environment. Planted trees decorated the setting: "They help relieve the barrenness of the commercial street we are located on and help lift our hearts a little, as well as those of our often dejected guests" (newsletter, June 1993). Fresh flowers on the table served also to underscore the honor of the guests dining at Loaves & Fishes.

> And we put a lot of emphasis on cleanliness: clean dining room, clean kitchen and clean bathrooms. Indeed, people who own restaurants often tell us that our kitchen and dining room are cleaner than theirs. Cleanliness is simply a sign of respect that we extend to our guests. We put fresh flowers on the tables each day, and decorate our dining room (we have two) to create an atmosphere of peace and beauty. Tiny symbols, but very important in our eyes to show the sincerity our commitment to treat our guests as part or our extended family. (Newsletter, October 1993)

Hospitality wedded to charitable action entailed attention to beautifying the setting for charity recipients. The constructed environment underscored that the volunteers and staff offered the food as a gift.

The personalist hospitality practiced at Loaves & Fishes involves the staff extending hospitality not only to the guests but also to the volunteers. As the newsletters of the early 1990s documented, Loaves & Fishes grew substantially,[6] at times causing the staff anxiety about maintaining the organization. For example, the Thanksgiving 1991 newsletter opened with "HELP!" in large, bold type, followed by the confession, "We are running a little scared these days at the enormous increase in hungry and homeless folks coming to us daily." This despair and the concurrent growth in the organization led to greater bureau-cratization—manifested in more counting, and increased regimenta-tion, of guests and volunteers alike. Yet throughout this process the staff continued to extend hospitality to the volunteers. They indicated that the volunteers, through their committed work, relieved their anxiety: "We know better than to be anxious about such things because this work of feeding the hungry and sheltering the homeless in Sacramento is not our work. It is your work and God's work" (newsletter, Thanks-giving 1992).

### Social Justice: "With Sadness not Hostility"

The work of personalist hospitality also tied the volunteer to the practice of social justice. The renouncing of selfishness, so important to personal-ist hospitality, encouraged the volunteer to take responsibility for pro-moting social justice. Volunteers received moral guidance on war, the economy, housing and work for the poor, and harassment of the poor by police. The consideration of social justice issues and their relation to in-dividual action ranged from abstract and oblique to specific and directive.

The August 1991 newsletter illustrated how personal responsibility and social justice become bound up in the shedding of selfishness:

> We worry sometimes that our marvelous volunteers will be over-whelmed by the constant increase in the flood of hungry families and single people coming to us for a decent meal and for other help. It has to be said bluntly: the self-centered values in our nation and state must change drastically if hunger and homelessness are to be elimi-nated. Meanwhile our state government has just eliminated emer-gency housing funds for the homeless, and has cut back the monthly income for indigent mothers with babies and small children.

Many newsletters strongly condemned the government. For example:

> The smell of injustice permeates our land. Why must decent people be abandoned to live on the streets in increasing numbers? . . . We want to cry out to our country and ask why in God's name we are al-

lowing this to go on, and to grow even worse. People need jobs and housing, not welfare and soup kitchens. (Christmas 1991)

Another newsletter accused the government of downplaying the economic crisis: "This has not been called what it is, a depression, but rather a recession as if this state of affairs is only temporary" (October 1993).

In keeping with Catholic Worker pacifism, the newsletters bore witness to the suffering of war. For example, although the staff did not condemn the Gulf War outright, they did testify to the hardships it caused:

> In the midst of a lot of distressing discussion about whether the U.S. and the U.N. need to go to war in the Mideast, we must bear witness to the reality here in Sacramento that many more hundreds of our brothers and sisters and their children have been thrown into the sea of unemployment. . . . Something is terribly wrong. (Christmas 1990)

The war in Bosnia gave proof that shedding the "sinful 'old person' " did not necessarily come easier to Christians, even at the time of the Resurrection (newsletter, Easter–Spring 1993).

Whereas the economy and the war were treated more abstractly in the newsletters, local injustices concerning the homeless warranted requests for specific direct action from individuals. For example, the staff requested help in addressing the lack of housing for the poor and police harassment of the homeless in Sacramento. In the Christmas 1991 newsletter Loaves & Fishes staff began organizing support for their proposal to build one thousand cottages, with a proposed rent of $200 per month. The housing would cost the city $40 million—which paled next to the amount the city spent on its new Convention Center and parking plaza. The emotional framing of the letter decried anger: "It will be with sadness not hostility that we undertake this crucial effort on behalf of the dispossessed in our community." Readers of the newsletter received both encouragement to participate in several letter drives supporting the building of the cottages and a special four-page brochure covering the cottage project. The staff asked community members to petition the local government to waive building fees for the cottages.

Social justice work for the Loaves & Fishes community also included petitioning for the right of homeless people to sleep on the banks of the Sacramento River. The organization challenged the local community to a more radical vision of the poor's right to use public space. Staff encouraged telephone calls to the mayor and the chief of police on behalf of the right of the homeless to sleep on the riverbanks during the warmer seasons when the city no longer provided public shelter.

> The homeless of our city continue, in many cases, to be treated as criminals *precisely because they are without homes.* A city "anti-camping" ordinance is now being used by the Mayor and the Police Dept. to issue citations to individual homeless folks who dare to be caught sleeping in a sleeping bag or blanket on the ground. It doesn't matter where, because every inch of ground in Sacramento has been designated illegal, and everyone unrolling a blanket or sleeping bag anywhere is now "camping." (Newsletter, August 1993; emphasis in original)

While the staff provided moral guidance on social justice issues, participation in advocacy work remained a choice left to the volunteer. Many volunteers limited their work to feeding the guests, but others also gave donations. For not only did the volunteers enter into the Loaves & Fishes "community" by practicing personalist hospitality in the dining room and by advocating local social justice, many also entered the organization by providing donations that contributed to its ongoing work.

### Donation Gathering: "Your Generous Spirit"

In keeping with its Catholic Worker roots, Loaves & Fishes did not accept government funds. The staff used the newsletter to request donations (of both money and goods) and to thank the community for donations.

In asking for donations to help with the building of the new dining room, the staff reported, "We sometimes feel embarrassed to be always coming to you in a begging posture. But we don't mind doing it when it is for the most neglected among our brothers and sisters" (newsletter, Easter 1991). The repeated metaphor of begging placed Loaves & Fishes, not the poor and homeless, in the position of thrusting a "tin begging cup" (February 1993) toward the domiciled community. "We continue to rely totally on your generosity, especially this time of the year, which is also our low income time of year. . . . So we must continue to beg your help in whatever way you can give it" (August 1991). Begging was couched in terms of the legitimacy of serving the poor nutritious, pleasing food in keeping with the implicit respect of personalist hospitality. For example: "We will not serve slop. The poor deserve better than that. We know you agree with us" (September 1991).

In addition to money, the staff requested expensive, frequently used items such as diapers, toothbrushes and toothpaste, coffee (decaffeinated preferably), and paper napkins. At the holidays they requested chocolate and candy treats, as well as white, one-size-fits-all athletic socks. When the library opened, a special request for reference books accompanied the newsletter. In the September 1991 issue, the staff suggested the growing of "Victory Gardens," similar to those planted in the early 1940s to help the war effort: "Perhaps it's time to go to war against hunger here in Sacramento."

The newsletter accompanied its monthly requests for help with descriptions of the activities and building projects at Loaves & Fishes. It reported large donations, but anonymously. Those least able to give received the greatest acknowledgment, as in the following reprint of an anonymous letter from a senior citizen to Loaves & Fishes.

> I can't get to you with any of the things you mentioned. I hope this check will help. I am 75, live in subsidized housing so you know my income is very small. But thanks to God and SSI I do have food and a roof. Who knows when I too could be dining at your table. God bless you and your work. (Easter–Spring 1993)

All supporters constituted the Loaves & Fishes Bank of Faith (newsletter, May–June 1992).

Most newsletters closed with thanks for previous donations. For example: "Thank you for hanging in with us. . . . We very much depend on your support to carry on in the face of so much suffering and hopelessness" (June 1993), and "May God bless you for your caring spirit" (February 1993). These expressions of gratitude often highlighted the need for continued support. For example, the February 1994 newsletter closed with the statement, "Thank you for your continuing generosity, which is our only means of monthly survival." In explaining a summer drop in donations, the October 1993 newsletter acknowledged, "We wish that we could tell you that your contributions will help end homelessness, but sadly they cannot. . . . We are there to care for them in your name, in whatever way we can. They are, after all, our dear guests. God bless."

Thus, through the newsletter, the staff, as moral entrepreneurs, spread their vision of charity. This ideal emphasized selfless giving, love for the poor, and social justice. As moral crusaders, the staff articulated an ideal to which they challenged all to aspire. The working arrangements of holiday fund-raising and volunteer coordination most troubled the relatively pure articulation of charitable ideals found in the newsletter.

## Sentimentalizing Holiday Giving

At Loaves & Fishes the hope of the Resurrection and the renunciation of selfishness shaped the moral vision most profoundly at the holidays. Volunteers citywide gave money, food, and labor. The staff attempted to make use of as many volunteers as possible, as this excerpt from the Easter 1994 newsletter demonstrated:

> Are we too late in writing you for Easter or is Easter too early for us
> this year? By the time you receive this letter asking for your help
> with our annual Easter Day Dinner, there will only be a week or so
> left for you to respond to our appeal for food and volunteers. We
> apologize for not giving you enough notice but this year—at least so

far—has just been a blur. At times we seems so overwhelmed with
the human suffering of so many hungry and homeless folks—people
who are literally at their wits ends—that we lose touch with our time
cycles.

But the reality of Spring and new growth will not be denied. In
every cement and asphalt crack in our Loaves & Fishes complex on
North C St. (the old warehouse and industrial area north of downtown Sacramento) grows a weed or a blade of grass determined to
live and take its rightful place in the sun. And a new hope springs
eternal among our hungry guests as well. The darkness and gloom
of the winter is at last over, the days are balmy and the night chills
are gone. And we too hope and pray that this year will be a better
one for our guests and for you too, our loyal friends and supporters.

### Holiday Donations: "So Grateful"

Just as Loaves & Fishes relied on volunteer labor for its charitable works,
so it depended almost solely on public contributions for its operating
budget. Monetary contributions from the public rose fairly steadily from
$1,208,808 in 1990 to $1,764,927 in 1994, according to tax records.
These documents show Loaves & Fishes' financial dependency on the
goodwill of individuals and church groups.[7] Just before Christmas 1993,
LeRoy Chatfield, executive director of Loaves & Fishes, talked quite
openly to Brian Ono, a reporter for a local television station, about the
dependence of the organization on holiday donations: "Our collections
this Christmas season, compared to last Christmas, we're down about 17
percent as of this date." Ono responded, "And that amounts to about a
$50,000 shortfall." Chatfield added that the shortfall could result in cut-
ting back services in 1994 (Ono 1993). The volunteer director echoed
the importance of holiday donations when she matter-of-factly told me
in an interview, "Of course, we survive on the money we get *during* the
holidays, as does The Salvation Army and other places."

By Thanksgiving 1993 Loaves & Fishes experienced a 15 percent
decrease in monetary donations and thus joined a nationwide trend.

Within this milieu, called "compassion fatigue" by the popular press, soup kitchens and food banks nationwide reported a Thanksgiving decline in donations that reached 40 percent in some locations (Smolowe 1993: 29). Loaves & Fishes' final 1993 tax report showed $1,671,428 in public donations; a 15 percent decrease for the year, estimated on overall contributions, would thus be a loss of $250,714. It appears, however, that by the end of the year Loaves & Fishes recouped its losses.

The personalizing of the needs of the poor through pictures and stories, as well as Loaves & Fishes' grateful stance to their Bank of Faith, appeared to be successful fund-raising strategies. The Thanksgiving 1992 newsletter opened with the message, "Greetings! We feel so grateful this Thanksgiving, grateful that we are able to personally help the folks who are considered to be the least in our society, and grateful to you and for your involvement." Much of the newsletter described current projects (tours of the organization's cottages for the homeless and petitioning city government on behalf of the cottages), as well as directions to Loaves & Fishes. It also requested donations of food items and told potential volunteers that they could ask green-capped street monitors for directions to the volunteer parking lot on arriving at the Loaves & Fishes complex.

Across the bottom of the Thanksgiving 1993 newsletter, a biblical proverb framed the giving experience: "If you shut your ears to the cry of the poor, you yourself will call and not be heard. Prov. 21:13." The same issue encouraged volunteers to respond by giving food, money, and time. Those who called the organization and signed up to volunteer received a sheet directing them to their shift. The explanation of the volunteering experience prepared the holiday volunteer for the somewhat rigid structure of this day.

> Please understand that this is a huge undertaking involving 150 volunteers. Typically, the day is highly chaotic as well as fun for all. We have scheduled three waves of volunteers to assist on the holiday. When you are thanked and hurriedly told that your shift is over, please be understanding.

Volunteers played an important and highly choreographed role in the provision of the holiday meal. Staff organized the welcoming of the holiday volunteers down to the name tags. Patty, the volunteer coordinator at Loaves & Fishes, explained to me in an interview that the staff tried to reserve the holidays for new volunteers rather than use the monthly volunteer groups or routine volunteers. She spent time before the holidays soliciting food donations as well as planning how to share any surplus with other organizations.

> And what I do is I get on the phone and I call everybody I can think of. I add new names to it every year and I watch the newspaper real carefully, and I will say this what we have, can we share it with you? Do you want it? We always give stuff to various groups. . . . We *shaaaare* this work, and we don't look at it as a competitive thing at all. Yes, we always have way too many volunteers. What I do is I call the agencies I can think of and I say, "When are you doing you holiday meal?" and then we try to [organize the volunteers] around that.

She explained the volunteer coordination carefully and was obviously concerned about finding a place for the holiday volunteers to participate. She told me that the organization has made its holiday meal use of volunteers into a "fine art."

I told Patty about my often futile attempts to steer holiday volunteers toward working more mundane shifts. She responded patiently, "And people get angry at you. They say, 'Well, I guess you don't need any help,' and you have to try and be as gentle as you can and there is always the, 'Well, we are open 364 days of the year, is there another day that you would like to come?' But I keep a long waiting list." As I continued to press the issue of holiday volunteers, telling Patty that I found "irony" in the single-minded desire of the holiday volunteers to give on such specific days, she responded carefully and quietly, "But you need to take people when they are willing to give help too. And we do try to accommodate a whole lot of people."

The staff sometimes expressed frustration with the sudden desire of community members to help on the holidays. Patty's patience with the holiday volunteers sometimes gave way to frustration. In my field-notes I recorded her description of holiday volunteering to other volunteers at Our Lady of Assumption while preparing food for a non-holiday meal.

> I told Patty about my friends who hoped to volunteer on Thanksgiving, and Patty explained that they get many calls from people hoping to volunteer on that day. They work people in shifts, so that as three come, three are sent home for instance. She had told a story earlier of how as some people arrive, they become cranky and disgruntled if they aren't given a position serving but instead are sent to do dishes. Some will say, "But I am here to serve." Patty clearly felt impatience. As we talked over the Harvest Casserole, Patty acknowledged their desire to help, but said there are 364 other days in the year.

The following Thanksgiving, 1994, the kitchen manager encouraged a local government office to donate money instead of one hundred fifty frozen turkeys because Loaves & Fishes had already received enough sliced turkey for at least two meals. The office representative responded that they would rather give food. (The kitchen manager explained to me that they "bartered" with the Sacramento Food Bank to hold the frozen food and that the Loaves & Fishes staff considered asking Folsom Prison to help with the cooking.) Later that same day one of the staff members told a television reporter, "I say this with some caution, but we need help every day of the year."

*Thanksgiving 1993: "Your Concern and Your Contributions"*
The 1993 Thanksgiving meal at Loaves & Fishes demonstrated how the staff mediated between the moral rhetoric of personalist hospitality and the demands of organizing a surplus volunteer pool at the holidays. The holidays placed Loaves & Fishes in the position of begging for resources for the daily work of feeding the urban poor; yet, as beggars, the staff felt compelled to welcome all contributions, regardless of their im-

mediate usefulness. Their gratitude on behalf of the poor could be heard in the Thanksgiving 1993 newsletter:

> More homeless and hungry people come to us all the time. More
> hungry mouths mean that we find ourselves constantly serving more
> and more meals. We are grateful this Thanksgiving that together,
> you and we are able to keep up with this rising tide of suffering men,
> women and children. Your concern and your contributions make it
> all possible, for which we want to say to you, especially during this
> Thanksgiving Day season, *thanks so very much*. And keep them com-
> ing. (Emphasis in original)

Loaves & Fishes traditionally served its Thanksgiving meal on the Tuesday before Thanksgiving so as to not interfere with the meal at The Salvation Army on Thursday. This production celebrated the holiday with an unusually rich and labor-intensive meal. Workers from a local hospital had picked up the plastic knives and forks (used only on holidays in place of flatware) and then returned it wrapped in orange and black napkins, with the silverware packages tied with a patterned autumn rib-bon. The Loaves & Fishes newsletter had requested turkeys (precooked and presliced in aluminum pans), pies, and socks and candy for the holi-day meal. The guests were to receive potato rolls, served with putter pats, pickles and olives as a garnish, canned fruit cocktail with marshmallows, yams, turkey, gray, cranberry sauce, a slice of pie, and apple juice and cof-fee. And as each guest left the dining room, a Loaves & Fishes worker would give him or her one pair of white tube socks and a bag of candy.

People wishing to volunteer were told to call the volunteer phone line and sign in. Whereas a routine meal at Loaves & Fishes required the work of 21 volunteers, 110 volunteers participated in the serving of the 1993 Thanksgiving meal. On Monday night the staff, with the help of 35 volunteers, stayed until 11:00 P.M. to do food prep. Many of the staff then returned at 6:00 the next morning to coordinate the 75 vol-unteers who worked in three shifts to serve the Thanksgiving meal. The volunteers and staff were assisted by a local caterer who parked his catering truck outside the kitchen to prepare gravy and yams (and keep the turkey warm) for the meal.

On the morning of the meal the caterer's truck obscured the volunteers' entrance to the kitchen. Patty stood outside in dark blue pants, a medium blue slightly longish T-shirt, and tennis shoes, directing new volunteers to the kitchen. The staff scheduled three shifts of volunteers to increase the holiday volunteer participation. The first shift, scheduled from 7:00 to 10:30, sliced turkey off the bone and began food preparation. Of the twenty-two volunteers who had signed up, thirteen showed up and two others joined in as walk-ins. When new volunteers appeared, their names were checked against the list, their phone numbers were recorded if they were not on the list, and they were given a name tag. The staff confirmed that volunteers parked in the volunteer lot, and women with handbags received directions to return them to their cars for safekeeping. The staff turned away several walk-in volunteers during the second shift, with a thank you and an invitation to come back another time. All volunteers wore color-coded name tags; red, black, or green lettering indicated what shift a volunteer worked so that the staff would know when a volunteer was scheduled to leave, thus creating room for the next shift of volunteers. The volunteers, probably prepared by the letter they received in the mail, seemed to accept this organization easily and without much surprise, although it underscored their less than essential contribution to the meal preparation.

Patty, Chris Delany, and some return holiday volunteers repeatedly commented on the efficient organization of this Thanksgiving meal. Yet Patty said that she would not relax until it was over and the last dishes were put away. She explained that she always felt more "frazzled" when she directed a large pool of volunteers. Patty also cautioned me, and perhaps herself as well, that something would probably go wrong or someone would get angry. She would be proven correct. For example, the preceding year a volunteer had reportedly gotten out of line, and LeRoy gave him a twenty-minute lecture; the volunteer asked to return this year and was accepted back on a probationary basis.

Few of the volunteers knew each other. Some had volunteered on other Thanksgivings. Some were disappointed because The Salvation Army staff told them over the telephone that they did not require any more volunteers that holiday. Some of the women wore dresses and low heels in keeping with the festive occasion. Others, however, wore T-shirts, turtlenecks, or sweatshirts, and worn walking shoes more common to the routine volunteers. The unusually large number of volunteers contributed to the festive and somewhat chaotic environment. The volunteers were chatty, asking each other what they did and where they came from. Many discussed their work, and one distributed business cards. Many of the first-shift volunteers left by 9:30 A.M., because there was little other food preparation, short of adding marshmallows to the fruit salad or filling the water pitchers.

My familiarity with the working arrangements of volunteers at Loaves & Fishes identified me as a staff member to many of the guests and the other volunteers. Patty asked me if I would use my knowledge to help coordinate the holiday volunteers. In her words, "The new volunteers are task-oriented." So I helped to find work for the volunteers. I steered a young woman to putting the salt and pepper shakers on the table and asked another to help me clear the tables of water pitchers so that the schoolchildren responsible for the table settings could finish decorating. I emerged as something of an expert at volunteering and found myself explaining how one could call the volunteer line to volunteer at other times of the year.

The second shift, which gathered at about 10:00, consisted of thirty-six of the forty-one signed-up volunteers and two walk-ins. Following staff directions, they gathered at tables in the dining room, some with the coffee they had been offered. Patty gave a talk about volunteering. She told them about the need to fill all the positions, not just serving, and explained that they might need to leave as other volunteers arrived.

She provided an overview of how Loaves & Fishes works and told them that they were welcome to come back if they liked this experience. Chris joined Patty, pointed out the location of the bathrooms, and then told the volunteers twice, "We like to be really nice to our guests."

As the time to serve the meal approached, the excitement in the dining room peaked. The poignancy of the holiday meal combined with the chaotic kitchen, crowded with talk and volunteers trying to figure out their assigned tasks, brought some volunteers to tears. The import of the meal escalated with the arrival of local reporters from ABC, NBC, and CBS for live coverage. A local female reporter, her face heavily rouged, dressed in a professional raincoat over slacks and low heels, disrupted the meal production. Chris stood in front of the camera as the reporter interviewed her. Chris told the camera people that they were not to film the guests without their consent. The reporter's cameraman requested a shot of Chris standing near the food, and so, standing next to the food rack, loaded with pumpkin pies, Chris began evenly, "It takes a lot of food to produce a Thanksgiving meal such as this one." She went on to carefully list the quantities of food amassed for the meal; she repeated this presentation for the other reporters.

Bishop Francis A. Quinn, a much-loved leader among Catholics in the area and an ardent supporter of Loaves & Fishes, arrived just a few minutes after we began serving. He put on an apron and was led to the serving of the turkey in the main dining room. Patty took the job of removing the already established meat server, a portly man in his fifties, who looked displeased as he lost his place on the serving line. Patty explained that the bishop would serve the meat now. Earlier Patty had told me that if there were extra volunteers, the job of serving the rolls and butter could be split to absorb another volunteer on the food line. The displaced meat server received a piece of pie and then moved to the serving of the rolls, where he appeared to regain his sense of usefulness.

Shortly after 1:30 a college-age woman discovered that her leather backpack had been stolen. She lost several hundred dollars worth of books, her credit cards, and about $100 in cash. She was aggravated and despondent. Chris talked with the executive director, who told her that Loaves & Fishes would reimburse the young woman for her lost items. Patty looked distraught and said that this could be a very expensive Thanksgiving. Chris comforted her by patting her on the cheek.

The third shift of volunteers settled into their work. Of the forty who had signed up, twenty-two arrived. This brought the total number of volunteers to seventy-five. The volunteers were more racially diverse than on the routine days I volunteered. There also appeared to be more mothers and daughters than usual. I saw some parents with adolescents; the usual prohibitions against children applied. Earlier a woman with her approximately seven-year-old daughter came and convinced a staff member that, despite the rules against children under fourteen volunteering, her daughter would sit quietly in the women's and children's dining room. Shortly thereafter Chris saw the winsome child sitting quietly and objected first on the basis that the girl might be upset by what she saw and second that the child would take a seat that could be used by a guest. The woman volunteer and her daughter left, the woman appearing disappointed and a bit frustrated but understanding.

Some volunteers continued to serve food while others helped to take the emptied aluminum pans outside to waiting guests. One man collected them for recycling; others patiently waited for one pan, of the right size, for their own cooking use. Some guests asked for pans of specific sizes, and the volunteers tried to fill these requests.

I was worn out from the day. The kitchen was both more exciting and more chaotic than usual. I was troubled by how many holiday volunteers scrambled to work on the serving line yet did not come back to help during the remainder of the year. I thought about giving and wondered about how the more I volunteer, the less substantial my gift seems. I wondered for the first time if my volunteering was becoming routinized. I began to think about what it would mean to think of myself as a routine volunteer. Two days later I would spend Thanksgiving at The Salvation Army serving another holiday meal.

## An Abundance of Giving

Holidays were an extraordinary experience at Loaves & Fishes. They required intense mobilization of staff to coordinate the volunteers and flood of donations. Volunteers received their greatest voice at the Thanksgiving to Christmas nexus when the media descended on the kitchen to observe community members feeding the poor. The holiday volunteer experience happened within what William Bunis, Angela Yancik, and David A. Snow (1996) identify as a time of heightened romanticism and the sentimentalization of caring. Bunis, Yancik, and Snow tracked newspaper coverage of the homeless in both the *New York Times* and the *London Times* as well as volunteerism in an Arizona agency serving the homeless, over a five-year period, to provide evidence that sympathy and gestures of goodwill toward the homeless follow a seasonal cycle, with a peak beginning at Thanksgiving and cresting at Christmas. They argue that their findings provide support for widening "spans of sympathy" (Lewis, cited in Bunis, Yancik, and Snow 1996: 387) for the misfortunate based on the cultural support for sympathy during this holiday season.

> Considering the link between major holidays, such as Christmas and Thanksgiving in the United States, and sentiments regarding social problems, it is reasonable to argue that major holidays function as both positive and negative ritual activities. Perhaps the holiday season propels society to confront itself—myth versus reality, prosperity versus poverty—such that the "moral communion" restores collective strength. (Bunis, Yancik, and Snow 1996: 391)

At Loaves & Fishes (and, as we shall see in the next chapter, at The Salvation Army), the serving of food to the poor took on a highly ritualized character during the Thanksgiving and Christmas holiday season.

Holiday volunteering worked to reveal to me the mundanity of the working arrangements of committed year-round caring. The holiday volunteers were but one part of a richer, more complicated story of volunteering. The volunteer experience of the committed volunteers, whether Alternative Sentencing Program or In-house volunteers at

The Salvation Army or religious group or unaffiliated volunteers at Loaves & Fishes, emerged out of working arrangements marked not by sentimentalized festivity but rather by commitment and steadfastness. This caring required sustenance from sources other than the widened span of sympathy provided by the sometimes fervent convergence of the media, patriotism, and religious ideals at the Thanksgiving to Christmas holiday season.

In contrast to the holiday volunteers, the routine volunteers practiced caring as a duty and obligation not tied to the symbolism of holidays. The holiday volunteers labored in working arrangements in which radical Christian ideals had been stretched to make room for politically diverse and often inexperienced large numbers of workers. The routine volunteers functioned within an environment saturated with a diluted form of personalist hospitality.

## CREATING PERSONALIST HOSPITALITY

The routine expression of personalist hospitality revealed itself in the mundane working arrangements of the kitchen and dining room. The volunteer orientation sessions provided a window into the ideal daily working arrangements of Loaves & Fishes as organized by the staff. These sessions officially brought volunteers into the organization, providing them with an introduction to the moral rhetoric of charitable action. The volunteer appreciation dinner, also called the volunteer thank you dinner, celebrated the year's accomplishments and the work of the volunteers. These formal events, as well as more mundane interactions involved in doing personalist hospitality, taught the moral rhetoric of charitable action to the committed volunteers.

### Volunteer Orientation Sessions: "The Whole Picture"

Individuals who called the volunteer telephone line received an invitation to come to Loaves & Fishes for a two-hour introductory session. In 1993 the orientation was offered four times a month and was attended by 690 prospective volunteers. Of those, 135 signed up to volunteer in the dining room or other programs (newsletter, February 1994). In an interview I asked Patty how many of those attending the orientation sessions would actually end up volunteering. She replied, "I would say three quarters of them. We get a lot of students doing papers, we get a lot of people who are thinking about donating money, and then we get a lot of people who just read the newspapers."

Along with twenty others, I attended a volunteer orientation session on a Wednesday during spring 1993. The staff had sent confirmations as well as a pamphlet on the cottage proposal. Three high school–age Asian-American boys; a white woman and a Hispanic woman, both college age; two middle-aged white MediCal eligibility workers; several young adult women; and several individuals of retirement age, most of them female and all of them white, attended this orientation session. Patty conducted the tour of Loaves & Fishes' philosophy and programs.

The first half of the orientation took place in the activities room above the kitchen, with the attendees seated around a large table. Patty explained that, because the area was removed from the guests, it was a discreet place to talk. Patty stood at one end of the table, addressing us as "class," and began by describing her own experience with Loaves & Fishes. She was from a middle-class background and first came to the kitchen as a volunteer and then quickly became a group leader in the dining room. She laughingly recounted her reaction on first encountering cockroaches in the old Loaves & Fishes' kitchen and told of her initial nervousness about cooking a casserole for several hundred guests.

Patty gave each of us a copy of the "Philosophy Statement of Loaves & Fishes," which read in part:

> Loaves & Fishes is a non-profit organization providing service in a spirit of love, hospitality and generosity to all those who come for assistance. . . .
>
> We are motivated to serve in Loaves & Fishes out of compassion for the poor and disadvantaged. Through our actions we hope to

communicate our respect and love for all who come to Loaves &
Fishes for assistance. . . .

We value collaborating with diverse groups in the work of Loaves
& Fishes and actively seek to involve volunteers from a variety of
backgrounds. Within the guiding principles listed above, we respect
the individual spirit and expression of each of the groups.

Patty's volunteer experience, intermingled with reading from the philosophy statement, let us know that those of us from the middle class might feel uncomfortable in the volunteer role but that we would receive support and guidance. Any gift we might make would be appreciated.

Patty recounted how the Delanys began Loaves & Fishes. They established Loaves & Fishes with only four rules: No booze, no drugs, no violence, no threats of violence. From the beginning, to maintain its independence, the organization was committed to accepting no government money.

Patty personalized her story by telling us that when she learned of the Catholic Workers in the fifth grade, she associated them with communists. Many of the prospective volunteers smiled at this. Patty explained that initially the St. Vincent de Paul Society funded the Delanys, and she gave us insights into the Delanys' lives, telling how Dan, the "fiery Irishman," had previously worked as a Fuller Brush man.

As prospective volunteers, we learned of some of the programs: Dining Room, Maryhouse, Mustard Seed, Mercy Clinic, Friendship Park, Service Center, Hope House, Brother Martin's Ministries, Loaves & Fishes Savings and Trust Account, Guest Health Outreach, Our Daily Bread, the Guest House, and Low Rent Housing. As Patty explained each program she described the opportunities for volunteer participation. She repeated that at Loaves & Fishes they "try to hang loose."

Patty explained how each program benefits the homeless. Of the jail visitation program, Patty said that approximately 15 percent of the guests end up in jail at any one time but that for a volunteer "maybe [this program was] not as rewarding as some other things." However, Dan Delany refers to this program, she told us, as "the jewel in [the organization's] crown." In addition, volunteers help to organize people to attend services for unclaimed bodies. Patty explained that at one time the deceased may have availed themselves of the meals offered by Loaves & Fishes.

After Patty's presentation, she took questions. Then she told us that we could choose to come on a tour of Friendship Park or stay near the kitchen if we might be uncomfortable. Most of us accompanied her. As we approached the park the volunteers began to clump in groups and grow quiet. We walked along as Patty described the available services. Most of the guests were relaxing or talking, but most of us, including me, experienced the walk through the park as voyeuristic and awkward.

Patty emphasized throughout the presentation the theme of voluntary giving. Latecomers to the orientation received information that writing papers about Loaves & Fishes was "okay"[8] and that there are "no pressures to feel you have to volunteer." The tour closed with repeated assurances that we were not to feel obligated to volunteer but that she hoped we would speak well of Loaves & Fishes. After the orientation, I received a form letter in the mail inviting me to give of my time and detailing nineteen possible volunteer positions.[9]

An interview with Patty approximately one year after this orientation session further illuminated the volunteer coordinator's work as a moral entrepreneur. She helped to manage the emotion work that welcomed the volunteers into the working arrangements of feeding the urban poor.

> The volunteer orientation sessions? I started those about two years ago. Just over two years ago. And it was really because so many people wanted to volunteer and what we would do is just shuttle them all into the dining room and people would be *nervous* to go around and they never got to see Maryhouse or the Park or the Library. And, we felt that wasn't very *welcoming*, you know that they needed a chance to get the *whole* picture, so that they would feel kind of like a part of Loaves & Fishes.

It probably works out best if the volunteers start out small. I am always real careful to say that most volunteers come once a month, because we don't want them to burn out and think, Oh Lord, it's Tuesday and I have to be at Loaves & Fishes. And I try to encourage them to do that, and if they are at all timid, to start in the dining room and get a feel for it, where you are with a bunch of other *middle-class* people and there's the counter in front of you. And see how comfortable they are?

The staff stretched the ideal of Catholic Worker hospitality with its emphasis on face-to-face personalism to make room for the middle-class volunteers. Nonetheless, Patty echoed Chris and Dan Delanys' concerns when she cautioned, "With growth, we are going to lose our charm."

The orientation sessions efficiently welcomed many prospective volunteers and visitors. Many of the volunteers I later met in the dining room had never attended an orientation session, but they were very useful for those who wished to come to Loaves & Fishes on their own, without an already established community.

### *The Volunteer Appreciation Dinner: "Shine Like Stars"*

In 1993 more than 375 people attended the annual volunteer appreciation dinner at St. Ignatius Parish Center. The Tuesday dinner, prepared by the same catering service that helps Loaves & Fishes on the holidays, celebrated Loaves & Fishes' ten-year anniversary. Volunteers paid $7 to attend.

Of the volunteers I interviewed, only a few of the older ones attended the dinner. They sat at tables with their volunteer group; the room was filled predominantly with white, retirement-age volunteers. Dorcy, the kitchen manager, Patty, and Chris Delany, dressed in matching floral skirts and tops, greeted the attendees. I sat with the members of Patty's church, Our Lady of Assumption, as she had invited me to join them. Because I was taking notes, a retired man seated next to me asked if I was a newspaper reporter; when I told him I was doing research, he inquired with interest about my project. Across from me sat

Catherine, a volunteer who joked with great enthusiasm about the wine and table decorations.

On entering, guests signed name tags, and Patty, Dorcy, or Chris escorted them to their tables. The church gymnasium bore witness to the festivity: the names of the dining room crews graced one wall; the tables were festooned with autumn-colored floral table runners above peach-colored plastic tablecloths; two bottles of wine adorned each of the long, rectangular folding tables.

The dinner reflected the efficient organization characteristic of Loaves & Fishes. At about 6:30 Chris Delany began the evening's presentation. First a Loaves & Fishes staff member spoke about the importance of signing the blue sheets we all received, which addressed the inhumane treatment of homeless people by the police. He spoke with quiet passion, urging us to appeal to the police.

In the next part of the program Chris gave out green and white ribbons to all of the team leaders who had worked at Loaves & Fishes for the preceding ten years. As Chris mentioned, most, if not all, of the ten to twelve teams were Catholic, and most were represented by retirement-age leaders. I noted that only four of the team leaders were men. After this the popular Bishop Quinn provided the before-meal blessing.

Chris returned to the stage after the buffet-style dinner. She received a framed portrait of herself and outgoing Bishop Quinn, and then delivered the evening's formal address. She opened by saying that Loaves & Fishes was founded by a "group of people who had a vision . . . [and] a lot of faith that vision would be carried out." The vision provided that the poor should be allowed "to rest, be sustained, physically and spiritually." She told us that in 1992 Loaves & Fishes served 260,000 meals and that this year, with the exception of March and August, that number had increased an average of 1,500 meals per month. She then referred to the biblical miracle of loaves and fishes as a metaphor for the volunteer work: "Miracles happen every day at Loaves & Fishes . . . to make it work for the brothers and sisters who are trying to hold their fragile lives together."

Closing on a contemplative note, Chris urged her listeners to consider the seriousness of homelessness as a social problem. She tied the "shamefulness" of homelessness to the "miraculous wonderful deeds" that must be done at Loaves & Fishes. Reading from her yellow notepad in a quiet, earnest manner, Chris reminded us of the food, shelter, and health care that all deserve. She appealed to us to work together for greater social justice. She closed by listing all the staff members and departments at Loaves & Fishes. Each group stood and was applauded. Before introducing Bishop Quinn, she expressed her happiness that today Loaves & Fishes is a more ecumenical organization that represents the diverse population of the country.

Bishop Quinn received a standing ovation. After saluting the ecumenism of Loaves & Fishes, he turned to his experience of seeing the homeless at Loaves & Fishes and doing corporal works of mercy. He expressed his own frustration at two men he saw frequently at Loaves & Fishes asking for assistance and said, "I know the frustration you must go through serving those who do not seem grateful." But, he reminded us, "to help those who are hurting is precisely what Christ did." In closing, the bishop praised the volunteers. He called the volunteers the "unsung Mother Teresas and Bishop Tutus." Blessing the audience, he declared, "Those who help the helpless will shine like stars for all eternity." Chris then brought the evening to a close.

### Mundane Working Arrangements in the Dining Room

Volunteers in the dining room learned personalist hospitality through the more mundane routine of preparing and serving food to the urban poor. But even before beginning their work, volunteers experienced the personalist hospitality of Loaves & Fishes as manifested in its use of street monitors. After leaving their cars in a gravel parking lot just half a block from the entrance to Loaves & Fishes, volunteers were unquestioningly welcomed onto the property by street monitors, who were easily recognizable in their green baseball caps and T-shirts. When I parked on a nearby street, however, the street monitors would ask me if I needed directions; entering the property from the parking lot made clear one's role as volunteer.

I often had the opportunity to experience the hospitality of the street monitors when I left Loaves & Fishes. One day, as I pulled out of the parking lot, for example, a street monitor started motioning me toward the Loaves & Fishes complex, and, not understanding, I rolled down my window. He came running over and asked, "Do you need a parking spot, ma'am?" I replied, "No thank you, I am taking off." He said, "Okay," and motioned me out, as if directing traffic. The street monitor seemed to be assuming the role of host as he directed me through the homeless people who were being brought onto the Loaves & Fishes property. Another day, as I drove onto the main street separating Loaves & Fishes and The Salvation Army, a street monitor who was standing with his colleague in a nearby empty lot raised his arm in a good-bye salute. Again I felt like a guest being escorted off the property. The staff modified radical personalist hospitality into working arrangements friendly to volunteers only partly committed to that vision.

The practice of meal preparation and serving socialized volunteers into the site-specific vision of personalist hospitality. Each group prepared its own special dish. For example, the Jewish community served chicken Mediterranean and the Unitarians and Charismatics made sloppy joes. While this rendition of personalist hospitality highlighted respect for the individual and choice, it nonetheless did not reflect the relative anarchy found in the accounts given of many Catholic Worker hospitality houses. Most significant, the working arrangements at Loaves & Fishes focused on providing comfort and welcome to the volunteers.

Volunteers appreciated the clearly delineated roles and duties in the kitchen. For example, a male volunteer with the Metropolitan Community Church, with whom I worked chopping cabbage, explained that he liked volunteering in the dining room, compared to his volunteer experience in a thrift store, because it was "more structured" and "suited [his] needs better." Staff relieved volunteers of the obligation to undertake the more difficult responsibilities of serving the guests. For instance, a staff member "takes the door" at Loaves & Fishes, thereby freeing volunteers from screening and admitting the guests for the meal. Staff members also worked on a dining room hospitality crew so that volunteers did not work in the dining room without their guidance.

Chris Delany explained that this modification of personalist hospitality developed after the volunteer hospitality program "fell apart." Dining room duties include wiping tables as guests leave, offering assistance with children, helping people with their trays, and replenishing the water pitchers on the tables. I know from experience that this can be an emotionally wrenching task. When working with the hospitality crew one day, I wiped the tables with a warm rag, helped a blind man with his tray, and assisted mothers with their trays. In the dining room I was struck by the differences between The Salvation Army and Loaves & Fishes. Loaves & Fishes looked more like a "dining room": the wooden chairs and tables, though several years old, were lovely; there were fresh flowers on the table, along with tiny salt and pepper shakers. Yet many of the guests at Loaves & Fishes were in worse condition than those at the Salvation Army. For example, one older man shook so badly he could barely feed himself. Some of the men smelled strongly of urine; when they left I wiped little puddles off their chairs. One man said something lewd to me and then grimaced, showing me his mouth full of food. A young pregnant woman threw up on her tray and then with some embarrassment continued to eat, carefully avoiding the part of the tray she had dirtied.

On a typical day in the dining room, many of the guests talked companionably among themselves while they ate. Families sat together, supervising small children, while other individuals ate alone, some bowed over their trays. I only saw one fight in the dining room. Two men pushed each other, food flew, and other guests retreated as the men grabbed at each other. The young son of one of them, cried, "Dad," and began to cry. One of the staff hospitality workers grabbed at one of the men, and street monitors quickly arrived to help separate the men. The staff escorted the men out, as others began to clean the floor. I found myself shaken and nervous, although as a volunteer among paid staff I had very little responsibility for managing the fight.

These examples begin to illustrate how, by weakening the principles of personalist hospitality, volunteers could remain quite separate from the emotionally demanding duties of serving the urban poor at Loaves & Fishes. The bureaucratization of the working arrangements in the dining room placed distance between many of the volunteers and their guests. (I return to the implications of these arrangements in chapter 3.)

Loaves & Fishes, however, continued to inspire feelings of community in its volunteers. For example, the group leader for the Unitarians, a middle-aged white real estate broker, told me that she likes Loaves & Fishes because it involves "people helping people" and builds "community." The staff also sees Loaves & Fishes as a community; when talking about police harassment of the homeless, Patty told the group from Our Lady of Assumption that Loaves & Fishes functions essentially as a "sanctuary."

Volunteers also joined in the caring community when they attended memorial services for homeless people, some of whom had no one to claim their bodies. These services occurred in the courtyard during the midmorning, and kitchen volunteers were invited to join the memorials. The courtyard, with its soothing fountain and beautiful flowering trellises, offered a peaceful site for the services. At one such service I heard the story of a man who was run down by a car as he traveled home to the Midwest. A Loaves & Fishes staff member told us that this man's body would be buried in a pauper's grave. He said that there was no category "homelessness" for cause of death but that such a category should exist. He explained that since 1989 Loaves & Fishes has been collecting these stories and that there are now about eighty of them. He told us that it was important that these stories be heard. We prayed together: "Let us pray. God, you who love John, just as you love all the fallen squirrels, we thank God for your understanding as you were homeless the three years before your death. We thank God that now John will have a home, beside you God." We said the Lord's Prayer together and the brief service was finished.

## CONCLUSION

The moral rhetoric of charitable action at Loaves & Fishes emphasized respect for the poor through giving. The organizational structure maximizes the labor of diverse church-based volunteer groups to feed the city's hungry. Within this setting, the staff stretched Catholic Worker principles of voluntary poverty and personalism into working arrangements that allowed middle- and upper-middle-class non-Catholic volunteers to choose participatory roles that felt most comfortable to them.

While Catholic Worker ideals infused the working arrangements, staff often outwardly expressed ambivalence about these roots. For example, in what seemed to be a move to create an open environment, the volunteer director declared at an orientation session, "We're not really religious, but its everywhere here." At other times staff members claimed religious motivations. At a spiritual retreat Chris Delany described the Loaves & Fishes' philosophy as based on the Gospel of Saint Matthew. This ambivalence toward Loaves & Fishes' Catholic Worker roots seemed to develop out of a struggle to both treat the guests as the Ambassadors of God and welcome large numbers of often uncomfortable volunteers.

Not only did the staff orchestrate the labor of the volunteers so as to maximize choice in duties and contact with the homeless, they also managed volunteers' emotions as they were made to feel welcome, needed, and appreciated. In this rendition of personalist hospitality, the staff attempted to respect the guests' emotions through careful maintenance of the precepts of personalism and took care of the volunteers' feelings as well. In our increasingly service-oriented market, workers manage both their own and their customers' emotions (Hochschild 1983). Similarly, staff at social service agencies such as Loaves & Fishes and The Salvation Army attend to the emotions of those they serve as well as of those they manage in the volunteer labor pool. Differences in how the staff cares for volunteers' and guests' emotions at Loaves & Fishes revealed how in this setting radical Christianity has been modified to include large numbers of more moderate volunteers. For example, Loaves & Fishes introduced volunteers into the organization through a two-hour orientation session and paid them tribute with an annual honorary dinner. The organization attempted to achieve a workable balance, addressing the desire of the volunteers to feel that they made an important contribution but avoiding overburdening them with the responsibility for either the production of the meal or the plight of the homeless. This allowed the volunteers to feel good about their contribution to feeding the urban poor without making a commitment to the more radical tenets of the Catholic Worker philosophy.

At Loaves & Fishes the moral rhetoric of charitable action highlighted dignity, respect, and choice for both the guests and the volunteers. The growth of Loaves & Fishes, however, posed a challenge to its Catholic Worker ideals. The staff felt concern that the greater bureaucracy and regimentation of the organization might cause Loaves & Fishes to lose touch with its Catholic Worker roots. The working arrangements of charitable action at Loaves & Fishes mediated between the radical Christian philosophy of the Catholic Workers and the organizational demands to recruit and manage a large volunteer workforce to provide for the daily needs of the urban poor in Sacramento.

These tensions between the anarchist politics of caring for the poor and the bureaucratic institutionalization of kitchens for the poor surfaced in the years shortly following my fieldwork as John Cardinal O'Connor of New York announced on the occasion of what would have been Dorothy Day's one hundredth birthday in 1997 a movement for her canonization. In O'Connor's words, "If anybody in our time can be called a saint, she can" (Elie 1998: 44). In Day's own words, often repeated in this dispute by those Workers and advocates who believe the Church is attempting to co-opt Day's work and testimony, "Don't call me a saint—I don't want to be dismissed that easily" (Elie 1998: 44). An unlikely candidate for canonization with her admission of having had an abortion and a child conceived out of wedlock and her avowed commitment to not just helping the poor but also changing the social conditions that cause poverty, Day and her vision of radical charity nonetheless continue to inspire committed and occasional volunteers and activists alike.

CHAPTER 2

# Administering Salvationism

*Evangelism and Alcoholics Anonymous at*
*The Salvation Army*

The Salvation Army differed significantly in its structure and working arrangements from Loaves & Fishes. For example, rather than operate independently, the Shelter Services Center in Sacramento was part of the large, internationally organized Salvation Army social services complex. The Shelter Services Center, also unlike Loaves & Fishes, bid for government contracts. With this funding, The Salvation Army ran the Sacramento "overflow" shelter at Cal Expo and participated in city-run neighborhood restoration projects. Furthermore, drug and alcohol treatment figured prominently in the social services provided at the Shelter Services Center.

This chapter shows how the conservative Salvationist moral rhetoric of charitable action sedimented into the working arrangements of evangelical social welfare work at The Salvation Army Shelter Services Center in Sacramento. It traces the organizational moral rhetoric of charitable action through Salvationist writings, including the early works of William Booth and Commander Frederick Booth-Tucker (who came to the United States just after the turn of the century), the *War Cry*, and participant-observation and interviews with staff members at the Shelter Services Center.[1]

At The Salvation Army, my volunteer role and social location made me peripheral to the daily working arrangements,[2] and I found the moral rhetoric of charitable action at The Salvation Army more opaque than at Loaves & Fishes. I was not In-house, a court-ordered volunteer, male, or working class. I felt welcomed, however, and learned about the life stories of the other workers in the kitchen, just as they learned about my life story. I needed, however, to ask more searching questions of the staff to unveil the moral rhetoric of charitable action.

## THE ROOTS OF SALVATIONISM AT THE SHELTER SERVICES CENTER

The Salvation Army came into existence in 1878. At that time William Booth renamed the Hallelujah Army, a volunteer-staffed Christian mission of eighty-eight social workers, founded in the mid-1860s by Booth and his wife, Catherine, The Salvation Army (Collier 1965: 66). Even before the organization was renamed, Booth had carried the title General in the Hallelujah Army (Fellows 1979: 17). In the preface to his 1890 publication, *In Darkest England and the Way Out*,[3] Booth laid out his program for the salvation of the despairing masses:

> And yet all the way through my career I have keenly felt the remedial measures usually enunciated in Christian programmes and ordinarily employed by Christian philanthropy to be lamentably inadequate for any effectual dealing with the despairing miseries of these outcast classes. The rescued are appallingly few—a ghastly minority compared with the multitudes who struggle and sink in the open-mouthed abyss. Alike, therefore, my humanity and my Christianity, if I may speak of them in any way as separate one from the other, have cried out for some comprehensive method of reaching and saving the perishing crowds. . . .

If we help the man it is in order that we may change him. . . . My
only hope for the permanent deliverance of mankind from misery,
either in this world or the next, is the regeneration or remaking of
the individual by the power of the Holy Ghost through Jesus Christ.

This program, named by Booth "the Salvation Army Social Campaign,"
established the social service agenda of The Salvation Army in the
United States.[4] Booth (1890: preface) outlined his program as a militaristic directive, entitled "The Scheme of Social Selection and Salvation." The Salvation Army has since been variously characterized as
"evangelical social welfare work," "evangelical social Christianity," and
"gospel egalitarianism" (Magnuson 1977: v).

In 1880 Booth's program, which he described as aimed at recovering
the "sinking classes" (1890: preface), arrived in the United States. The
first shelter for homeless men opened in 1888 (McKinley 1986: 7). By
1890 410 corps operated in thirty-five states (McKinley 1986: 2). Yet
the United States was but one site of recruitment for The Salvation
Army. *The Salvation Army Year Book, 1994*, reported that as of January
1992 The Salvation Army operated in ninety-eight countries and other
territories, using 136 languages. The Army employed 16,455 active officers, 460 auxiliary captains, and 1,411 cadets; it also employed 76,677
full-time employees without rank.

Throughout its history The Salvation Army has espoused the practice
of charitable action as a buttress to its work of evangelizing the poor. The
Mission Statement of The Salvation Army proclaims this vision of charity:

The Salvation Army, an international movement, is an evangelical
part of the universal Christian church.

Its message is based on the Bible. Its ministry is motivated by the
love of God. Its mission is to preach the gospel of Jesus Christ and
to meet human needs in His name without discrimination.

General Booth conceived of The Salvation Army as tending to the
material and spiritual needs of the poor. A Salvation Army report of
1899 proclaimed:

The Salvation Army is the evolution of two great ideas—first, that of reaching with the gospel of salvation the masses who are outside the pale of ordinary church influences; second, that of caring for their temporal as well as spiritual necessities. In the one hand, it has carried to the people the Bread of Life, while in the other it has borne to them the bread that perisheth. (Booth-Tucker 1972)

The Salvation Army motto, "Heart to God and Hand to Man," captures the complexity of this salvation project. Present-day spokespeople for The Salvation Army underscore this union of evangelizing and addressing human misery. The Reverend Billy Graham, an ardent supporter of The Salvation Army, said of the Social Service Center in Cleveland, "This is truly Christian in action" (Gariepy 1990: 17). In 1988 General Eva Burrows announced to the ecumenical congress, "Our mandate is evangelism and compassion" (Gariepy 1990: 20).

The passion of The Salvation Army's evangelical social welfare work is revealed in a rallying cry delivered by Booth shortly before his death.

> While women weep as they do now,
>     I'll fight!
> While little children go hungry, as they do now,
>     I'll fight!
> While men go to prison, in and out, in and out,
>     I'll fight!
> While there is a drunkard left,
> While there is a poor girl left upon the streets,
> While there remains one dark soul without the light
>     of God, I'll fight!
>       I'll fight to the very end!
>           *(Gariepy 1990: 16)*

This call to battle reflected a larger cultural movement to masculinize Protestantism beginning in the mid-1800s. Muscular Christianity emphasized the virility of Protestantism along with the development of character and put men's work roles in the center of a religious identity (Bederman 1989; Bendroth 1993).

The Salvation Army's military model, with its chain of command (including military titles) and local bands and banners, further underscored its patriarchal roots. In 1878 the organization issued its first volume of *Orders and Regulations for The Salvation Army*. The group divides itself up into regions, with local headquarters that traditionally work from "citadels" or "forts," and when Salvationists die, they receive recognition for being "promoted to glory."

A Salvation Army pamphlet, *This Is the Salvation Army*, answers the question, "Why a Salvation Army?"

> Because Salvationists believe that the organization, discipline, mobility and esprit de corps of a military body can, and should, be adapted to a militant Christian movement, they know from experience that the evil in the world will not yield to pious exhortations, but needs to be out-fought and out-lived by people who are single-minded in their Christian charity.
>
> The aim of the Salvationists is to fight the good fight, guarding against temptation, but aggressively winning men for God on the front lines of human need.
>
> Like the military, the Army moves to meet emergency situations when the need arrives, reaches people where they are on a day to day basis, shapes young lives and mends broken ones. Their goal? The world for God. (The Salvation Army n.d.)

The Salvationist historian Henry Gariepy (1990: 20) celebrated the military model with his proclamation, "[The Salvation Army] wages war with the two-edged sword of evangelism and compassion. It yields weapons of prayer, the Bible, faith and love in action."

The Salvation Army calls itself a church. For example, Commissioner Kenneth L. Hodder, writing in the *War Cry*, expressed "delight" that General Eva Burrows circulated a letter before her retirement in 1993 that made it clear to all officers that The Salvation Army is a church. In Hodder's (1994: 5) words, "We know The Salvation Army is a movement. It's an Army; it's an organization; it's an agency. It's all these things and many more. But The Salvation Army *is* a church in form and in function. . . . We are Christian social ministers." William Booth (1890: preface) intertwined Christianity and social work through the practice of charitable action: "Alike, therefore, my humanity and my Christianity, if I may speak of them in any way as separate one from the other, have cried out for some more comprehensive method of reaching and saving the perishing crowds."

In short, The Salvation Army church wages a spiritual war on secular terrain to save souls. This convergence of social work and Christianity points to the complexity of the salvation proffered to the poor. The Salvationist historian Edward McKinley (1980: xi) explains that while the "Army is fiercely evangelical," the Salvationists believe that before people can be evangelized, they must first be fed. The Salvation Army extends physical salvation to make possible a spiritual moral regeneration.

In *In Darkest England*, Booth (1890: 110) proclaims, "We talk freely about Salvation, because it is to us the very light and joy of our existence." He aimed his Salvation Campaign at all members of the poorer classes:

> The Scheme of Social Salvation is not worth discussion which is not as wide as the Scheme of Eternal Salvation set forth in the Gospel. The Glad Tidings must be to every creature, not merely to an elect few who are to be saved while the mass of their fellows are predestined to a temporal damnation. (1890: 36)

Booth believed that a "Social Lifeboat Institution" (1890: 43) would allow The Salvation Army to rescue those who might sink, if left on their own. But first food and shelter must be extended.

> But what is the use of preaching the Gospel to men whose whole attention is concentrated upon a mad, desperate struggle to keep themselves alive? . . . And you will have all the better opportunity to find a way to his heart, if he comes to know that it was you who

pulled him out of the horrible pit and the miry clay in which he was
sinking to perdition. (Booth 1890: 45)

Physical salvation enables spiritual salvation. In Booth's (1890: 44)
words, "All material help from without is useful only in so far as it develops moral strength within." The ultimate goal is spiritual salvation:
"I must assert in the most unqualified way that it is primarily and mainly
for the sake of saving the soul that I seek the salvation of the body"
(1890: 45).

Booth ordered The Salvation Army to pay particular attention to
drunkenness, which he considered a base social problem.

> I will take the question of the drunkard, for the drink difficulty lies
> at the root of everything. Nine-tenths of our poverty, squalor, vice,
> and crime spring from this poisonous tap-root. Many of our social
> evils, which overshadow the land like so many upas trees would
> dwindle away and die if they were not constantly watered with
> strong drink. (1890: 47)

This moralistic view of the drunkard demanded that the Salvationists
devote themselves to changing the drunkard's behavior so that he would
resist temptation. In Booth's (1890: 85) words, "If he is a drunkard, he
must be made sober; if idle, he must be made industrious." In an un-
dated public address from the late nineteenth century, titled "The Salvation Army as a Temperance Movement," Commander Booth-Tucker
(1972) extolled, "Every Salvationist whom you meet, every worker in
our ranks, every office, every bandsman, every member is a teetotaler.
Abstinence is a condition of membership. . . . The keynote of our temperance work is conversion."

The Salvationists did not, however, characterize the work of self-
disciplining and assisting others as limited to any one class of person.
The Salvationists understood charitable work as significant to their own
spiritual salvation. A Salvationist publication from Christmas 1899 ex-
pounds this view.

It is impossible to exaggerate the value of the moral reformation thus wrought amongst the degenerate classes. Not that the work is by any means confined to them. Indeed, the bulk of our ordinary congregations is made up of the respectable working classes. No effort, however, is spared to induce every convert to go forth to the rescue of others. In fact the words Saint and Soldier are made to be synonymous. No sooner is the sinner saved than he is trained to systematic warfare and taught that his very soul's salvation depends on his becoming the savior of others. (Booth-Tucker 1972)

General Booth believed that all people should be guided into self-discipline and personal responsibility. He found hope in the "eagerness" of most men and women to engage in work (1890: 39). Discipline compromised an organizing principle of The Salvation Army: "We have, in the recognition of the importance of discipline and organization, what may be called regimented co-operation" (Booth 1890: 90). Work held great value for the individual as well in General Booth's estimation: "A man's labour is not only his capital, but his life" (1890: 32). Booth aimed to establish "a Workshop or Labour Yard" in connection with every shelter. These labor yards served the important function of providing those seeking help with the ability to earn a small amount of money for their bed and board. Booth (1890: 105) wrote, "This is a fundamental feature of the Scheme, and one which I think will commend it to all those who are anxious to benefit the poor by enabling them to help themselves without the demoralising intervention of charitable relief."

"The Salvation Army in the United States," a report dated Christmas 1899, documented that the organization operated a workingmen's hotel in Sacramento (Booth-Tucker 1972).[5] By the time of my fieldwork, The Salvation Army ran the Adult Rehabilitation Center, an administrative office, and the Shelter Services Center, in addition to overseeing numerous programs, most notably the Neighborhood Abatement of Refuse (NABORS) project aimed at rehabilitating and reclaiming poor neighborhoods and the city-commissioned overflow meal and shelter for the city's homeless population. Just as Peter Maurin's program for the Catholic Workers took strongest hold in the cities, so did General Booth's plan for the "city colony" gain the greatest support there (McKinley 1986: 45–46).

The ideological roots of the evangelical social welfare work practiced at The Salvation Army Shelter Services Center in Sacramento carried forth the beliefs of General William Booth and the early Salvationists. The working arrangements at the center emphasized the practice of moral regeneration through temperance and disciplined work. While the Shelter Services Center in Sacramento seemed to be less evangelical than other Salvation Army centers,[6] the staff paid great attention to drunkenness and the importance of the work ethic in raising people out of poverty. As will be seen, the Sacramento Salvation Army Shelter Services Center, with its work to instill discipline and self-responsibility, did not stray far from the tenets of charitable action established by the early Salvationists.

## SOWING SALVATIONISM

The framing images of Salvationism could be seen in operation at the Shelter Services Center. In contrast to Loaves & Fishes, where the volunteers could learn the beliefs and ideology of personalist hospitality through reading the newsletter or attending either an orientation session or a volunteer appreciation dinner, volunteers at the Shelter Services Center—mostly court-ordered or In-house male residents—received socialization into the principles of Salvationism through mandatory work requirements.

### MANAGING SALVATIONISM

This section draws on interviews with two staff members at The Salvation Army Shelter Services Center in Sacramento, as well as participant-observation, to discuss the working arrangements of charitable action managed by the staff. Dave and Kevin, both white and in their middle to late thirties, came to The Salvation Army as homeless substance abusers. At the time of my interviews both men were working toward counseling degrees in substance abuse, and Kevin had just received a promotion to join Dave as a substance abuse counselor. Both men worked as volunteers in the kitchen before coming to supervise volunteers themselves. Neither wanted to become a Salvationist, and both followed a trajectory through The Salvation Army that differed quite radically from that available to most of the homeless at Loaves & Fishes.

By the time I met Dave, he worked in a noisy office off the entryway to the reception desk. Enrolled at a local state college, he was working on a program in chemical dependency studies and, on completion, planned to transfer to a small, local college to work on a B.A. in psychology. Typically Dave wore slacks, a casual dress shirt and tie, sometimes a jacket, and a gold bracelet and necklace. He combed his blond hair back. He often visited the kitchen in the morning for a sweet treat and some coffee.

Kevin's arrival at The Salvation Army followed a similar pattern; he was first ordered by the court to the Drug and Alcohol Rehabilitation Center (also called the Adult Rehabilitation Center, or ARC). On his graduation from that program, the Shelter Services Center hired him to work in the kitchen. Depending on whether Kevin was working in the kitchen as a cook or in the front office as a counselor, he changed his dress. In the kitchen Kevin wore the white pants and shirt of the kitchen staff, often personalized with a blue bandanna and a red shirt underneath his white kitchen shirt, tennis shoes, a clean white towel tucked under his belt, and his comb stuck in his back pocket. On the days he worked as a counselor, Kevin wore slacks, cowboy boots, casual dress shirts, and often slightly humorous, funky ties, with his comb stuck in his back pocket and his neck-length brown hair pulled back in a small ponytail.

Interviews with these two aspiring substance abuse counselors demonstrated Salvationist ideology in action. This ideology interwove traditional Salvationist concerns about saving souls with the concerns of

Alcoholics Anonymous (A.A.)[7] and the importance of work. In short, this "course of regeneration" (Booth 1890: 92) infused A.A. principles with the discipline and camaraderie of hard work in the hope of Salvation.

### Salvation: "A Course of Regeneration"

The Shelter Services Center revealed itself to be ideologically similar to General Booth's envisioning of "Harbours of Refuge":

> These Harbours will gather up the poor destitute creatures, supply their immediate pressing necessities, furnish temporary employment, inspire them with hope for the future, and commence at once a course of regeneration by moral and religious influences. (Booth 1890: 92)

The less strenuous emphasis on evangelism at the center, compared to the program at other Salvation Army sites in Sacramento, was manifested in the Salvationists' tolerance of a "liberal" understanding of the Higher Power in its A.A. program.

These differences resulted in tensions between the Salvationists and civilians (often formerly homeless) and the struggles over evangelizing and administering social welfare. Kevin located the conflict, not in differing understandings of God by the Salvationists, but in how the Salvationists managed these two programs.

> The Salvationist view of religion is still the same for all Salvation Army. It's just that problem over there is that you have a different Major running the program. Just to give you an example, he believes in one God and one God only, and there's only one to way find God, and if you can't find that God that way, then there is something wrong with *you*.

Kevin believed that only by working the steps of A.A. would the men he encountered come to appreciate God as defined by the Salvationists.

> See, what it is in A.A. is that we all grow to understand God as we work those steps. But the guys I get are all brand new in the *waaalk*

of the sobriety, so you are not ready to say that guy on the wall is God, you're ready to say you've got to look inside your heart and see what he thinks he can believe in. And that's where the steps help.

Kevin believes that by forcing a definition of God on the men new to the program, "all you get is more anger and resentment." Thus, Kevin explained, "I don't teach that, I don't believe that." While forced participation in meetings and a limited definition of God are contrary to A.A. principles, the organizational moral rhetoric of charitable action and A.A. principles fostered an ideology demanding that the poor take personal responsibility for their plight.

*Drunkenness: "That Big Hole Inside of Myself"*
Both Dave and Kevin experienced A.A.-inspired self work as their salvation. Dave, the resident manager at the center, explained his experience when he first arrived as a homeless person with a substance abuse problem:

> I, back then, when I was here as a client, I shortly after, I was one of the ones that did get *hired*. I never volunteered though, okay, but I got hired as a cook, that was my trade and I cooked in the kitchen, but I was still, still using, even then. And I, in fact, I used to smoke cocaine in the bathroom in the kitchen. Okay, I have been thrown out of here for being drunk before, you know, and finally I just, you know, just got tired of living that way, and I could kind of see that big hole inside of myself. You know, and I went into a recovery program, you know, that's what I did. But whenever I look at the new clients coming in, that's, I see myself, I see myself. You know, I see myself a couple of years ago. I see the hopelessness that I *felt* and the having all the problems and none of the answers, you know, that type of thing. And, in fact, I think all of us would try to let the clients know that there *are* some answers, that it's going to require some *work* on their part, but there are some answers, you know. And our success rate I think is pretty good too. A lot of people leave here.

In recounting his salvation, Dave used A.A. imagery—"that big hole inside of myself," "I see myself," "having all the problems and none of the answers"—to tell the story of his own regeneration through working the program of A.A. and The Salvation Army. Similarly, Kevin maintained his commitment to the ARC, where he had taught the "first days of recovery" program for more than a year and a half. In his words,

> That involves me, teaching a class once a week where we basically
> expose them to the dangers and the problems that drugs and alcohol
> causes in our lives. And then, from that, I try to tailor it so maybe
> they can hopefully look at themselves as maybe having a problem,
> rather than other people having a problem.

Dave's roles as resident manager and counselor complicated his enforcement of the no-drinking policy. In his words, "If we smell alcohol on their breath, while they are living here, they will be *terminated* [spoken gravely] from the program." If a drunken individual came to Dave's office for counseling, however, he suggested that they leave the property for the time being. Dave acknowledged this role-playing as "almost contradictory," by explaining the wearing of a "different hat" and being "more of an enforcer" in his role as resident manager.

Dave's and Kevin's role-playing illustrated the significance of Alcoholics Anonymous ideology to the working arrangements at The Salvation Army. As drug and alcohol counselors attending college for certification in substance abuse counseling, each played an important role in managing the moral rhetoric of charitable action presented to others coming to The Salvation Army. Dave and Kevin interviewed the incoming In-house members of The Salvation Army and oversaw the Alternative Sentencing Program. Both men, when employed in the kitchen, supervised the In-house volunteers, the ASP volunteers, and "outside" volunteers such as myself (although such volunteers were rare).

Both Dave and Kevin worked into positions of authority at The Salvation Army; their skills as substance abuse counselors appeared to be central to this success. Kevin explained their counseling technique to me:

> If a guy has an addiction problem, Dave and I will sit him down and
> see how he feels, and if he says I, I, which is common, I don't like
> A.A., or I don't like people telling me I'm drunk, then we will try to
> get to the real reason, whether he has some kind of *feeaar* or resent-
> ment, and then we will suggest another meeting, or we will suggest
> something more. But it's not like you are going to have to go or you
> are not going to be able to stay.

At this center, in keeping with A.A. principles, the residents choose
whether or not to attend A.A. meetings.

Kevin's experience at the Salvationist Adult Rehabilitation Center illustrated how The Salvation Army's working arrangements differed by
location. At the ARC the staff required residents to attend three A.A.
meetings a week. The ARC's Major, using a program of "Christian
Concepts," taught that A.A.'s Twelve Steps originate in the Bible. Kevin
expressed difficulty with the Major's strict Christian definition of the
Higher Power as God, saying, "That's where the Major and I get into a
hassle."[8] Kevin told me that if someone wanted their Higher Power to
be a doorknob, that was fine with him. He understood this difference to
reveal the importance of actual participation in A.A. meetings such as
he had done to understand the meaning of the steps.

> Basically what it boils down to is that if you're not an alcoholic you
> don't understand that way of thinking, and the Major [at the ARC] is
> not an alcoholic. Whereas Howard [a Salvationist at the Shelter Ser-
> vices Center] came down this road of addiction so he understands it.
> And I think this is where the problem lies.

Nonetheless, Kevin felt saddened at leaving the ARC: "But they are
wonderful people. . . . That's why I will have a hard time when I do
switch my schedule."

*Work Ethic: "To Take Care of Business"*

As formerly homeless men converted to Salvation Army civilian employees, Kevin and Dave learned, and now administer, the Salvationist

ideology. While not uncritical of The Salvation Army, both men generally supported its work ethic. They saw The Salvation Army as a support institution within which they could practice their dedication to
both the homeless and A.A. Kevin humbly explained to me that when
he transferred to The Salvation Army, it was the first time he had lived
outside of an institution in many years:

> But I have lived on my own since I came here in November. It's the
> first time in seven years I have ever lived on my own. I have always
> been in jails or some kind of institution, so it's a *big* step for me. I
> love being around the people here, because it reminds me of where I
> have come from, and I am very comfortable here. It's, as far as a ca-
> reer, I don't know.

Both Kevin and Dave found a niche at The Salvation Army as "civilians" engaged in the work of drug and alcohol rehabilitation. The
working arrangements of the Shelter Services Center allowed both men
to practice, although not without certain tensions, A.A.'s Twelfth Step:
"Having had a spiritual awakening as the result of these steps, we tried
to carry this message to alcoholics, and to practice these principles in all
our affairs" (Alcoholics Anonymous 1970: 28). Their stories revealed
the convergence of a Salvationist work ethic with the rhetoric of Alcoholics Anonymous. Kevin explained, stuttering a bit in his earnestness,
that neither he nor Dave intended to become Salvationists: "We are just
*employees*, that's all we are called, we're employees. And, and for guys
like me and Dave, Howard allows us to teach the Twelve Steps and
that's what we do." Both men intended, however, to advance their education, and both favored the expansion of The Salvation Army Shelter
Services Center. Kevin planned to become a certified alcohol and drug
counselor (CADAC), and Dave intended to take over more of the counseling and do less of the other intake procedures. Kevin considered
leaving The Salvation Army eventually: "I would like to stay with them
[The Salvation Army], but the pay, I won't be able to afford a family, I
won't be able to afford to live, but for me today and the next few years,

I am fine where I am at." Both Kevin and Dave spoke of their hope that Sacramento would house a Salvationist Harbor Light Center, a rehabilitation center that allows persons with drug and alcohol problems to live on site for six months, thus granting them more time to reassemble self-sufficient lives.

The A.A. rhetoric of moral reform converged easily with the Salvationist work ethic rhetoric. For example, from Monday through Friday the In-house must be off the property from 8:00 A.M. to 4:00 P.M., as the resident manager explained, using an A.A. expression, "to take care of business." The In-house were encouraged not to volunteer in the kitchen, as this allowed them to stay on the property, unless they convinced the staff that without having something to keep them occupied they would use drugs or drink. Volunteering all the time in the kitchen constituted "putting all their eggs in one basket," as Dave explained, using yet another expression common to A.A.

Dave explained the kinds of people who volunteered at The Salvation Army.

> Basically, we get four groups of people. We get people who are sent by the courts, to do community service hours, of course we get In-house clients. We get groups, meaning church groups, certain civic groups that want to come and volunteer . . . usually it's, like, a periodic thing. Like we have groups that come every Fourth of July.

Dave reinforced my own experience: very few people fit the fourth category of volunteers, those, like me, who are unaffiliated with any group. We and the church-based volunteers received the least amount of disciplining. The In-house and ASP volunteers both experienced imposed discipline.

Kevin explained to me that the kitchen staff tried to avoid treating the volunteers too authoritatively, yet those volunteers who were uncooperative received explicit instructions.

> Well, first what I try to do with them, if they are off the street, this is a kitchen, are you aware? What would you like to do? I want to

see where their perception is at. You know we get some real big, bulky guys in here, and usually the attitude cases that don't want to be here, and we will put them out in the freezer lifting boxes so they can work off some of their stress and their frustration, and then they feel a little better. And then you get the guy who is like me, that did, did drugs all his life and is used to doing dishes, so we will put them on the dishwasher [we both laugh warmly]. It is very seldom that we point at a guy and say, you are going to do this [mocking an authoritative tone].

Kevin clearly enjoyed the volunteers he met in the kitchen; the volunteers clearly liked him. He told me, thoughtfully, "Volunteers are interesting."

At The Salvation Army the volunteer role in the kitchen could bring status and material benefits for the In-house volunteers, yet these benefits could not be taken for granted. Dave explained:

Also, there are certain little perks of going in there and volunteering. You know, the food, you get quantity and quality, the quantity especially is unlimited if you are a volunteer [laughing] and at least among the clients that are living in In-house there is a certain *status* kind of thing that is attached to, you know, being a volunteer, plus rumor has it that if you volunteer in the kitchen, you get hired eventually [spoken grudgingly], so that helps, although we let them know that isn't necessarily the case.

The volunteers at The Salvation Army, especially the In-house, worked under rules that imposed boundaries on their autonomy.

As Dave explained to me, "We got major rules and we got minor rules. The major ones are the *real* important ones. Those are the ones that somebody could get terminated for." The major rules included no drinking at all while living In-house, no drugs on the property, no violence, no stealing, and no disregarding the eleven o'clock curfew. With regard to the curfew, if an individual disobeyed this rule the first night he lost his bed. If someone violated the curfew later on, the staff wrote the transgression down; a second violation led the staff to ask the person to vacate. The In-house could receive passes ahead of time for "taking care of business." The minor rules included taking a shower, keeping beds made, no smoking inside, and no food in the dorms. Kevin stated, "*Violence* is kind of like the central issue of this," meaning that the other major rule violations could lead to violence.

We don't take, I mean, if somebody just pushes somebody, I don't care how minor it is, *it's major.* We don't have problems here, we don't have fights here. Because we cut it off before it ever gets started, and threats, they make a threat of violence, even something like, why don't you come off the property and we'll handle it [mimicking a swaggering tone], you know, that's a threat. Okay. And they are gone. We are not going to play that. *Theft*, and the reason we enforce that so much is because it could lead to violence.

Dave and Kevin illustrate how at The Salvation Army the social category "homeless" began to fray at the edges with the selective incorporation of the client population into volunteers and then sometimes into staff. Homeless people who demonstrated their willingness and capability to assume a disciplined work ethic might earn privileges and prestige not granted to the vast majority of people who came to Loaves & Fishes for their daily meals. Implicit in The Salvation Army moral rhetoric of charitable action and A.A. ideology lay the belief that, although life may have treated you unfairly, only you could take steps to address this misfortune. Thus the Salvationist ideology and the A.A. program converged in a moral rhetoric of charitable action wherein the homeless faced expectations to work toward their own salvation through self-disciplining.

## Organizing Holiday Giving

As at Loaves & Fishes the holidays demonstrated moral ideals in the site-specific vision of charity while simultaneously challenging the mundane working arrangements of the organization. Two important differences underlay this comparison, however. First, Loaves & Fishes officially celebrated more holidays and consequently brought in more holiday volunteers, and second, kitchen workers at The Salvation Army expressed more ambivalence toward the holidays and the holiday volunteers than did the staff at Loaves & Fishes.

*Holiday Donations: "Sharing Is Caring"*

Both Loaves & Fishes and The Salvation Army depended on the Thanksgiving and Christmas holidays for the bulk of their donations. The Salvation Army, however, relied also on government contracts. For example, during this time the Sacramento County Department of Human Services awarded the Shelter Services Center the contract to operate the city's overflow shelter for homeless people unable to find food and shelter elsewhere. In 1994–95, the contract paid The Salvation Army approximately $70,000 per month (Guyettte 1994: 13). The Salvation Army nationally benefited greatly from private donations; in 1993 it reported more private donations than any other charity nationally (*Sacramento Bee* 1994: A18). But in that year The Salvation Army, along with Loaves & Fishes, found that its monetary donations fell significantly, by approximately $10,000 (Hayward 1993: B1).

During the Thanksgiving–Christmas holiday season, The Salvation Army sent its workers to storefronts to ring bells and solicit donations in their kettles, proclaiming the Salvationist holiday motto: "Sharing Is Caring."[9] In 1993 The Salvation Army took out newspaper ads with the headline "Hunger Hurts," and Pacific Gas and Electric included a filler in its customers' monthly bills soliciting donations to help The Salvation Army with energy emergencies, with the promise to provide matching donations up to $2 million. In the same holiday season a Salvation Army office near Sacramento was robbed of nearly $5,000 in kettle collections. The *Sacramento Bee* and local television stations covered the loss; a month later close to half the amount had been recovered in donations.

Thanksgiving at The Salvation Army received local television coverage with members of the local NBA team, the Sacramento Kings, helping to serve the meal. The *Bee* wrote of the Thanksgiving meal:

Tradition took a holiday on Thanksgiving Day in Sacramento, where Kings waited on paupers at The Salvation Army. . . . But the holiday spirit was just as joyful at the compound in a warehouse district on North B Street. Several players from the Sacramento Kings shuttled coffee and desserts to tables where guests clapped between bites to thunderous hymns sung by The Salvation Army's 15-member gospel choir. (Dávila 1993: B1)

Nonetheless, news coverage of Loaves & Fishes exceeded that of The Salvation Army during the holidays, as well as during the rest of the year.

### *Thanksgiving 1993: "Aware of God's Blessings"*

Thanksgiving at The Salvation Army demonstrated the ideological importance of practicing evangelical social welfare work for the Salvationists. Salvationists joined with the Catholic Workers in emphasizing the importance of individuals transcending selfishness and materialism to give to others. For example, the bimonthly *War Cry* ran a story on Thanksgiving in a November and a December 1993 issue. One story, "The Habit of Thanksgiving," argued that giving thanks should be part of religious practice: "The road to thankfulness lies in your own soul. When you are thankful, you are aware of God's blessings" (Brinson 1993: 6). The other story, written by Major Mrs. Betty Israel, described how the author and her husband had prepared a Thanksgiving meal for locals in the Virgin Islands and received a gift of $100 from an unknown man for the provision of the meal. Major Mrs. Israel wrote, "To meet someone just once, at just the right time, with just what we needed, is something of a mystery. Unless, of course, it was a miracle" (1993: 21).

Both articles did not celebrate Thanksgiving as a national holiday but rather pointed to the importance of giving thanks and seeing Christ in all Christians. While the Christian themes of seeing God in the poor and the worth of transcending selfishness linked the holiday visions of charity at The Salvation Army and Loaves & Fishes, the working arrangements of the holiday reflected differences in their visions of charity.

By 9:30 on Thanksgiving morning volunteers were slicing turkey and folding plastic silverware into dinner-size napkins. The dining room contained twenty-five tables, each set for five. In contrast to the Loaves & Fishes staff, The Salvation Army staff did not sign in volunteers, or limit their numbers. Furthermore, the front desk staff asked volunteers to sign a liability release form as they entered the building. The kitchen staff told all the volunteers to put on hairnets, to which some volunteers responded with obvious discomfort while others good-naturedly laughed. As a group the volunteers came more frequently with family members; The Salvation Army, in contrast to Loaves & Fishes, permitted children to volunteer. Unlike other days at The Salvation Army, most of the volunteers were white. One young man served the meal while carrying a toddler on his hip. A white boy of perhaps seven helped a tall black In-house man serve the dessert by messily squirting whipped cream on top of the pie. In addition to these volunteers, some members of the Sacramento Kings, sporting their NBA jackets, helped to serve the meal.

The Thanksgiving meal consisted of precooked turkey (meat that was not sliced was pulled off the bones by about a dozen volunteers, most of them men), instant mashed potatoes (made just before serving), frozen corn, gravy (made in one batch in the large soup vat), and pumpkin pie (mostly store bought). Servers brought the meal to the diners and ensured that each place setting included a Styrofoam bowl of green salad with ranch dressing. While some volunteers brought the meal to the tables after going through one of several lines where the food was dished up, others circulated with coffee and fruit punch.

The staff wore white chef's outfits and paper chef's hats, thus marking the formality of the holiday. Raul, in charge of the kitchen, directed formerly In-house civilian employees in the supervision of the holiday volunteers. Major John stood by the door to the dining room watching the proceedings and giving orders to Raul.

I joined the volunteers folding napkins around the plastic knives, spoons, and forks for stacking onto baking sheets. Tina, an African-American In-house volunteer of approximately my age, and I became authorities as people turned to us because of our apparent knowledge of The Salvation Army and the staff. Later Raul officially put me in charge of folding the nearly fifteen hundred place settings. As we worked I talked with a white, recent college graduate who followed her boyfriend to Sacramento from the East Coast. She wore jeans and a mustard-colored wool blazer; he wore a red fraternity jacket. She told me that she had called The Salvation Army about a month ago because, with no family in the area, she wanted to do something like this for the holiday. She seemed surprised to learn that The Salvation Army serves meals daily; I explained that she could volunteer at The Salvation Army or Loaves & Fishes at other times, but she showed little interest. She told me that what she saw on this busy, chaotic day was "great." Her boyfriend came over, and they joked around as they folded the napkins. She told him that she was hungry and that she wished they had eaten breakfast. As the serving approached, she told me that it looked like there were plenty of volunteers and that they were going to leave.

Behind us, at the food prep table, stood three middle-aged women, one black and two white, all wearing slacks and blouses. They were alone for the holidays and volunteered because they thought those with families might not have the time. They discussed their health, and one shared her pain over her disrupted family relations. As we all worked madly folding silverware, a young black man dressed in maroon sweat pants over jeans and a red and black turban, took orders for coffee or fruit punch from the volunteers.

As we neared serving time, a white Salvationist couple from the Core office (The Salvation Army headquarters in Sacramento), perhaps in their early fifties, came into the kitchen in their dress uniforms. The woman ate a piece of turkey off of a plate and as she did so joked that now the rest of us, meaning the volunteers packing the kitchen, would know that they could do this too.

At about 11:15 Tina left to join the choir setting up in the dining room, and I organized putting away the silverware so that the volunteers could gather in the dining room for a talk. The staff and the In-house mostly remained in the kitchen while the volunteers gathered. Major John spoke, standing atop an overturned milk crate so that he could be heard by the approximately one hundred volunteers crowding the dining room (usually only from five to ten volunteers assisted the staff). He thanked us for coming to The Salvation Army. He told us that some of the people coming to the meal would express more grati-tude than others and that we should extend an even bigger smile to those who express less gratitude so that they might leave warmed.

Next Major John organized the dividing up of duties. First he asked for fifteen volunteers to work in the kitchen, indicating that perhaps "the far corner," where I and other In-house committed volunteers stood, might be best for this duty. Next he asked for eight volunteers for the serving line in the dining room and eight for the line in the outside courtyard. Most of the volunteers wanted to work as servers; some worked bringing plates, some juice and coffee, and some cleared and re-set the tables. Then the Salvationist said, "Thank *you*," as he expressed his gratitude to the volunteers for making the meal possible. He sug-gested that we pray, and several young white men with crewcuts said loudly, "Yes, let's pray."

We served no more than six hundred people; even fewer came to the winter overflow meal. Many men came in by themselves and ate bowed over their plates, some asking for foil to take their leftovers with them. Unlike at Loaves & Fishes, the staff permitted giving out aluminum foil for this purpose. Volunteers and staff threw away the aluminum turkey pans, however, rather than let the homeless take them for their camp-fires and makeshift kitchens as at Loaves & Fishes.

The dining room was a blur of motion, with the servers moving around the tables, bringing plates and drinks. The volunteers hurried from table to table asking if the diners would like more punch or coffee. A white woman in her thirties, dressed in jeans and a sweater, leaned over a table of black and white children. She stopped them from eating and told them to bow their heads and say Grace. Later she chided a black Burns security guard to wait his turn in line for food.

In the small room off the dining room where the visiting Salvationists usually eat, the choir sang gospel songs. Some of the volunteers
gathered, waving their hands in praise of God and clapping and swaying
to the music. A black woman in her twenties, dressed warmly, left her
place at a table and edged closer to the singers. Wiping tears from her
cheeks, she edged even closer, so that she was practically among them as
she sang and listened, her eyes closed.

Serving was nearly finished by 2:00, but food kept trickling in. Most
of the deliveries, especially later in the day, were by men. Some
brought more turkeys; one man and his son brought eight spaghetti
squash in a large Igloo cooler; a staff member told me that they would
probably be thrown out. Yet this man was thanked as warmly as all the
others and wished a happy holiday. The entire back of the kitchen was
stacked with canned and boxed goods. Later I learned that the staff put
in frozen storage an estimated four hundred cooked turkeys.

Before leaving, I helped to make a green salad for the In-house dinner. I told Danny, a cook, who was hurriedly cleaning, that I felt badly
leaving him when things were so crazy, but he replied, "What do you
mean? It's always crazy around here."

### Ambivalence and Charity

The measured empathy of the Loaves & Fishes staff toward the holiday
volunteers contrasted with the more obvious ambivalence of The Salvation Army staff members. Dave described the holiday volunteers as
parts of "mega-groups": "Like on certain holidays, certain churches and
all will come, Thanksgiving is a big one, we have mega-groups that
come during that time, that's in fact, so many that we hardly know what
to do with the volunteers." Kevin, a cook at the time, explained to me
that the holiday volunteers, in his estimation, have different motives
than many of the other volunteers: "On the holidays is when we get
people in with the stories of, you know, my brother was helped out by
The Salvation Army in such and such city and state, so every year in his
honor I come and help out." Kevin noted the particularity of some of

these volunteers in an unusually mocking tone: "You know, because a lot of people, like you saw at Christmastime, they want to 'serve,' that's all, 'serve,' but some people just like to do nothing but prep."

Kevin's assessment of the holiday volunteers reflected the ambivalence of many of the other kitchen staff. In an interview Kevin told me quietly and without much anger, but some sadness, "See that's the kind of volunteering that I have little problem with, it's like, I want to be seen giving a plate of food to a homeless person, and it's like, that's not what it's about." Yet Kevin does not dismiss the holiday volunteers outright: "Yeah, I was kind of glad to be excused from that day, because I don't understand enough yet, because I don't really understand how they do all that, and that's fine, I mean, I am sure that serves a purpose."

## DOING SALVATIONISM IN THE KITCHEN

In-house residents, ASP volunteers, and occasional "outside" volunteers join the kitchen staff (who are mostly formerly In-house) in doing Salvationism. Volunteers learned both the mundane working arrangements of the Shelter Services Center and the moral rhetoric of charitable action of Salvationism through their adherence to the kitchen rules. Both the A.A. rhetoric of moral reform and the Salvationist work ethic rhetoric emphasized redemption through adherence to rules. As the environmental psychologists Denis Wood and Robert J. Beck (1994: xvi) found, the rules governing the use of space may be more "explicit and easy to collect" than the behaviors "implicit" in the use of particular space. Thus their "environmental ethology" allows us to describe how rules operate in action rather than as "aspects of personality" (3).

Volunteers at The Salvation Army vied for parking in the busy front parking lot, or they parked behind the Social Services Complex and requested an escort past the dorms and sitting rooms to the kitchen. Rather than use staff as security guards, a function served by the Loaves & Fishes street monitors, The Salvation Army employed security guards from a private security company. These Burns security guards wore uniforms similar to those worn by the police. Two guards often stood in the front parking lot, talking among themselves and greeting new arrivals. The use of Burns security guards to patrol the fenced-in property underscored how the Salvationists used the built environment to control its morally suspect clients. While by no means a prison, aspects of the constructed environment at The Salvation Army mimicked the disciplining with its attention to timetables, gestures, surveillance, and a precise system of commands described by Michel Foucault in his classic work, *Discipline and Punish* (1979).

Yet the guards and staff appeared to enjoy each others' company. The guards ate meals with the staff and residents, and many chose to be positioned at The Salvation Army.

> The Latino Burns guard entered the dining room and told us that he was applying for a job elsewhere. When [an ASP volunteer] asked, he told us that he earned *cinco* [Spanish for "five"] an hour and that at the factory he would earn more but that he had worked at The Salvation Army a year ago and chose to return because he liked this place.

The guards offered direction to newcomers and explained to kitchen volunteers that they must be buzzed into the kitchen by a front desk worker.

Unlike volunteers at Loaves & Fishes, kitchen volunteers at The Salvation Army were required to sign in. Furthermore, they had to abide by the requirement to wear a hairnet or paper chef's hat. Whereas volunteers at Loaves & Fishes typically introduced themselves with both first and last names, volunteers and staff in The Salvation army kitchen usually just used first names. Kitchen management, however, were sometimes addressed by their last names only, as in the case of the resident manager. As Dave told me, "I use Longmuir [in referring to the resident manager in the kitchen], rather than Dave, in keeping with the other workers' usage of last name in place of a first name. Some workers refer to him as Longmuir, others as Dave Longmuir." The Burns security guards, the sign-in sheet, and the use of last names for superiors underscored the local hierarchy at the Shelter Services Center.

The staff planned the menu without the contribution of the volunteers. Rather than highlight individual choice, as at Loaves & Fishes, the staff emphasized adherence to kitchen rules. The cooks more often used recipes, especially when baking.[10] Rather than ask the volunteers how they would like to cook the meal, the staff most frequently gave them orders.

Whereas at Loaves & Fishes staff and volunteers stepped just outside to smoke, the Shelter Services Center intended to ban smoking on the property. Dave explained that the ban on smoking enforced the sobriety doctrine of the Salvationists.

> Committees and stuff, that we meet statewide, like, for instance, our administrator here, Howard, is involved in the drug and alcohol roundtables. It's like a brainstorming meeting, they have about once every three months, to kind of set policy on drug and alcohol programs, and this is Salvation Army–wide, including the ARC and everything else, although it does tend to affect us, because the ARC right now has a no smoking policy, no smoking on the property, so since they are doing it, we are saying, well, okay, we will do it too.
> Right, right. That's kind of what we are working towards right now.

The proposed ban on smoking at the Shelter Services Center further inscribed the self-disciplining and sobriety of Salvationist moral rhetoric into the everyday work environment of the kitchen workers.

In spite of the strict rules, a feeling of camaraderie and fun often dominated the Shelter Services Center. Unlike the relative quiet of Loaves & Fishes, The Salvation Army kitchen often rang with the sound of music. After one morning especially memorable for the high spirits of the kitchen workers, I recorded in my fieldnotes, "We worked to music; the radio now fixed with a thermometer as an antenna. We listened to the Beatles, and some of the men joined in with 'I think I'm going to be sad.' " On another day, Rod Stewart singing "Have I Told

You Lately How Much I Love You?" elicited catcalls from some of the men. The staff required that the radio be turned off before the front office staff entered the kitchen for lunch. Also, the radio was turned down or off when the resident manager came to the kitchen on business. The music offered a reward for hard work, but its management also underscored the required respect for front-office workers.

The working arrangements of the Shelter Services Center grounded the moral rhetoric in practice. Abstinence, discipline, and self-help were encouraged with the no smoking and drinking policy, the strict work schedule, and rewards for hard work. Music and camaraderie appeared to ease the rigidity of these rules.

## COMPARING WORKING ARRANGEMENTS OF CHARITABLE ACTION: LOAVES & FISHES AND THE SALVATION ARMY

In response to my question about whether The Salvation Army had any sort of working relationship with Loaves & Fishes, Dave explained,

> The Salvation Army, *weee're* the big kids on the block. We have more funding sources than most of the other service providers in Sacramento. *Because* of that I, at least *I*, feel like there is a lot of resentment from the other facilities. Now, I won't say that we don't work together 'cause we do. On a daily basis, not only Loaves & Fishes but all the other organizations. But I feel like there is an underlying resentment towards *us*.

After he delineated the programs on which the The Salvation Army and Loaves & Fishes collaborated, such as Mercy Clinic, Friendship Park, and, with the most admiration, the Jail Visitation Program, Dave went on to thoughtfully criticize Loaves & Fishes' lack of rules for its guests.

> They don't seem to give the clients a whole lot of guidelines, you know, they just kind of let them do their own thing. And we tend to give a little more structure, I think. I don't know, we're, you know, there's a fine line between helping somebody and enabling somebody.

You know, and I think that's the bottom line, we kind of see things a little bit differently on that issue. But we work with them a lot.

Although Dave's view was that Loaves & Fishes' practices enabled the homeless, Chris Delany had a different view, which I heard her explain at a spiritual retreat: "We are just trying to help people survive from day to day." In response to The Salvation Army's plan to provide a one-year rehabilitation program, Chris declared that they needed to "get real" in their expectations about homeless people. On another occasion the volunteer coordinator explained that many of the Loaves & Fishes guests do not like to go to The Salvation Army. In her words, "Our guests tell us that it reminds them of prison." In the same orientation session, however, she acknowledged nonetheless that the "pecking order" at Loaves & Fishes served best those with children. "We don't offer as good services to the men," she said.

As we shall see, many of the men who embraced Salvationism endorsed its rigid hierarchy and portrayed Loaves & Fishes as a good organization for its treatment of women and children and the elderly but inappropriate for men. These same men often described the minimal rules at Loaves & Fishes as morally bankrupt. Dave, the resident manager, concurred; he criticized Loaves & Fishes' lack of rules for its guests but suggested to me that it provided good services for women and children and the elderly. I recorded in my fieldnotes a story told to some volunteers by the kitchen manager that illustrates how some men perceived the Loaves & Fishes dining room as a feminine setting.

> Dorcy [the kitchen manager] told the volunteers of a homeless man who had just died, for whom Loaves & Fishes staff had provided identification. This 84-year-old man had lived on the streets, poor, since the depression. . . . She said that he wouldn't take handouts from women and that perhaps only once had come into the dining room. He ate out of dumpsters, and sometimes the staff would send

a man outside to serve him milk and bananas, a favorite of his. Other times, they would drop $1 bills near him.

The muscular Christianity practiced at The Salvation Army Shelter Services Center provided assistance in a manner much less troubling to a traditional masculine identity. It appeared that for many of the Salvationist clients, Booth's (1890: 106) words still rang true: "This is not charity; it is work for the workers, help for those who cannot help themselves."

At The Salvation Army staff (often formerly In-house homeless) and volunteers (often serving community service hours) worked together to feed the urban poor. Within The Salvation Army vision, all volunteers and staff adhered to a work ethic that emphasized the importance of discipline to self-transformation. Within this predominantly male, working-class setting, many of the men battled alcohol and drug problems; the principles of Alcoholic Anonymous and The Salvation Army structured a moral rhetoric of charitable action wherein individuals struggle to help others out of poverty and despair through hard work and service to others. The Salvation Army's militaristic structure was at odds with the personalist hospitality valued at Loaves & Fishes, and even with the antibureaucratic principles of A.A.[11]

Workers at The Salvation Army and Loaves & Fishes used the constructed environment to communicate symbolic messages about the moral worth of the poor, with very real consequences for the daily lives of charity recipients. Symbolic boundaries may be used to cultivate inequality (Lamont and Fournier 1992), but boundaries can also be constructed so as to challenge inequality, even within the parameters of an unequal relationship. That is, at The Salvation Army boundary maintenance clearly underscored the limited entitlements of the poor. Extensive rules, surveillance, and curtailed physical freedoms upheld a conservative vision of the poor as needing discipline. At Loaves & Fishes, in contrast, a landscaped courtyard, flowers on the dining tables, and campaigns for the poor's right to camp on public land constructed a progressive vision of the poor as entitled, rights-bearing members of our society.

Just as individuals use art in their homes to communicate taste and beauty allegiances (Halle 1993), students use objects to ease their transition from home to college (Silver 1996), and workers use keys and calendars to sculpt boundaries around work and home (Nippert-Eng 1995, 1996), charity workers used the built environment to uphold particular visions of charity. These territories of the self, with vastly different aesthetics, conveyed meaningful moral and social messages about the homeless self.

The working arrangements of Loaves & Fishes and The Salvation Army lend support to Arthur Stinchcombe's (1965) thesis that the structural arrangements of an organization at its founding may remain fairly stable over time. That is, their working arrangements remained fairly faithful to those established by their intellectual founders. Yet the working arrangements of the Shelter Services Center seemed more fateful for The Salvation Army volunteers than were the Loaves & Fishes' working arrangements for the routine volunteers. At The Salvation Army the institutional arrangements for volunteer experience were more trenchant; they often determined whether or not the volunteer would fulfill a court-ordered service or whether a homeless volunteer would find work and even shelter.

## PART TWO

# *Constructing Moral Selves*

·  ·  ·  ·  ·

Identifying how moral rhetorics of charitable action functioned at Loaves & Fishes and The Salvation Army provides one way to understand the differences between these two charitable agencies. The following chapters explore how volunteers and staff committed to the vision of charity at Loaves & Fishes and The Salvation Army used and experienced these organizational rhetorics as they engaged in moral selving. An analysis of these two types of moral selving lends meaningful insights into the relationship between volunteers and the ideological contexts of the two organizations.

These chapters draw attention to those volunteers who *felt* ideologically committed to the organization's moral rhetoric. The self-conceptualizations of these volunteers revealed them to be sentient moral actors. The phenomenology of the volunteer moral experience allows us to understand how individuals experienced the working arrangements. More specifically, how did the situationally available rhetorics of charitable action allow the volunteer to experience and talk about volunteer work as a moral practice?

Moral selving is best traced through the experience of the committed volunteers at both Loaves & Fishes and The Salvation Army. The routine volunteers (either religiously or nonreligiously based) at Loaves & Fishes and the drafted volunteers (both In-house residents and ASP volunteers) at The Salvation Army committed themselves to self-betterment through adherence to the site-specific moral rhetoric of charitable action.

An examination of experience turns our attention to emotions. The visions of charity found at Loaves & Fishes and The Salvation Army entailed specifiable emotional expectations, guided by the framing rules and feeling rules (Hochschild 1979) that governed the moral selving of the routine and drafted volunteers. Framing rules constitute the guidelines by which we make sense of a situation, whereas feeling rules entail guidelines that explicate the appropriateness of an emotional response.

Hochschild (1979: 566) holds that "rules for managing feelings are implicit in any ideological stance; they are 'the bottom side' of ideology." Thus, although The Salvation Army and Loaves & Fishes both met the same organizational goal by serving the homeless food, the framing rules of personalist hospitality and Salvationism and the feeling rules implicit in these moral rhetorics reflected how the two different visions of charity entailed dramatically different moral selving.

The work of moral selving is deeply emotional but not only about experiencing or managing emotions. Rather the focus is on creating a better person. This directs the individual not simply inward but outward; at Loaves & Fishes the volunteers strive to treat the poor with more compassion and love, whereas at The Salvation Army volunteers and workers alike labor to be more responsible toward others. What we see in both settings is what the anthropologist Catherine A. Lutz (1988: 213) calls "the tandem development of emotional and moral maturity." While granting the importance of emotion rules and culture in determining emotions, Lutz (1988: 213) argues that emotions "are first, in a sense, about values and commitments felt." Volunteering in programs for the poor requires the individual to engage personally with both the ethical and emotional consequences of political ideologies about the right ordering of social welfare.

Moments of tension with the moral rhetorics illuminated their power in guiding volunteers' moral selving. Volunteers in each setting entered fairly easily into the practice of charitable action with relative strangers to build moral communities but in time came to struggle with particular aspects of the working arrangements. This exploration of the volunteers' affinity with the moral rhetorics and the decision to struggle with their most troubling aspects takes us closer to answering the following questions: How are particular volunteer selves experienced? What does it mean to be a volunteer within these contrasting moral rhetorics of charitable action? How is the volunteer's moral self constructed? What are the possible complications and contradictions in sculpting a moral self in each setting?

# CHAPTER 3

# Moral Selving within
# Personalist Hospitality
## *Gratitude, Commitment, and Witnessing*

Moral selving as an analytic category developed out of my interviews with volunteers who spoke of their commitment to work in ethical terms. These volunteers revealed that they are dedicated to creating themselves as more virtuous, and often spiritual, persons. They wedded reflection to active participation in the social world. Not only did they feel welcomed by the personalist hospitality at Loaves & Fishes, many felt steadfastly dedicated to its (re)creation. Thus they engaged not only with the urban poor but also with their own moral understanding of the poor. This engagement often led them to strive to reconcile precepts of personalist hospitality with their efforts at self-betterment.

As we saw in chapter 1, the Catholic Workers' practice of personalist hospitality emphasizes the importance of individual responsibility in the provision of charity. In the Christian interpretation of personalist hospitality, the guests are seen as the Ambassadors of God. Personalism directs the Catholic Workers to nonbureaucratic, respectful treatment of their guests, which posed an emotional dilemma for many volunteers, who found it difficult to treat all guests as the deserving poor. The moral rhetoric of charitable action at Loaves & Fishes mediated between the radical Catholic Worker philosophy and the emotional dilemmas of middle-class, ecumenically and politically diverse volunteers. Nevertheless, the Catholic Worker roots endured as the staff emphasized dignity, respect, and choice to both the guests and the volunteers.

Here I show how the organizational rhetoric of charitable action at Loaves & Fishes guided the volunteers' moral selving, although seldom perfectly. For example, the volunteers adhered to the Catholic Worker practice of calling those being served "guests." When interviewed, however, many volunteers revealed their difficulty and discomfort in accepting the Catholic Worker understanding of all the guests as Ambassadors of God deserving of charitable love. The routine volunteers' struggle to align their emotions with the feeling rules of personalist hospitality illustrated how powerfully the Loaves & Fishes vision of charity shaped their moral selving. Their choice to wrestle with charitable love, rather than dismiss it or cynically adhere to it, demonstrated the embeddedness of volunteers' moral selving within personalist hospitality.

*Gratitude, commitment,* and *witnessing* emerged as key themes in the routine volunteers' accounts of their experiences at Loaves & Fishes. Although the volunteers did not always use this precise language (they more frequently used the words *gratitude* and *commitment* but rarely used *witnessing*), they certainly spoke often of and about these themes. None talked of moral selving per se, but, as this chapter explores, the committed volunteers' experience of work at Loaves & Fishes was laden with a concern for moral self-betterment. Some seemed to be more driven than others to volunteer out of a commitment to self-betterment, but for all the work intersected with concerns about helping others and bettering their selves.[1]

Moral selving both mirrored and shaped the volunteers' connection to a wider community. Some volunteers encouraged others to participate in their volunteer work; some hoped to model caring for others for their children; others volunteered out of acknowledgment of their own economic vulnerability and gratitude for the good fortune of having homes. *Gratitude* for economic security, *commitment* to the work of feeding the urban poor, and *witnessing* the sacred in one's life emerged as interconnected themes, resonant with personalist hospitality but concurrently a product of the volunteers' moral selving.

## DOING PERSONALIST HOSPITALITY: STORIES OF MORAL SELVING

As I first listened to the routine volunteers' accounts of their decision to come to Loaves & Fishes, I looked for external considerations that might explain why these individuals made this choice.[2] In most volunteer accounts an orientation to volunteering could be traced back to the volunteers' life stories. All but two of the routine volunteers came to Loaves & Fishes with volunteer experiences that dated back to childhood or their young adult years. Nonetheless, the initial decision to work at Loaves & Fishes often depended on fortuitous contact with other volunteers; only one sought out Loaves & Fishes on her own. Yet, as I listened more attentively to the volunteers, they seemed motivated by a need to create a self in keeping with particular moral ideals.

Gained primarily from interviews, the routine volunteers' stories described how these mostly white, mostly middle-aged and older, middle-class volunteers desired to take meaningful action to help the poor. The Loaves & Fishes vision of charity served as the ideal from which the routine volunteers strove to create a *more* authentic self.[3] In short, the practice of charitable action at Loaves & Fishes involved action in the service of moral coherence guided by the tenets of personalist hospitality.

The routine volunteers talked about themselves and their work in terms similar to what Victor Gecas (1982: 3) has called "self-concept," an overarching image of oneself "as a physical, social, spiritual, or moral being." This understanding of the self accords with John Dewey's ([1908] 1960: 172) formulation of the moral self wherein "all voluntary action is a remaking of the self, since it creates new designs, instigates to new modes of endeavor, brings to light new conditions which institute new ends." Action and the construction of moral selves became inextricably linked in this understanding of "what *kind* of self" (159) the individual hoped to shape.

Gecas builds motivation into his analysis of the self-concept with three self-based concerns: self-esteem, self-efficacy, and authenticity. Although all three are linked, Gecas understands self-esteem, the drive to feel good about oneself, as less relevant to the moral domain. Self-efficacy, the drive to understand oneself as a causal agent, and authenticity, the drive toward meaning, however, link together as individuals work to be "moral agents" (Gecas 1991: 179). Within this formulation, "authenticity is a function of commitment to systems of meaning in society, particularly to various identities embedded in systems of values and beliefs" (178). This understanding of the self as motivated from within resonates with Dewey's formulation of the moral self as actively striving toward the production of a particular *kind* of self in relation to others.

In analyzing volunteers' accounts of their experiences at Loaves & Fishes, I found that moral selving at Loaves & Fishes wedded self-efficacy to a drive toward authenticity. Moral selving can be understood as self-guided work on what Michael Schwalbe terms the "moral self." Schwalbe's (1991: 281) model "help[s] us see better the social embeddedness of individuals as moral actors." The moral self comprises "a set of self-related cognitive elements": an impulse to role-take, role-taking range, understanding of the self as containing moral characteristics, and a feeling of self-efficacy (288). The ability to imagine others' feelings and thoughts provides a capacity, role-taking, through which the actor can assess conflicting values and interests with concern for their impact on others. Role-taking range expands through social experience in diverse contexts. Self-conceptions of virtue may be the most particular to individual biography. Self-efficacy suggests that the moral self is more than just cognitive; it is also based in action. Some routine volunteers struggled to change their judgments of the poor, but all worked to take action based on their moral beliefs. In short, their commitment to feeding the urban poor represented the wedding of self-efficacy and authenticity as self-motivations to create a more caring person.

Schwalbe's (1991: 293) model "implies a link between the moral self and moral culture as providing the symbolic resources drawn upon to construct self-conceptions of virtue." In this case participation in personalist hospitality provided symbolic resources for use by the routine volunteers in moral selving. The role-taking range of the volunteers expanded as they watched other volunteers, and often more significantly the staff, interact with the guests. We will see how they learned this moral culture—new to them—through interaction with others.

A useful metaphor for understanding this interactive moral selving among the routine volunteers is offered by Peter L. Berger and Thomas Luckman (1967). Although they attempted to understand instances of "alternation," instances of total transformation that involve subjective experiences of resocialization, their approach is applicable to the more gradual cases of transformation I found at Loaves & Fishes.

> A "recipe" for successful alternation has to include both social and conceptual conditions, the social, of course, serving as the matrix of the conceptual. The most important social condition is the availability of an effective plausibility structure, that is, a social base serving as the "laboratory" of transformation. This plausibility structure will be mediated to the individual by means of significant others, with whom he must establish strongly affective identification. (Berger and Luckman 1967: 157)

Below I describe how the kitchen and dining room at Loaves & Fishes operated as the laboratory of transformation while the tenets of personalist hospitality constituted the recipe for moral selving. This recipe for transformation either confirmed or challenged volunteers' beliefs and values and ongoing day-to-day interactions outside of Loaves & Fishes. Although the themes of gratitude, commitment, and witnessing were interwoven in any given volunteer story, considering each separately allows for an analysis of how the different tenets of personalist hospitality composed the recipe for moral selving at Loaves & Fishes.

## Gratitude: "Giving from an Attitude of Abundance"

> Thank you for sharing your resources with Loaves &
> Fishes. Joy is your reward for giving from an attitude of
> abundance, not scarcity, with faith that your own needs
> will be provided for as well.
>
> *Note, October 1994*

The above message of gratitude typed on a notecard and signed by a Loaves & Fishes volunteer acknowledged my small monetary donation. Many of the volunteers expressed affinity with this sentiment, not surprising as this theme dominates American culture—both secular and sacred—as well. For example, Catherine, a mother of six who helped to care for her grandchildren, felt gratitude that her children were housed and fed. "Thank God it is not my kids standing in line, but you never know when something could fall through for one of them. I just, I'm *real* thankful for what I have." Catherine began volunteering at Loaves & Fishes with the "girls" from Mass after her mother died. The feeling of gratitude and well-being obligated many of the routine volunteers to fashion a self in service of others. Like Catherine, other volunteers' pursuit of authenticity involved charitable action to help the less fortunate.

Lori had done volunteer work all of her life. A mother of a young child and residential real estate agent, Lori worked long hours yet had come to Loaves & Fishes as the cheerful and energetic Unitarian group leader for five years. Her commitment to volunteering was based on gratitude and giving back to the community. She explained,

> I think that for myself I have been given a lot, and I complain sometimes, business is slow, and how am I gonna make the mortgage payments this month, and I got bills, and I'm working too hard, and all that's true, but I have been given a lot. You know, and maybe it's just the ability to stay sane in an ever more insane environment.

Self-disciplining entered into Lori's moral selving as well. In earlier years the temptation to just "hang outside the burrito store drinking beer" enticed her. Rather than merely enjoy what she had been given, Lori felt compelled to volunteer in gratitude to the community that sustained her.

Herb, a part-time staff attorney at the Legal Center for the Elderly and Disabled and group organizer of the Jewish community at Loaves & Fishes for several years, described his lifestyle as "quasi-hippie." Even with his job cutback and a new baby, Herb appreciated the relative wealth of his lifestyle.

> You know with the kind of job that I had, gave me the luxury, I don't know if you call it a luxury, but since I work part-time, Mondays I don't go to work, so I am free to do this. I assume that my responsibility to my family might be to figure out some way to make some more money and it may be that I will get a job that won't give me the flexibility.

Herb struggled with conflicting demands but believed that while he had the time and energy he should help those less fortunate. His understanding of gratitude contained, in his words, "a *social* orientation to social action."

Like Herb, Dan's gratitude for others' well-being motivated not only his volunteer work but also his paid work. A retired Jewish social worker who came to California in 1967 to work for the State Department of Mental Hygiene, Dan volunteered about thirty hours a week organizing the resettlement of Russian Jews in Sacramento and participated in the Jewish community day at Loaves & Fishes. Dan traced his gratitude to his childhood experience of the depression when he lived in an orphanage and then in a "hospital" for the "maimed and paralyzed" where his parents worked: "Our family never came out of the depression. . . . This has been my milieu all my time. I was in such a facility myself, my folks working in a facility which was philanthropically supported, and I went into this work."

The most elaborated expressions of gratitude came from two Christian volunteers who experienced feelings of inauthenticity before the personal transformation of "finding God." As a youth, Tony, a father and bricklayer, felt the "desire" to enter the seminary and become a priest. After the suppression of that desire by "family, friends, everything," he joined the Marine Corps and later took a job in business. He described this lifestyle as "pretty much a self-centered type." After experiencing a religious transformation, he created a life that felt to him truer to his Catholic values. He explained, "And I just thank God, I just thank God that I am not in a position, so I am able to give a little bit, a little bit, in love, not just to soothe my own guilt, but in love, to me is quite rewarding." In keeping with these ideals, Tony expressed his gratitude by feeding the poor at Loaves & Fishes for the past two and a half years.

Charlie, formerly an In-house resident at The Salvation Army and middle-aged African-American, joined the Jewish Community several years later, stirring and lifting the heavy meat trays served at lunch. Charlie felt gratitude to The Salvation Army for taking him in when he was "a *lost* puppy there." He got "dry" at The Salvation Army. Volunteer work allowed Charlie to express his gratitude for the help he received, and to witness God.

> This is why I am so *grateful*, the least I can do is volunteer, do something that might help somebody. I know which side my bread is buttered. And I know: I can't pay $50, $50, $50, $50, but *I can give up my self.* And that's the most valuable thing anybody has got. Yeah. So, I like doing that.

These volunteers worked to express their gratitude for abundance, both material and spiritual, in their lives. Such expressions of gratitude can be understood in Hochschild's terms as an "economy of gratitude" wherein "the summary of all *felt gifts*" resulted in an obligation to help others (1989: 96; emphasis in original). Volunteers' expressions of gratitude resonated with the philosophies of personalist hospitality, since they believed that abundance should be shared with others. Yet, as we shall see below, some volunteers were quite ambivalent about whether the guests should extend gratitude to them for their charitable work.

In a social psychological study of volunteers in a soup kitchen, Michael Stein (1989) identified an emotional economy in which volunteers expected gratitude from the guests. At Loaves & Fishes the idealism of personalist hospitality officially relieved the guests of the duty to express gratitude. The staff, however, as I recorded in my fieldnotes, tried to extend gratitude to the volunteers.

> Dorcy, the kitchen manager, offered us lemonade and this was refreshing. As we moved tubs of chili out of the cooler, she stopped to tell me that I had gone "the extra mile" this day. We were pleased to discover at the end of the day that she had saved us ice-cream sandwiches and this was all I ate, in the car, as I drove back to Davis.

Frequently, after a demanding day, I received a warm "Thank you, honey," as I left Loaves & Fishes. Nonetheless, not all volunteers felt satisfied with this radical vision of charity that absolved the poor of the obligation to thank volunteers and staff for their charity. The attempt to put feelings into action led the routine volunteers much less unequivocally toward a commitment to the work of feeding the urban poor at Loaves & Fishes.

## COMMITMENT: "THE CORPORAL WORKS OF MERCY"

> The Spiritual Works of Mercy are: to admonish the sinner, to instruct the ignorant, to counsel the doubtful, to comfort the sorrowful, to bear wrongs patiently, to forgive all injuries, and to pray for the living and the dead.
>    Corporal Works are to feed the hungry, to give drink to the thirsty, to clothe the naked, to ransom the captive, to harbor the harborless, to visit the sick, and to bury the dead.
>    ... It is by the Works of Mercy that we shall be judged.
>
> *Day*, By Little and By Little

The moral rhetoric of personalist hospitality expressed by Dorothy Day upheld a self-motivated commitment to feeding the urban poor. In keeping with this vision, the staff at Loaves & Fishes banned state-ordered Alternative Sentencing Program volunteers and made room for the large volunteer groups drawn to weekend volunteering. Loaves & Fishes had experimented with the ASP volunteer. When I asked Patty, the volunteer coordinator, if there were religious reasons why Loaves & Fishes no longer used ASP volunteers, she responded thoughtfully, "Well, I think we would say more *moral* convictions, that we want people here who want to be here, rather than are *forced* to be here." The use of ASP volunteers contradicted the Catholic Worker philosophy that highlighted the worth of a freely chosen desire to give to the poor. Patty's account of why she found working with volunteers uniquely rewarding illustrated the Catholic Worker concern that volunteers be self-motivated:

> The other places I did not work with volunteers. It was a job. And everybody was very good and did a wonderful job [spoken brightly], and really there were people who were very motivated to help other people, but there is just something extra *special* about people coming in and saying, "I want to do it, no I don't want to be paid."

Patty also worked to keep the volunteer role open to as many members of the community as possible, excluding those who might feel pressured or coerced into the role. This could be a difficult task, as illustrated by her description of the desire of many volunteers to work only on the weekends.

> And the weekends are a problem, we have fewer guests here and a *lot* more volunteers. So it would be really hard to accommodate them on the weekends. We have no trouble getting groups for the weekend. During the week it is a little more difficult.

Yet the staff accepted weekend volunteers based on their willingness to give, just as they worked to accept the outpouring of giving on the holidays.

Similar to the members of the communes and utopias studied by

Rosabeth Moss Kanter (1972), Loaves & Fishes staff worked to gain the commitment of their volunteers. Kanter identified the primary problem of utopian communities as how to organize their members so as to accomplish the goals of the organization and sustain member involvement. "Commitment links self-interest to social requirements. A person is committed to a relationship or to a group to the extent that he sees it as expressing or fulfilling some fundamental part of himself" (Kanter 1972: 66).

As we shall see, the routine volunteers expressed their commitment to feeding the urban poor in the routinization of their work. This commitment can best be understood by examining their dedication to the work of feeding the guests, or personal commitment; the building of a reference group; and the work of maintaining the volunteer groups. By fall 1992 more than fifteen hundred volunteers served in fifty-one "volunteer crews" that worked in the kitchen and dining room ("Bulletin Board," Loaves & Fishes fall 1992). Without the intimacy of the group experience, this mobilization might have easily degenerated into bureaucratic impersonality. The groups provided a context rich with camaraderie within which volunteers learned personalist hospitality. The work of maintaining these groups fell mainly on the group leaders, who are the most vivid exemplars of the committed volunteers.

### The Personal Commitment

Volunteers spoke of a personal commitment to the work of feeding the urban poor. For example, Lori, the residential real estate broker, mother of a toddler, and group leader for the Unitarians and Charismatics, explained, "That it was probably the first thing, steady thing, that I took on as a program, here in the valley." Volunteering at Loaves & Fishes allowed Lori to shape a moral self that modeled caring for others in her community:

> Okay, now you're a parent, you *really* have to do things *right*, you
> have to make an example, you have to make a *difference*, you know,
> you're a *home owner*, you're a part of a *community*, and a lot of that

too I got from my parents. Real, *strong sense* of community, doing the right thing at the right time.

For her, Loaves & Fishes became a "very important" way of structuring her commitment to her new community.

Similarly, Miguel, a young Mexican American who had been a volunteer with the Metropolitan Community Church for one year, expressed his commitment to helping those less fortunate through action: "I'm just helping out my fellow man, and I just have this attitude that if we all did that the world would be a hell of a lot better. You know, sometimes, not just look the other way when somebody falls down." Although the Metropolitan Community Church began to loosen its tie to Loaves & Fishes in 1994, the majority of the church's volunteers, Miguel included, maintained their commitment to the work of Loaves & Fishes, deciding to rename themselves the Gay and Lesbian Community volunteers and to continue to prepare one meal each month. Lori's and Miguel's concern for social responsibility and voluntary work, or authenticity and self-efficacy, illustrated how volunteers felt motivated to commit themselves to feeding the urban poor in their community.

Many volunteers came to Loaves & Fishes after retirement, or when they were temporarily unemployed. I recorded in my fieldnotes that Liz came to Loaves & Fishes with the Metropolitan Community Church while on disability from her job in a warehouse. Although she was doing something useful while on disability, she felt sheepish about volunteering only once a month. I also noted that Joe, a retired defense worker, volunteered with the Catholic Workers.

Joe worked competently chopping the red leaf lettuce and the iceberg lettuce. When interrupted by Chris to grab a tub, he was prompt and cordial. I was impressed by what a hard worker Joe was. He arrived before me, and worked taking trays during the meal—demanding work. I noticed later when he was taking trays that he had sweat beads on his reddish, sun-freckled, balding forehead.

For others, familial obligations had forestalled a personal commitment to the works of mercy. Both Catherine and Elizabeth delayed volunteering at Loaves & Fishes until their caretaking duties for their mothers ended. A committed volunteer, Catherine believed her volunteer work shaped a "better" self: "I think it makes me a better person by going down there and working for them. And having compassion for them."

Elizabeth's decision to volunteer after her mother's death revealed a more active strategy to become involved at Loaves & Fishes than was evidenced by many of the other volunteers. Initially she volunteered at a shelter for the homeless in Sacramento. There Elizabeth was troubled by the decision-making role assigned to her as she managed limited bed space for the homeless: "If I were being paid and in a capacity where I had some real say about what happened to people, you know. As a volunteer, you don't have any real say." Elizabeth phoned the Sacramento volunteer hotline and learned of Loaves & Fishes' need for volunteers. She intentionally volunteered with the Cathedral group and the Unitarian/Charismatics, because these two groups often needed extra volunteers. On Easter she left Loaves & Fishes shortly after her arrival to give the holiday volunteers the opportunity to work. Her commitment to feeding the urban poor reflected a sensitivity to balancing organizational needs with a drive to be true to her commitment to help others.

For both Charlie and Pete, the commitment to the work of feeding the urban poor developed out of deeply personal experiences with helping institutions. Charlie was formerly In-house at The Salvation Army. He learned the importance of volunteer work through participation in A.A. meetings: "They said never say no, always make yourself available." Charlie transferred his focus from A.A. to God when he began attending church two years after leaving The Salvation Army. He quit A.A. meetings, having "put all of [his] eggs in one basket. The basket called Jesus Christ." He became what he called "a *delivered* alcoholic."

This commitment to Jesus provided both meaning and structure to Charlie's life as he struggled to stay sober: "I was just so grateful that people had helped me and I had found the Lord, and it had turned my life around. You know, it gave some structure once I didn't have all the hours of drinking." Charlie also served meals with his fellow church members at the Union Mission in Sacramento.

Pete's experience with his wife's mental illness structured his commitment to the guests at Loaves & Fishes: " 'Cause I used to spend a lot of time in state hospitals with my wife. Of course I had to have her committed, and so I used to spend my weekends there, and so I know, and it's very sad, these poor things have nothing to turn to." Before he began volunteer work, Pete had little experience with homeless people. In his words, "I have always tried to help the underdog to a degree, and this was my first exposure to the homeless." After doing the dishes every Monday for several years, Pete regularly encountered some of his "steadies" as he walked to Loaves & Fishes from the Sacramento Light Rail. His work at Loaves & Fishes fulfilled a simple desire to keep busy and help others. "But just so long as I'm busy, that's all I can do. All I want, 'cause all I want is my health and peace of mind and keep busy, and that's it."

For both Dan and Herb, Judaism guided the commitment to feeding the urban poor. Although Dan gave far more time to his volunteer work in the resettlement of Russian Jews in Sacramento, he took seriously his commitment to Loaves & Fishes. He explained, "I try to not fail to come for fear that I would have been not personally missed, but as another resource, I would have been leaving others in a bind. So I come regularly. It's on my calendar." Dan hoped to pass this commitment to routine caring on to the grandson he and his wife raised, so he brought the boy with him to Loaves & Fishes on school holidays. Dan acknowledged that his grandson thought preparing food at Loaves & Fishes was "boring," but he felt that "it [was] sensitizing him well."

Herb believed an authentic commitment to the work of feeding the urban poor involved the self in action. As coordinator of the Jewish Community Relations Council, he responded to a request from Loaves & Fishes to locate free louse shampoo for its guests.

> They wanted it donated, so I decided at least this was something relevant. I just had the feeling that some of the people in the organization [the Jewish community], that they just talked and wrote checks and that was the extent of the involvement. And the Community Relations Council is supposed to be involved in the community.

Herb located the shampoo from a company "back East," and then, "being very good recruiters at Loaves & Fishes," the staff invited the Jewish community to participate in the dining room.

Herb developed a "philosophy" of volunteer action to merge Jewish beliefs with a theory of action.

> It's a combination of the Jewish thing, about *tikkun olam,* which means "to heal the world." It is consistent with the Jewish person. Just writing checks and arguing, no matter how well intentioned, is not enough. It is not a complete participation in the world.

He also helped Dan move furniture for Russian Jewish immigrants. "I *enjoy* getting together with some other people and hauling a chair. There's something real about it." He valued hands-on volunteer experience as an element of both political and spiritual action. Herb explained that "Judaism, at least that strain, is consistent with my personal beliefs."

A seemingly insincere, or inauthentic, commitment to the work of feeding the urban poor on the part of some volunteers could result in staff sanctions. For example, after Frank, a young Hispanic man, left a car sales position, he decided to volunteer daily for two to three months in the kitchen. Over time he expressed irritation with the repetition of directions he heard as a frequent volunteer, and then he began to position himself as an unofficial group director while spending much of his time socializing with other volunteers. As I recorded in my fieldnotes,

Rob, the group leader of the Metropolitan Community Church, spoke with Dorcy, the kitchen manager, about his frustration with Frank.

> Rob was clearly annoyed at Frank's presence the last day the MCC [Metropolitan Community Church] volunteered. Apparently Frank was directing the Metropolitan Church volunteers and Rob wanted Frank "out of his face." Dorcy said that Rob seems to see himself as the "ambassador of Loaves & Fishes." She said, looking at me and telling me, "You are getting the inside scoop," that this is how they think of Frank and that they had a talk with him about his behavior and acting appropriately.

The routine volunteers' commitment both reflected and shaped their moral selving. In contrast to the holiday volunteers, practicality, not sentimentality, underlay this commitment to the corporal works of mercy. Their desire to legitimate spiritual and political virtues motivated this commitment and guided their moral selving. In the words of the Catholic bricklayer who volunteered with the Jewish Community, "I am a firm believer that we should take whatever motivates us to be there once a month, twice a month, we should make a concerted effort to apply that same motivation to our everyday life." Commitment among the routine volunteers to the corporal works of mercy dramatically revealed the wedding of self-efficacy and authenticity as self-motivations. That is, the routine volunteers strove in their moral selving to link action with the moral importance of feeding the urban poor.

### *"Reference Groups" for Doing Personalist Hospitality*

We have seen how personal commitment on the part of individuals manifested itself in the habitual work of feeding and serving the urban poor. Some volunteers rooted this commitment in a spiritual commitment to charity. Others sought authenticity in Christian works of mercy. And for still others, Judaism structured the spiritual basis of moral selving.

I draw here on the work of Tamotsu Shibutani (1955) to describe how fellow routine volunteers at Loaves & Fishes composed a "reference group" that guided the process of moral selving. "Reference groups . . . arise through the internalization of norms; they constitute the structure of expectations imputed to some audience for whom one organizes his conduct" (Shibutani 1955: 565). The kitchen manager oriented new volunteers to the group leader. Within these groups, volunteers learned to regard the work of Loaves & Fishes as infused with moral good through the shared experience of feeding the urban poor.

For some volunteers, such as Catherine (who carpooled to Loaves & Fishes with seven or eight of "the girls" after Mass), volunteering both provided a time with old friends and offered an opportunity to meet new acquaintances from her church. In her words, "There's a lot of them, that you see at church, but you don't know who they are, but now that you work with them, you know who they are." Pete, who came to Loaves & Fishes every Monday, noted with pleasure, "I have met so many nice people. I have made lots of friends." Pete explained that he now sees these "nice people" around town. Similarly, Tony, a Christian bricklayer, felt welcomed by the Jewish community.

> As a matter of fact, it's been two, two and a half years now that I have been attending once a month, and I have come to know some of the people on a real personal level. And I consider some of them to really be my dear friends, my brothers and friends. I love them dearly. And they have invited me to various functions.

These loving feelings fostered in Tony an emotional attachment to the Jewish community.

These reference groups functioned as the significant others so important to the conversion experience described by Berger and Luckman (1967: 51–52). The volunteer groups intertwined "sociability" and a shared commitment to the work of feeding the poor. Sociability, defined by Georg Simmel ([1917] 1950) as a form of association in which individuals' pleasure becomes shared and status differentials fade, made the work of volunteering satisfying. Over time the routine volunteers established a sincere camaraderie.

For the routine volunteers, even talk of sociability revealed a moral substrate. The Jewish community organizer, Herb, explained,

> I just like talking to the people. I like the opportunity. I think there is a more genuine kind of interaction when you are working together. I mean, if two people are stirring up potatoes, you can talk about Israel, or welfare, or gossip about somebody even. There is something, there is some *authenticity*, about having a relationship when you are doing physical work together.

Herb noted that as an organizer he could "float," thereby maximizing his opportunity to interact with different volunteers.

Stories of discomfort with the volunteer groups rarely surfaced. A middle-aged gay man tried volunteering once with a Lutheran church group. I recorded in my fieldnotes,

> Fred told me that as he sat folding napkins with the Lutheran church someone asked him about coming to Loaves & Fishes and he explained that usually he came with the MCC. . . . At a woman's look of confusion, he explained [that he meant] the Metropolitan Community Church for Gays and Lesbians. This woman looked taken aback; the dining room and kitchen grew absolutely silent, and quickly the woman in the seat next to him slid out of her seat and into the next one over. . . . Fred told the story not as if angry or resentful, but rather a bit sadly, and as if he lost an important opportunity.

Fred said that, in contrast to the MCC, he did not find the Lutheran group to be very much fun.

Dan also said that he enjoyed the sociability of Loaves & Fishes, though it remained heavily textured with a moral commitment to the work itself:

> Why I came to this? Well, to be part of the community's *witness*, so to speak, and it's easy enough and there's a satisfaction, you are fill-

ing a need, and there's a satisfaction with working with *compatriots* in our community, and I guess in all honesty, there's an element of a certain need for recognition. My involvement also fills, feeds, personal needs, and I think that is pretty well recognized in the whole area of volunteerism. It has got to be something that *satisfies*.

For all the routine volunteers, sociability faded in importance to the work itself. Dan maintained that none of the routine volunteers worked solely for the sociability: "It might be for some, a couple of them, who are otherwise not involved in the constituent organizations, but it doesn't fulfill a need, that sort of need for me." Herb cautioned against deriving self-satisfaction from working at Loaves & Fishes:

> But *really* I think it is just a stopgap and really not social action, it's not the kind of thing that we can get really *self-satisfied* about, feeding the poor. Isn't it great to feed the poor? No, it's stinking to have people coming in empty.

For the routine volunteers, the sociability of volunteering was less important than the collective, morally engaged work of feeding the guests.

Yet friendship networks and sociability may have helped to maintain a commitment to steadfast volunteering. Catherine saw other volunteers at Mass, where they discussed the material needs of Loaves & Fishes. Miguel called other volunteers to remind them of their commitment. Herb received telephone calls from other volunteers about their availability for work. Pete ran into other volunteers as he traveled throughout Sacramento. When I worked next to him on the line, Miguel would jokingly intercede in the sometimes lengthy flirting directed at me. He would ask the men who were holding up the line talking to me, "Are you flirting with her?" They would sometimes reply yes, sometimes no, but regardless they would move on, much to my relief. Only half of the routine volunteers said that sociability was important to their volunteering, and the others did not frame the importance of this work in terms of friendship or sociability. From my own experience as a volunteer and from my interviews, it seemed likely that sociability works as an unspoken, underlying reward to sustain the work of volunteers.

The shared practice of personalist hospitality taught the volunteers appropriate guidelines for managing their own and others' moral selves within a Catholic Worker vision of charity. Just as the "social shaping of emotions is as much an interpersonal and public process as it is personal and private" (Cahill and Eggleston 1994: 301), so too is the shaping of moral selves distinctly social. The volunteer group experience contains the components of an "interaction ritual" (Collins 1990) wherein participants in face-to-face interaction focus on a task with an awareness that others are paying attention, share collective sentiments, and consequently generate feelings of moral solidarity. These feelings of moral solidarity and heightened emotionality remained with the volunteers outside of Loaves & Fishes, increasing the commitment of some volunteers to the additional work of maintaining the group.

### Maintaining the Group

Many routine volunteers, mostly group leaders, became involved in the recruitment of other volunteers. Herb, a group organizer for the Jewish community, mailed out reminders of the upcoming volunteer days and placed notices in the Jewish community newspaper, the *Jewish Voice*, and local temple newspapers. The postcard reminders exclaimed, "Do a Mitzvah!" Herb told me this publicity was very successful: "Early on I was recruiting, or letting people know about it. Now, usually people ask me because they hear about it, or they hear about how I am involved in it. We like to keep a continual stream of volunteers because there is attrition." Herb was able to pass on the more demanding aspects of group maintenance when he enlisted the Jewish Community Center to advertise its involvement with Loaves & Fishes and to coordinate a monetary donation for the meat.

Miguel brought in a volunteer from his same-sex couples group. He also took responsibility for helping with the Metropolitan Community Church telephone list to remind volunteers of their upcoming day at

Loaves & Fishes. Lori, group organizer for the Unitarians and Charismatics, commented ironically, "Originally, I started coming with the Unitarians, and have since dragged, *brought* several of my associates: title people, lenders, insurance people." When I asked, "How do you get them to come?" Lori responded unabashedly,

> I tell them that they are making money on the community. From the community. And that they should give something back to the *community*. I give them a little bit of guilt, from my father's side of the family. You probably won't get a client down here, but *you will give the community back* just hopefully what you have earned. But really, it is community, and what goes around comes around. I mean, *I honestly, honestly believe that*. And it feels good.

Lori believed that professional members of the community, not just students and seniors, should donate time to this work. Herb, Miguel, and Lori thus served as liaisons between their religious communities and Loaves & Fishes, thereby maintaining the commitment to the work of feeding the poor.

As this new volunteer recruitment shows, the group organizers functioned as extensions of the Loaves & Fishes staff in the "invisible labor" of "sociability work" (Daniels 1985). Unlike the female "high society" philanthropically oriented volunteers studied by Arlene Kaplan Daniels, however, male volunteers at Loaves & Fishes took responsibility for this work too. Sociability work involved the volunteers not only in the creation of personalist hospitality but also (and paradoxically) in the bureaucratization of the volunteer experience.

The bureaucratization of volunteer recruitment and management rested most heavily on the group leaders. Thus Lori's organizing duties contributed to the "mechanical" feel of her volunteer work. Rob, a leader of the MCC, asked Miguel to help him make reminder calls to the volunteers. Although Herb delegated some of the organizational work of being a group leader to the Jewish Community, he felt, nonetheless, that he had some responsibility for being there.

It is tiring and it sort of, it's a test, every month. You know, can I do it? Will I finish? Or will I be exhausted or sick? You know, it's a little bit of strain. I would like to continue doing it, but maybe let somebody else take the reins at some point. I think I am ready to, but I haven't done that yet.

A personal commitment to the work of feeding the poor at Loaves & Fishes and the routinization of maintaining a volunteer group provided a structured volunteer framework for many of the routine volunteers. In *Beyond Caring* (1996), a study of how nurses manage the suffering and death they encounter on a daily basis, Daniel F. Chambliss argues that routinization transforms the moral ambiguity of their work. He identifies four phenomenological tasks as critical to the routinization process: the learning of geographic surroundings, the learning of a specialized language, the learning of technique, and the learning of "types" of patients. These four learning tasks are certainly essential components of the recipe for learning personalist hospitality. Yet the routine volunteers' immersion in the organization was fluid and often affected by contradictory images of types of homeless people. As they struggled with witnessing at Loaves & Fishes, we see most clearly how the progressive politics of moral selving fell short of a complete transformation of the liberal or conservative images of the homeless held by many volunteers. Yet because "morality is rooted in collective life" (Chambliss 1996: 185) and the routine volunteers feel great commitment to Loaves & Fishes, they engaged with the progressive politics of treating the homeless as the Ambassadors of God, even if only to abandon the personal connection implicit in this belief.

## WITNESSING: "A REVOLUTION OF THE HEART"

The greatest challenge of the day is: how to bring about a revolution of the heart, a revolution which has to start with each one of us? When we begin to take the lowest place, to wash the feet of others, to love our brothers

with that burning love, that passion, which led to the
Cross, then we can truly say, "Now I have begun."
*Day*, Loaves and Fishes

Catholic Worker philosophy teaches that *witnessing* God in one's life involves performing not only corporal works of mercy but also spiritual works of mercy. Day wrote in 1940 of her conviction of the need to perform spiritual works: "Food for the body is not enough. There must be food for the soul" (1983: 91). At Loaves & Fishes the vision of charity encouraged the volunteers to imbue corporal works of mercy with spirituality, to build an ecumenical community on this practice, and to grant the guests sacred status as Ambassadors of God. Although few volunteers approached the spiritual aspect by preaching to others, many described the volunteer experience as spiritually meaningful. Less ambiguously, the routine volunteers embraced the building of ecumenical community on the foundation of their commitment to corporal works of mercy. For some, the building of an ecumenical community originated in deeply held spiritual practices, whereas for others this ideal sprang from moral commitments not linked to religiosity. Granting all the guests sacred status as Ambassadors of God most challenged the volunteers to achieve "a revolution of the heart." Many faltered in their moral selving as they confronted this vision of charity.

### Spiritual Works of Mercy

Some volunteer groups joined hands in prayer prior to serving.

    We stood in a semicircle, holding hands. Rob [the MCC group leader] began the prayer, asking God and sweet Jesus that our services not be needed anymore.

*Fieldnotes*

At Loaves & Fishes it was common practice to say a prayer before serving the meal. The volunteer coordinator often led us in the Lord's

Prayer. For these volunteers and others, feeding the urban poor was inseparable from a spiritual commitment.

Pete felt that his work at Loaves & Fishes witnessed his belief in God: "I live the Golden Rule. And try to help anyone I can and so on and so on." The routine work of caring witnessed his belief in God and his commitment to helping the less fortunate isolated in institutions. Catherine said that volunteer work shaped her Catholic self.

> I feel Catholic when I am sharing things, so maybe in that respect it does [seem Catholic], and we are all down there sharing and giving, like the good Lord says, "Do for my brother and you are doing for me," which is part of our image too, you know, of being a good Catholic, the Ten Commandments, and things like that.

Participation in the evangelical group at Loaves & Fishes gave Tony and Charlie an opportunity to witness God in communion with others. Tony, who volunteered with the Jewish community, found in Loaves & Fishes "a winning formula."

> Just the concept alone, the scriptural concept of Loaves & Fishes and the multiplication of Loaves & Fishes, feeding a multitude. When I go there, I experience firsthand the miracle. Firsthand. You can't tell me there aren't miracles. There are miracles everywhere. I look at Loaves & Fishes and I think, this truly is, this whole program uses people, just looking at people when people are willing, when people have been touched and are sensitive, look at what happens.

Charlie was one of the few volunteers at Loaves & Fishes who witnessed God through his ministry to other volunteers.

> Okay, the reason I do it now is because I *feel* I can't give the Lord any money for, you know, what he does for me, so I *feel* by working, letting him work through me, in helping other people, who, you know, are in this situation, that it's a way of ministering to people, not just saying, well, the Lord is the answer and all of this, but actual action.

Charlie compared his presence at Loaves & Fishes with the Jewish Community to having been one of the few black men in his church.

> I was in the back praising the Lord, and talking about the blessed hope and [a Jewish woman] said, "Do you guys really believe that?" And I said, "Wow!" The Lord sent me here to minister, to evangelize. I feel everywhere I go, I am there for a reason. There's only about two black guys in my church. And I asked the Lord, why am I the only black guy in this church, you know? Why did he put me here? Yeah, and then he told me so that I can evangelize *them* and they can evangelize *me*. Yep.

Charlie's commitment to the Lord and evangelizing structured his life. He volunteered at Loaves & Fishes to become a better Christian: "I'm still growing, you know, I'm not done here yet." Charlie spoke of church attendance, ministry to others, and performing corporal works of mercy in moral terms.[4]

Both Tony and Charlie appeared to experience themselves in a "conversion" process, "a radical reorganization of identity, meaning, life" (Richard Travisano, cited in Lofland and Skonovd 1981: 375). Tony understood himself to be on a spiritual "journey" away from "a pretty much self-centered lifestyle."

> And the fuel tank was on empty, spiritually, emotionally, it was the real only time in my life, the first meaningful time, where in all sincerity I cried out for help. No strings attached. No compromises. And such is the leaven that we read about, leaven works through the entire batch, and it takes time, change takes time. Conversion takes time. It's a process that we live. Day in and day out. And so here I am right now.

Tony devoted his life to this spiritual journey and his relationship with God. He echoed Tony's use of the conversion motif when he described his attendance at church about two years after leaving The Salvation Army: "It was no thunderbolt, or anything like that. It was a gradual thing." Moral selving for Charlie meant a steadfast commitment to serving God. This commitment included spiritual growth, the practice of charitable action at Loaves & Fishes, and spreading the word.

Whether or not it was stated explicitly, moral selving for all the routine volunteers seemed to be analogous to a conversion or an alternation (Lofland and Skonovd 1981; Berger and Luckman 1967). The volunteers strove to create a reworked moral self. Unlike Tony and Charlie, however, most of the routine volunteers did not see themselves as undergoing a total change, as in the conversion or alternation experience; moral self-betterment generally involved a commitment to gradually fashioning an idealized moral self.

The power of personalist hospitality to shape the moral self rested for many of the routine volunteers in its sacred qualities. Victor Turner's ([1974] 1982) work on ritual analyzes its power in shaping the sacred world. In this case, some of the volunteers' accounts suggest that they experienced themselves as leaving the mundane world behind as they entered the sacred, ritualistic world of Loaves & Fishes. This work appeared to function as a transitory or intervening phase that led to incorporation of elements of personalist hospitality in the volunteers' moral selving. Although Day (1978: 17) wrote that "conversion is a lonely experience," the shared intimacy and sociability of personalist hospitality at Loaves & Fishes provided an atmosphere of camaraderie for the routine volunteers within an ecumenical community.

### Building an Ecumenical Community

Even among volunteers for whom witnessing the sacred held less meaning, building an ecumenical community gave spiritual meaning to doing charitable work. The "Philosophy Statement of Loaves & Fishes" (see chap. 1) affirmed the organizational commitment to this ideal: "We value collaborating with diverse groups in the work of Loaves & Fishes and actively seek to involve volunteers from a variety of backgrounds. Within the guiding principles listed above, we respect the individual spirit and expression of each of these groups" (January 1991). Loaves & Fishes upheld this commitment with the inclusion of the gay and lesbian church, the Jewish community, and a wide range of Christian faiths, as well as nondenominational groups. The routine volunteers appreciated this affirmation of a spiritual community bound together in feeding the urban poor. Even those who felt detached from their religious roots voiced support for building an ecumenical community.

For Lori, witnessing God faded in relation to community building and the routinization of being a group leader. She admitted somewhat uncertainly that her work at Loaves & Fishes felt less "spiritual" and "just more mechanical" than previous work in another Christian kitchen in spite of the Unitarian support and frequent mention of Loaves & Fishes at Sunday meetings.

> It doesn't really seem like the Unitarian. No, I don't know if that's true. That's a good question. I guess I do feel like I'm having fellowship with the other Unitarians, although it doesn't seem like a Unitarian event so much to me. I mean, I don't think of it so much in contact with doing something with the Unitarians as doing a thing because we're a group of concerned people. It doesn't seem like we're doing it for that reason.

Lori speculated that her position as an active group organizer demanded most of her attention and left little time for introspection about the spiritual meaning of the experience.

Only one of the routine volunteers did not speak of witnessing God in the consideration of volunteer work. Miguel, raised a Catholic, attended neither the Metropolitan Community Church nor a Catholic church. He characterized himself as "agnostic, leaning towards atheist." Although he chose not to participate in the prayer led by the MCC group organizer before serving, he respected others' witnessing: "I watch myself, because I realize that it is a Catholic organization. I watch what I say a lot of times." Miguel, however, praised the ecumenical community at Loaves & Fishes.

Jewish volunteer participation dramatically revealed the range of witnessing and the importance of spiritual community building at Loaves & Fishes. Herb and Dan, then active members of the Sacramento Jewish Council, worked to establish the Jewish community's involvement at Loaves & Fishes. Dan initially attempted to involve the Jewish community on Sundays: "It seemed an ideal thing for the Jewish community to do." He sought to fulfill a need for Jewish involvement in the larger community. He believed the Jewish community belonged at Loaves & Fishes "to do their fair share in the community."

Not only did the Jewish community embrace the building of an ecumenical community with their enthusiastic participation at Loaves & Fishes, they also welcomed a Christian volunteer, Tony. When Tony asked if it would be appropriate for him to volunteer with the Jewish community, his friends told him that he did not need a "membership card." The staff, as recorded in my fieldnotes, worked to make the group feel comfortable.

> The kitchen manager commented on how quickly we were serving the food. I heard one of the staff members comment on how this was a day from hell. At one point, Chris Delany said, "Thank the Lord of Israel," and, seeing me watching her, laughed and said that she couldn't say "Praise be to God" with this group. We both laughed.

Dan valued participation at Loaves & Fishes to counteract negative perceptions of Jews.

> Some who are truly not appreciative of the Jewish community would say, you know, that we look, that we only look out for our own. If they are kinder they say, they look after their own, meaning it's a positive quality. Sometimes we are accused of being clannish, we always stick together, but then we butt into everyone's business. But you could say that our attitude is, there but for the grace of God go I.

Dan understood the Jewish community to compose "another ingredient" in the recipe for moral selving at Loaves & Fishes.

Herb shared Dan's commitment to building an ecumenical community. Not only did he hope to improve popular sentiments about Jews, he also felt that witnessing God should involve hands-on charitable action.

It was something I felt was important to the Jewish community,
'cause I know that the Jewish community, that the individuals in it
are very socially oriented, but a lot of the participation is by check-
book, and I think, yeah, this is the Community Relations Council
and if we are worried about our relation with the other folks, if there
is a feeling that the Jews are upper class or Jews once they make it
don't participate, I think that there is something very valuable about
a hands-on experience, in both directions. So, I thought that was a
good exercise for the people and also good for our image and I
*pushed* it.

Herb also clearly valued the participation of non-Jewish volunteers.
"The fact that they participate means that in their souls we are all kind
of resonating in the same way, and I like that too." Dan and Herb understood the Jewish community's involvement at Loaves & Fishes to
provide an opportunity for visible social contributions in a Christian-
dominated world. Routine volunteering afforded Dan and Herb the opportunity to practice Judaism and to participate in ecumenical community building.

The Jewish community members focused on the importance of community building in a predominantly Christian world as the witnessing
of God. Jewish religious and cultural history makes primary the importance of *tzedakah*, encouraging charity understood at once as a free gift
and also as a ritually mandated obligation, both to the Jewish and to the
non-Jewish community.[5] Scholars of Jewish philanthropy have concluded that giving reinforces Jewish identity through the practice of
tzedakah (Rimor and Tobin 1990).

The Jewish volunteers I encountered at Loaves & Fishes lent further
evidence in support of the finding that giving strengthens Jewish identity. The Jewish community participation at Loaves & Fishes illustrated
how volunteer work created links with a wider community while rein-
forcing group identity.

While the working arrangements of personalist hospitality encouraged an ecumenical community, they simultaneously challenged volunteers to merge the corporal and spiritual works of mercy in face-to-face loving interaction with the homeless. As we shall see, volunteers' difficulties with this challenge seemed less a function of religious affiliation and more often a result of political orientation.

### The Ambassadors of God

The framing rules of personalist hospitality teach its adherents to treat all the poor with equal dignity, respect, and love and not to bifurcate the poor into the categories "worthy" and "unworthy." Many of the routine volunteers, however, felt that some guests, usually male, bore responsibility for their plight. Nonetheless, many of these same volunteers felt great admiration for the staff's treatment of the guests. The discordance between individual and organizational definitions of the worthy poor challenged many of the volunteers in their drive toward moral authenticity. Moral selving for some revolved around resolving contradictory and unsettling images of the guests.

The difficulty evidenced among some of the routine volunteers in extending charitable love to all the guests can best be understood when situated in historical context. American society has historically demarcated the deserving poor from the undeserving poor. Seemingly able-bodied laborers (especially men) and the idle have constituted the unworthy poor (Katz 1986: 18; Trattner 1989: 21–22). Women have been assigned the duty of caring for children, thereby relieving them of the primary duty of providing for the family (Sapiro 1990: 49) and making them worthy of charity. At Loaves & Fishes the routine volunteers participated in a progressive vision of charity that worked against this tradition; all the guests, in the tradition of the Catholic Workers, ideally became Ambassadors of God. Although the volunteers occasionally lapsed into victim blaming "cloaked in kindness and concern" (Ryan [1971] 1976: 6) when they sanctioned those wanting seconds or made inquiries of the guests deemed inappropriate by the staff.

The staff worked hard to socialize the volunteers into the feeling rules of treating the guests as the Ambassadors of God. For example, as recorded in my fieldnotes, when new volunteers arrived to augment the efforts of the Metropolitan Community Church, Chris Delany explained to them how hospitality worked in the dining room.

> Chris explained that Loaves & Fishes' philosophy comes out of Saint Matthew's judgment, "What you do for the weakest, you do for me," and that Loaves & Fishes is not here to judge these folks. She explained that many people are afraid of the "homeless *poor*" but that many of them are "wounded" and that Loaves & Fishes tried to extend to them "hospitality." If they wanted to, they could even attend a tour to see what Loaves & Fishes does for its guests.

As the following example from my fieldnotes illustrates, the staff interceded when volunteers challenged the guests' merit.

> Apparently, the group was not happy with the rules at Loaves & Fishes, and although they finished their shift, they left afterwards saying that they would not be back. Dorcy, the kitchen manager, told us of a woman whom she had to pull of the line, telling her that she could not question the homeless about coming through the line for seconds. Dorcy asked the woman if she had to explain herself at home when she wanted seconds, and the woman said no she didn't, but apparently she remained disturbed that not all of the homeless finished everything on their trays before asking for seconds. Dorcy, Miguel, and I talked about how it is not easy for the homeless to get seconds at Loaves & Fishes, and Miguel emphasized that for some this is the only meal of the day. Dorcy emphasized the importance of the volunteers being *gracious*.

This group withdrew its commitment to Loaves & Fishes after this experience. Rather than wrestle with the feeling rules of personalist hospitality, they simply rejected them. In contrast, the more committed routine volunteers did not reject the feeling rules outright but worked to feel comfortable within the parameters of the emotion culture of personalist hospitality.

For example, Dan and Lori valued Loaves & Fishes' charitable action, but both resisted accepting all the guests as deserving. The vision of charity espoused at Loaves & Fishes allowed Dan to practice Jewish charity. He explained to me that "the highest level" of giving on the Jewish "moral yardstick" involves helping people to take care of themselves, followed by giving before someone asks. In agreement with this principle, Dan appreciated that Loaves & Fishes required a minimum wage of $6 an hour for any job advertised in Friendship Park, as well as the hospitality in the dining room. "So, you don't wait to give them their food, when it's a handout, but you lay some food out there." Dan felt that Loaves & Fishes met the challenge of moral giving: "Loaves & Fishes is trying to make this place hospitable and nonthreatening, and you start putting up too many rules and you violate that. The folks have enough assault in the community, without having to get that." Dan's experience as a social activist allowed him to appreciate the personalist hospitality at Loaves & Fishes.

Yet Dan was discouraged as he tried to maintain a nonjudgmental standard of giving. He struggled with the dictates of his Jewish beliefs, further enforced by the hospitality practiced at Loaves & Fishes, as he became impatient with the guests he observed gathered just outside the kitchen door where he left the trash and used boxes.

> I see them milling about, waiting, and there's a lot of *banter* going
> on. From there and other encounters, I feel bad taking on a wee bit
> of an attitude, some of this is their own doing. I don't dwell on this. I
> don't want to use all of my energies to *prove* that. But the way I ac-
> commodate that is by telling myself that you have to recognize that
> everyone has a different threshold.

Dan initially drew on both his childhood experience of the depression and his social work expertise to rationalize the troubling choices some guests made about how to spend their time.

Lori particularly enjoyed serving the women and children, and images of the children remained her most salient memories of the experience of serving. She supported showing the children "kindness" to reveal "that it is possible to get help, and to get better from the help, more the hand up than the hand*out*." In short, Lori liked the "nonjudgmental approach" and the fact that Loaves & Fishes "has provided, at least close by, lots of other ways for you to help yourself." Lori labored to shape her moral self in accordance with the generosity given to all the guests by the kitchen supervisor and Chris Delany.

> I suppose if there is anything that I know I need attitude help with, it is, unlike the generosity that the kitchen supervisor and Chris feel, if you are young, relatively healthy, male, I mean, I know that it is not the most—what is the word I am looking for?—magnanimous opinion, but if you don't have a kid, any responsibilities, why not get out there and work?

Lori answered her own tentative question adamantly with "I don't get it." Although Lori favored self-help strategies coupled with a hand up, she acknowledged that people's stories might not always have been readily available to her. She admired the magnanimity the kitchen supervisor and Chris revealed in their practice of tolerance and worked to shape her moral self in accordance with this practice, even when her political assessment of some of the guests contradicted such an acceptance.

Lori's admiration of the kitchen supervisor and Chris suggested that she used their perspective to widen her role-taking range. That is, through her role-taking capacities, Lori incorporated the staff into her reference group. This expanded definition of who constituted the deserving poor troubled her sense of authenticity. As she witnessed the generosity practiced by the kitchen supervisor and Chris, she questioned her own moral judgments, action, and feelings. She wrestled with a change, not just in her demeanor, but in her emotions as well.

Similarly, Tony struggled to share Christian love with the guests, attempting to increase his ability to deal with them face-to-face. "The misery" he saw at Loaves & Fishes was difficult to accept. Although he admitted awkwardly that his attitude to homeless people was once much different, he still struggled in his encounters with the guests.

> I get behind those ovens and it's kind of like a buffer for me. I really don't have to, I mean, if I don't want to look out there, I don't have to. If I don't want to look out in the street, I really don't have to. It tears me up to see these people. Walking down the street, early in the morning. Just a little blanket wrapped around them. It tears my heart out. Where do you go with that emotion? That experience? How do you deal with that? Probably my best way of dealing with it at this point in time is just staying at the ovens, 'cause I really don't want to face them. It's there, and it exists, and I know it, but I am not ready to get that close to it.

The practice of personalist hospitality pushed Tony to interact more intimately with the guests, but he could not bring himself to come close enough to serve the guests their meal. Tony's moral selving thus involved the effort to look homeless people directly in the eyes.

> Painful, I think it's painful. And I am not to that point yet. I don't feel comfortable. I would like to [serve], but in all honesty [it's too difficult] to look into the eyes of some of those people. I get behind those ovens and it's kind of like a buffer for me.

Christianity taught Tony that we are all of one body, but many different parts. He strove to mold himself so that he would be able to look into the eyes of the homeless and share his love with them. He said, "Maybe in time, I will have a desire to serve."

> I don't think that I would feel *comfortable* serving. There is something, there is something, Rebecca, there is just something there that I haven't probably come to grips with, and I just don't feel that I would be doing it because it is a part of me. I just, you know, charity comes in different degrees. And long-distance charity is probably the easiest. You put a few bucks in an envelope and let somebody else do it. And that was pretty much *my* way of doing things, and so now I'm getting a little bit more, I'm beginning to get *closer*, and it takes time,

you just can't push somebody off into ten feet of water who has never swam before.

Tony's struggle with personalist hospitality most dramatically revealed the power of the moral rhetoric of charitable action at Loaves & Fishes to shape volunteers' "emotion work" (Hochschild 1979). He tried to manage his emotions to feel the loving acceptance of the guests that he believed his Christianity and personalist hospitality prescribed. His emotion work to change his feelings, and not just his demeanor, revealed the depth of his spiritual commitment to the vision of charity at Loaves & Fishes. Even concern with failure to successfully manage his emotions revealed the force of the moral rhetoric of charity in guiding his understanding of the appropriate emotional response. Tony's account of his struggle to feel charitable love for the guests suggests, in sociological terms, that he felt his troubled response to the guests did not match the "moral appropriateness" (Hochschild 1975: 290) dictated by the feeling rules of personalist hospitality. He then struggled to better align his emotions with the feeling rules.

Not all of the routine volunteers wrestled as dramatically with their feelings about the guests. For example, Catherine, a steadfast Catholic, saw herself as no better than the homeless to whom she served food. "I know what it is to not *have* a lot of stuff, and I don't look down on them because they don't have it. I feel sorry for them." Yet, as I recorded in my fieldnotes, Catherine did feel judgmental about the guests who smoked.

> As the two of us worked slicing tomatoes from a can for salsa, she told me, looking outside at some of the guests, that the only thing she had difficulty with in homeless people was their smoking. She cited the amount of money cigarettes cost and their proven detriment to one's health as her objection.

This did not affect her appreciation for the charitable love given to the poor at Loaves & Fishes, however. Miguel agreed with Catherine's view of the staff's treatment of their guests: "I especially appreciate that they are treated with dignity. You don't ask any questions." Miguel, raised in a lower-class immigrant family, believed everyone was vulnerable to poverty. "I guess that is part of the reason that I help. It could be any one of us."

As a former social worker, Herb appreciated that the staff's charitable love of the guests spared them the "earbanging" of proselytizing and "paternalism."

> I found it in the welfare department and in some of the places that made poverty a sign of some kind of a moral lapse, or moral deprav-ity. They wanted people to apologize for being poor. Or, admit what a horrible person they were, and then we will help you once you have debased yourself. Loaves & Fishes doesn't do that. Of all the places that I have ever experienced it is the most free of that, totally free of that.

Herb recounted that he felt "very happy" and "very impressed" with the Loaves & Fishes vision of charity. He noted that he supported their "social activism," especially the plan to build cottages for the homeless. He found nothing "inconsistent ethically" in his volunteer work there.

Pete, the weekly volunteer dishwasher, recounted his impatience with friends of his who wondered why the homeless did not find work. With outrage tempered by sympathy for what he understands as his friends' ignorance, Pete explained to me in an interview, "Well, my God, there's nothing out here. It's very sad." Charlie, formerly In-house at The Salvation Army, joined Pete in appreciating Loaves & Fishes' tolerance of the unemployed. He characterized "some of the staff" at The Salvation Army as "a little more arrogant." He appreciated how the staff at Loaves & Fishes accepted all the guests with the same warmth and respect.

Studies of volunteers in other private shelters illustrate how fre-quently staff expect volunteers to demand middle-class notions of ap-propriate behavior and manners from homeless clients. Doug A. Timmer, D. Stanley Eitzen, and Kathryn D. Talley argue that all too frequently such an ideology emphasizes strict enforcement of rules over stabilization of the homeless' precarious social position:

> The ubiquitous promotion of middle-class values, mores, and behavior in these shelters is apparently designed as an antidote to the culture of poverty, to the culture of homelessness. Shelter residents often resent the middle-class standards of orderliness and cleanliness, middle-class moralisms about appropriate behavior, the official shelter rules and regulations, and the rigid daily routine. (1994: 106)

At Loaves & Fishes the street monitors and hospitality crew shielded volunteers from the need to abide by even the minimal rules intended to preserve civility in the dining room.

Ethnographic studies of private shelters demanding strict rule compliance from the homeless suggest that volunteers often feel uncomfortable in their roles as rule enforcers. Although Gwendolyn A. Dordick (1997) focused her attention on the experiences of the homeless, not volunteers, her analysis of a private shelter reveals a social world in which volunteers served primarily as rule enforcers on behalf of the staff. One volunteer explained to Dordick, "I use the rules if they can help. But if they get in the way of what we are trying to do here, I really don't bother. . . . For the most part, I just use my own discretion" (1997: 165). The homeless retained space at the private shelter by demonstrating to staff and volunteers that they accepted the burden of responsibility for their plight through willingness to change their behavior. "Good relations with individual volunteers [were] thus critical to maintaining a secure spot within the shelter" (Dordick 1997: 178).

In a study of moral identity among shelter volunteers drawn primarily from a nearby university, Daphne Holden (1997) analyzed the difficulty volunteers faced in resolving the tension between sustaining virtue and acting as rule enforcers. They were treated with outright hostility when they attempted to uphold shelter expectations by monitoring the behavior of the homeless. The volunteers attempted to negotiate this contradiction by establishing an "egalitarian" moral identity. Thus the volunteers acted like friends to the homeless, compared themselves favorably to other types of volunteers, and—like the volunteer observed by Dordick—exercised considerable discretion in rule enforcement (Holden 1997: 127). As Holden convincingly argues, this egalitarian moral identity sidestepped a critical analysis by the volunteers of the inequalities implicit in the relationship between themselves and the homeless. In her words, "the trump cards remained in the hands of volunteers," who could decide when to treat the guests as equals and when to draw on the power of their status as volunteer (1997: 142).

The working arrangements of feeding the poor at Loaves & Fishes largely absolved the volunteers of the need to enforce rules. The staff imposed minimal social control and took on this task in their roles as street monitors, hospitality workers, volunteer coordinator, and dining hall manager. Furthermore, volunteers were spared the dirty work of cleaning up. They could, however, choose to help with dishes or to work in the dining room. For example, Miguel explained to me,

> I think I will do anything but dishes. I *haaaate* dishes. I don't mind mopping. I can wipe down counters, I'll slice and dice, I'll hand the napkins and trays, but I think I would rather serve the food.

Chris Delany and the kitchen manager occasionally entreated the volunteers to stay after serving to help with the cleanup. As I recorded on many occasions in my fieldnotes, many of those who did not participate in the cleanup seemed not to notice that the kitchen staff hired to do this dirty work generally were men of color; others interacted minimally but politely. The male volunteers who washed dishes and worked at the ovens usually interacted much more easily with the paid staff. The working arrangements at Loaves & Fishes allowed the volunteers to *choose* whether to enter into the potentially socially difficult and frequently dirty work of personalist hospitality.

In thinking about hospitality as a social form, Virginia Olesen (1994: 195) notes the importance of economic and social context in shaping the production of particular selves: "Shifts in societal ethos, egalitarianism, and market forces transform and retransform the form or provide circumstances in which the form is altered or appropriated." She argues that even the less-rationalized hospice form of hospitality (in contrast to domestic hospitality or the appropriated form evidenced in the airline cabin) has become more bureaucratized and less concerned with preserving uniqueness and connectedness. Personalist hospitality at Loaves & Fishes certainly seems to evidence a movement from resisting rationalization to using bureaucratization as a means to integrate volunteers with diverse attitudes to homeless into the daily workings of the kitchen and the dining room.

Elizabeth purposefully sought out Loaves & Fishes to free herself from the difficulty of playing rule enforcer in a shelter setting. Miguel enjoyed working the feeding line but adamantly declared his unwillingness to wash dishes. Pete chose to spend several hours each week washing dishes alongside the paid kitchen staff, leaving room on the food serving line for others. The staff had modified the practice of personalist hospitality to allow volunteer choice in participation, not only in the dirty work of cleaning up and the awkward work of monitoring the minimal rules, but also in accepting the poor as Ambassadors of God. While many volunteers never talked with me about the staff's work or the dirty and difficult work of feeding large groups of people, they did talk about their struggles with extending love and acceptance to all of the guests.

The willingness of all the volunteers to struggle with the Loaves & Fishes vision of charity evidenced the power of personalist hospitality to shape the volunteers' moral selving. Even when faced with the guests most troubling to them (seemingly able-bodied, young men), the routine volunteers strove to provide charitable love. For some, like Tony, this struggle engaged them in the work of faith-based moral self-betterment as prescribed by Christian visions of the poor; others, like Herb and Dan, struggled to serve within the precepts of Jewish traditions of caring for the poor. Lori's concern to match the magnanimity of the kitchen staff revealed more a secular-based struggle to accept a political vision of all the poor as deserving than an encounter with a faith-based ideology.[6] In short, whereas some volunteers felt comfortable working within the faith-based Catholic Worker vision of the poor as Ambassadors of God, others tried to reconcile this vision with their own religious beliefs, while still others struggled with the implications of the deserving poor more as a secularized political ideology than a faith-based teaching.

Not only did some volunteers want the guests to express gratitude to them as hosts, but, even more significant, they could not overcome their judgmental attitudes about the guests that revealed a bias against the poor. Rather than accept a form of hospitality that uncritically acknowledged the uniqueness of the guests and cherished connectedness among all participants, some volunteers drew on hierarchical co-constructions of guest and host and worthy and unworthy poor to uphold a stratified social world antithetical to the personalist hospitality ideology. These moments of moral incongruity revealed resistance to a Christian progressive vision of charity. Such contradictions foreshadowed the crisis of legitimacy Loaves & Fishes would experience in the coming years as local community members expressed dissatisfaction with its continued advocacy on behalf of all the homeless and consequent growth.

## CONCLUSION

> If we do not keep indoctrinating, we lose the vision. And
> if we lose the vision, we become merely philanthropists,
> doling out palliatives.
>     The vision is this. We are working for "a new heaven
> and new *earth*, wherein justice dwelleth." We are trying
> with action, "Thy will be done on *earth* as it is heaven."
> We are working for a Christian social order.
>                     *Day*, By Little and By Little

Gratitude, commitment, and witnessing revolved as interconnected themes in the moral selving of the routine volunteers. For these volunteers, the mundanity of feeding the poor took on a higher moral tone as they collectively aspired to self-betterment. Their commitment to the Loaves & Fishes vision of charity stood in stark contrast to the sentimentality that guided the holiday volunteers. Within the moral community of the routine volunteers, moral selving directed the volunteers not inward but outward in the direction of community and action.

This analysis of the routine volunteers provides a dramatic counterexample to the analyses of the many scholars who decry the moral eclipse of community by economic and political frameworks (Wolfe 1989), self-reliance (Bellah et. al. [1985] 1996), narcissism (Lasch 1978), or cynicism (Stivers 1994). In a study of suburbanites, M. P. Baumgartner (1988) documented the prevalence of "moral minimalism" as people sought to avoid conflict. This suburban moral order reflected the fragmentation of social ties and an ethos of restraint in dealing with strangers. Baumgartner's work lends ethnographic depth to Robert D. Putnam's (1995a, 1995b, 1996) much-touted argument that America's civil society has withered in the wake of declining social connectedness and civic engagement. The routine volunteers, however, provide evidence for Bellah and colleagues' more optimistic argument in *The Good Society* (1991) that moral order can be established by individuals taking control of their institutions.

Yet, as Wuthnow (1998b) argues, perhaps civic organizations should be understood at this historical moment as "porous institutions" allowing for the easy flow of people and resources both in and out of a community. Wuthnow suggests that while a membership model might characterize the participation of individuals in traditional voluntary organizations dedicated to charity and service, a networking metaphor captures better the experience of more recent participation in civic culture. Indeed, there is evidence suggesting that many experienced Loaves & Fishes in this way.[7] Others, however, clearly felt themselves to be long-term members of Loaves & Fishes. Indeed, in follow-up calls to inquire about their relationship to Loaves & Fishes several years after the fieldwork ended (see the epilogue), I documented volunteers with more than ten years' commitment to Loaves & Fishes. These long-term volunteers used the techniques of networking to recruit new members and to maintain the volunteer group. These long-term members, although not the norm at Loaves & Fishes, played a central role in helping to organize the hundreds of volunteers at Loaves & Fishes. They exemplified how, as Wuthnow points out, volunteers and paid professionals may exist in a symbiotic relationship.

Although the routine volunteers demonstrated remarkable social connectedness and civic engagement, they were not always sure of the best way to help the guests as they strove to feel charitable love for all of them. Their stories of volunteering are remarkably free of cynicism or narcissism. Although they admired self-reliance, the routine volunteers nonetheless valued action on behalf of the less fortunate. The attempt by some volunteers to square their more conservative framing of the worthy poor with the progressive moral rhetoric of Loaves & Fishes left them with discomforting feelings of inauthenticity. The staff organized volunteer labor so that these volunteers could choose to avoid the guests if they desired. The working arrangements of food preparation and serving maintained social distance and allowed the volunteers to evade their more troubled feelings. Many routine volunteers nonetheless felt compelled to wrestle with their ambivalence about personalist hospitality. These volunteers not only struggled with the demands of the etiquette and rhetoric implicit in treating all the guests with compassion but strove to feel compassion for all the guests.

Work in the kitchen could either reverse or underscore inequality between volunteer and guest. In the words of Candace Clark (1997: 229) in her nuanced study of sympathy, "Sympathy and other emotional gifts may contribute to both cohesion *and* stratification." In my fieldwork I observed how middle-class etiquette could be used both to maintain distance between guest and volunteer and to accord the poor equality by viewing them as guests. Through their work at Loaves & Fishes, many of the volunteers felt closer to Sacramento's poor and their need for political entitlement.

The volunteer role appeared to be an important social and personal commitment for all the routine volunteers. This commitment reflects the power of what Rebecca J. Erickson calls "self-values" in determining self-conceptions. Erickson (1995: 133) argues that "because some self-values are more important to one's sense of authenticity than others, they may help to explain the range of commitments we hold to particular role-identities." Although some of the routine volunteers had worked at Loaves & Fishes for five years by the time of my interviews, their personal commitment to feeding the poor, not the duration of the commitment, probably best explained their deeply moral regard for this work.

Participation by the mostly white, middle-class routine volunteers in personalist hospitality involved not only caring for the poor but also bettering their moral selves. They joined a desire for action, or self-efficacy, with the search for meaning, or authenticity, in their gratitude for economic security, commitment to feeding the urban poor, and witnessing the sacred. Some volunteers' visions of authentic ideals originated in deeply spiritual roots, while others' vision of a more caring world rested on social and political ideals. Yet for all of the routine volunteers the collective ceremony of ritualistic volunteering reinforced social sentiments and morality. Within this Durkheimian vision of collective action, the routine volunteers' practice of personalist hospitality and feeding the urban poor did "indeed remake their moral being" (Durkheim [1912] 1995: 363).

# CHAPTER 4

# Moral Selving within Salvationism

*Sobriety, Work, and Redemption*

Moral selving among the drafted volunteers at The Salvation Army exposed an organization that believed in mandated change. Whereas Loaves & Fishes entrusted the routine volunteers with self-guided moral selving, at The Salvation Army staff supervised the moral selving of the drafted volunteers. Here I examine what it meant for the In-house residents and Alternative Sentencing Program participants, most of whom were male, to become more virtuous, and often spiritual, persons. My analysis suggests that, like the routine volunteers at Loaves & Fishes, the drafted volunteers believed that constructing a principled self involved caring for others. Although many initially did not wish to be at The Salvation Army, those who became committed to the experience found it important to their self-betterment. Welcomed by the staff and other volunteers, they began moral selving by working within the rhetoric of Alcoholics Anonymous and Salvationism.

As we saw in chapter 3, The Salvation Army's practice of charitable action extended physical salvation to open the way for spiritual salvation. The military model of The Salvation Army structured a hierarchy wherein Salvationists and civilian staff extend "Heart to God and Hand to Man." New recruits and staff alike received disciplining into a work ethic that valued sobriety and productivity. Many of the volunteers were battling alcohol and drug problems, or the stigma of court-ordered volunteer hours. The principles of A.A. and The Salvation Army composed a moral rhetoric of charitable action highlighting self-control and personal responsibility to transform corrupt selves. In contrast to the social distance pervading relations between volunteers and guests at Loaves & Fishes, volunteers and staff at The Salvation Army strove to help each other and the homeless out of poverty and despair through hard work and self-discipline.

New recruits to The Salvation Army learned the strict rules of deference and demeanor, which, according to Erving Goffman ([1956] 1967), maintain local hierarchies. Goffman defines *deference* as honorific or privileged regard, which is often the result of membership in a high-status social category, whereas *demeanor* reveals physical deportment communicating desirable (or undesirable) traits. Goffman ([1956] 1967: 92) argues, "If an individual is to act with proper demeanor and show proper deference, then it will be necessary for him to have areas of self-esteem." The predominantly homeless and court-ordered volunteers at The Salvation Army, who suffered a lack of both material and symbolic resources, remained severely disadvantaged within the interactive negotiation of status.

Salvationist ideology provided institutionally based resources for moral selving wherein the volunteer recruits were expected to be sober, disciplined to work, and filled with redemption in all aspects of their lives. The Salvation Army functioned akin to what Goffman (1961) calls a "total institution." Although The Salvation Army did not operate as strictly as the locked-down mental institution that provided the setting for Goffman's study of the total institution, The Salvation Army did provide strict behavioral guidelines and monitoring of its homeless volunteers and to a lesser extent of the court-ordered volunteers. The institutionally based moral selving at the Shelter Services

Center resembled Goffman's description of the moral career within a total institution:

> Each moral career, and behind this, each self, occurs within the confines of an institutional system. . . . The self, then, can be seen as something that resides in the arrangements prevailing in a social system for its members. The self in this sense is not a property of the person to whom it is attributed, but dwells rather in the pattern of social control that is exerted in connection with the person by himself and those around him. This special kind of institutional arrangement does not so much support the self as constitute it. (1961: 168)

The Salvation Army staff worked to socialize the drafted volunteers, particularly the In-house residents, to an institutionally based morality. While the drafted and especially the ASP volunteers remained in contact with others outside the institution, the staff challenged them to align their moral careers with Salvationist principles of the moral self.

Whereas the committed routine volunteers at Loaves & Fishes wrestled with the political tenets of personalism, even the committed drafted volunteers often resisted the self-disciplining implicit in Salvationist redemption. Autonomy underlay the routine volunteer choice to struggle with personalist hospitality. At The Salvation Army many of the In-house and ASP volunteers resisted coercion to become sober and to practice self-disciplining through work; thus these recruits were left without many options for salvation. The drafted volunteers found honor and a strictly defined path to moral redemption. Although I offer some examples of out-and-out resistance and failed moral selving, I focus primarily on those who strove to shape their moral selving in accordance with Salvationist ideology. This analysis of the drafted volunteers who struggled to become sober and productive workers renders visible the linkages between Salvationist rhetoric and moral selving.

Whereas the routine volunteers at Loaves & Fishes ideally worked to express commitment to the work of feeding the urban poor, gratitude for economic security, and witnessing of the sacred in one's life, the drafted volunteers, to the degree that they agreed with the organizational rhetoric, worked to attain *sobriety*, self-discipline through *work*, and salvation through *redemption*. A successful moral career challenged the mostly male drafted volunteers to leave behind a stigmatized identity and adopt what Jessie Bernard (1981) has described as "the good-provider role." The good-provider role is mapped into sex-role segregation wherein men provide for women and children and women do caretaking work.

> The good provider was a "family man." He set a good table, provided a decent home, paid the mortgage, bought the shoes, and kept his children warmly clothed. . . . The good provider made a decent contribution to the church. His work might be demanding, but he expected it to be. If in addition to being a good provider, a man was kind, gentle, generous, and not a heavy drinker or gambler, that was all frosting on the cake. (Bernard 1981: 3)

The good-provider role upheld the Salvationist expression of muscular Christianity that centered men's religious identity and moral character around work roles.

Both the routine and the drafted volunteers revealed the embeddedness of moral selving in charitable action. The drafted volunteers, however, found it difficult to lodge their moral selving in a role not readily available to them in their stigmatized situation as In-house or ASP volunteers.

## DOING SALVATIONISM: STORIES OF
## MORAL SELVING

The drafted volunteers arrived at The Salvation Army with discrediting attributes experienced as stigma (Goffman 1963). The social status of being homeless, often unemployed, or sentenced to court-ordered volunteer hours spoiled their identity as competent, self-supporting, upstanding community members. Those who became committed to self-betterment entered into the Salvationist work ethic to remake themselves. By linking their self-concept to work roles played at The

Salvation Army, these volunteers salvaged their spoiled identity and masculinity through hard work and discipline. Predominantly working-class men of color with anxieties about "respectability," they resembled the men that Mitchell Duneier encountered at the Valois Diner in Chicago's Hyde Park:

> If respectability can be defined by the sociologist as a mode of life embodying conceptions of moral worth, it is defined rather more loosely in actual practice by a man's opposition to a number of human characteristics he disdains: wastefulness, pretension, aggressiveness, uncommunicativeness, impatience, flashiness, laziness, disrespect for elders, and perhaps most important a lack of personal responsibility. (1992: 66)

Similarly, moral selving at The Salvation Army entailed salvaging respectability by distancing oneself from these stigmatizing characteristics.

Furthermore, in the struggle to attain respectability, the drafted volunteers worked to repair their self-esteem.[1] Gecas (1991: 180) formulates the self-esteem motive as the "most responsive to the interpersonal domain," with others' judgments leading to potentially damaging or empowering self-evaluations. Within this realm, Gecas (1991: 180) asserts, "strategies of self-presentation and impression management come into play in the service of maintaining a favorable self-image." The drafted volunteers described below fit Gecas's model, as they welded a drive to recoup self-esteem through work to a desire to build self-efficacy through sobriety, work, and redemption. In contrast to the Loaves & Fishes routine volunteers' concern for what Gecas calls authenticity, the drafted volunteers expressed greater concern about salvaging self-esteem.[2]

The symbolic resources of Salvationism provided a recipe for moral selving emphasizing self-disciplining through work. The drafted volunteers learned this role through participation in the kitchen. The staff furnished the model with which the recruits could broaden their role-taking range. Those In-house and ASP volunteers most committed to the worker role, with its accompanying rules of deference and demeanor, were sometimes asked to join The Salvation Army staff.

## SOBRIETY: "OUR COMMON WELFARE"

1. Our common welfare should come first; personal recovery depends upon A.A. unity. . . .
5. Each group has but one primary purpose—to carry its message to the alcoholic who still suffers.

*From the Twelve Traditions of*
*Alcoholics Anonymous*

The thoroughness with which drafted volunteers' incorporated the Twelve Steps and Twelve Traditions of A.A. into everyday talk and practice recalled William Booth's (1890: 180) nineteenth-century ideological agenda for "effectual deliverance for the drunkard." Just as Booth understood that men should help their fellow men remain sober, so did many of the kitchen staff use A.A., and, more recently, Narcotics Anonymous (N.A.), principles to structure daily activities in the kitchen according to this communal endeavor. For example, the drafted volunteers frequently explained to the staff that they were "taking care of business" as they left the property. This A.A. phrase sufficed to legitimate suspect excursions "off property."

The staff tried to direct the drafted volunteers to A.A., N.A., or Adult Children of Alcoholics (A.C.A.) to provide a supportive environment for the building of self-esteem and self-efficacy. Kevin, a drug and alcoholic counselor explained, "If we can get them actively involved in that type of network, then we got a chance. They have a chance if they get out there." Dave, the resident manager, argued that almost all of the residents would benefit, as did he, from participation in one of these programs.

The major, *major* problem here is drug and alcohol issues. We administer the substance abuse inventory to everybody that comes in, and the positive results of that is about 90 percent. So it was even higher than what I had thought it would be. I am really *amazed*, and I know that, like in my case, I hitchhiked into Sacramento back in '91 and I was, or I *am*, an alcoholic, and when I got here I just, I mean, the bottle beat me to death, you know, and I didn't want to be here.

In keeping with A.A.'s emphasis on doing service work, chairing meetings, and helping others' maintain their sobriety, Dave believed that "people can most help themselves by caring for others."

The intake approach Kevin advocated to Dave when he first began counseling assumed that a client might be in denial of his or her dependency. As I wrote in my fieldnotes,

> Kevin told me that he told Dave about doing intake differently, by showing him his textbook, depicting an interview as the client telling the interviewer what he thinks is wrong with himself. . . . Kevin said that then they could see if the client was in denial.

This approach to alcohol counseling stretched the A.A. mandate not to "follow up or try to control its members" (Alcoholics Anonymous n.d.a). The staff, rather than trust the recruits with self-guided surveillance, monitored the drafted volunteers' demeanor for emotions deemed by A.A. to be counterproductive to maintaining sobriety: anger, resentment, and denial. This monitoring corresponded to the surveillance of the drafted volunteers within the Salvationist setting.

A.A.-based moral selving delineated clear interactional guidelines. For example, I heard the kitchen manager, Raul, a Chicano, tell another man of a lesson that he had learned. Raul told him that he had learned that you could not change anybody else. He emphasized this by repeating that you should just try to be happy yourself and let others be themselves. In this interaction Raul carried the message of A.A. to this new recruit, thereby practicing the Fifth Tradition: "Each group has but one primary purpose—to carry its message to the alcoholic who still suffers." He also reinforced the Twelfth Tradition: "Place principles before personalities" (Alcoholics Anonymous 1965: 55).

Interactions such as these support Norman Denzin's (1987a) observation that lessons about the "alcoholic self" teach the recruit a new language. The new recruit to A.A. learns this language and consequently what it means to be an alcoholic by participating in the social world of A.A. (Rudy 1986). At the Shelter Services Center, similar to the Skid Row therapeutic setting studied by Darin Weinberg (1996), volunteers and staff entered into a "treatment *community* rather than a treatment facility," in that socialization into what it means to be an alcoholic or a drug addict was provided not just by staff but also by other A.A. and N.A. participants among the volunteers. In Weinberg's terms, participants in such a community demonstrate their commitment to recovery through ideology avowal (adherence to program ideology) as well as through the more complicated ideology exemplification (avowance of the importance of ideology to one's everyday experiences). Participants in A.A. and N.A. at the Shelter Services Center entered into a therapeutic community struggling to be authentic to the principles of recovery. In their daily interactions they used the language of recovery to talk about appropriate behaviors.

At the Shelter Services Center this process was especially moralistic in the practice of the Fourth Step: "We made a searching and fearless moral inventory of ourselves." For example, Chris, a white cook, explained to Raul as he prepared a meal, "Don't you know, I'm an alcoholic, we always do things the hard way." The participants monitored both their own and others' emotional states for anger and resentment, defined by A.A. as particularly corrosive to the alcoholic. In another instance, recorded in my fieldnotes, Chris told Jerome, a black In-house volunteer, that he should attend a meeting because he seemed angry.

> There was meeting talk today as Jerome said he needed to go to a noon N.A. meeting. He recounted how mad he got last night when he couldn't find a meeting, and Chris said he thought there was an A.A. meeting near where he had been. Jerome said that would be okay, that he got clean at A.A. Chris made a comment about Jerome being angry and told him that he should go to a meeting at noon.

Later Chris joked with the lunch servers about seeing Jerome out there eating when he was "well and wonderful" and Jerome joked back that he wasn't sure he wanted to be "well and wonderful."

Jerome was ambivalent in his resistance to Chris's monitoring of his moral selving as he indicated that he was not sure that he wanted to be, in A.A. language, "well and wonderful." Chris, however, took seriously his obligation to "carry this message" to Jerome.

Monitoring emotional demeanor was a routine part of interactions between staff and volunteers, as I discovered when I returned to The Salvation Army after a few months' absence.

> I found out that Greg [a white cook active in A.A.] recognized me when he asked where I had been the last few months. I told him that I had been busy with school. He said that I looked good, and I said that I felt rested and that the last few months had been really good. He said, nonjudgmentally, that I had seemed very much more stressed when he last saw me. He said this just as an observation, not a judgment, and I did not feel that I had to respond or defend my apparent stress. (Fieldnotes)

Yet those known to be members of A.A. or N.A. did receive direct warnings about having an anxious demeanor, as an interaction between two cooks revealed: "Chris was kind of high-strung today, and later, as lunch approached, Raul told him several times to cool his heels, after doing an imitation of him behind his back, running around somewhat frantically (fieldnotes). Raul encouraged Chris to take some time out and calm himself.

The following interaction between two In-house volunteers is an example of how A.A. members received encouragement for presenting a calm demeanor.

> Jack sat down for a while and Tommy congratulated him on being more mellow. He told Jack that he seemed like a different person, that he didn't even recognize him. Jack explained that he was trying to learn to relax but that this was difficult after twenty-three years of

being a drug addict. Jack stood up and was laughing loudly as he noticed he had spilled enchilada sauce down his T-shirt. His laughter was loud and nervous; then he self-consciously covered his mouth with his hand and quieted down.

Tommy, a black kitchen worker, tried to give Jack, a white, support for his recovery by building his self-esteem. Tommy joined the team to support Chris's presentation of self as a recovering alcoholic, who, in sociological terms, possessed good self-esteem and was driven by self-efficacy.

While "taking five" or preparing a meal, A.A. members often told their stories. They refer to their life stories of when they were practicing alcoholics as "drunk-a-logues." Occasionally staff and volunteers at the Shelter Services Center would also use this term. These drunk-a-logues recounted not only "wild living" and "partying" but also the despondency caused by poor self-esteem. A.A., N.A., and work at The Salvation Army all contributed to the building of positive self-images. Celia, a black woman in her late thirties, did ASP hours at The Salvation Army to work off a sentence for a minor drug possession. She maintained contact with a nun at Loaves & Fishes whom she met through its jail visitation program and used all available resources in her struggle to live a sober life.

> God is going to help me do it. He's going to help me do it. He's going to help me do it. And I go to counseling too. I go to chemical dependency center, I take parenting classes, I take mental health classes, you know, reasserting yourself in society, and living a clean and sober life, free of all chemical dependency and drugs, alcohol, anything. Matter of fact the Lord delivered me from cigarettes on January the fourteenth.

Celia evidenced self-efficacy as she pieced together a network of support groups intended to build her self-esteem.

Because the Shelter Services Center could provide only a short-term community for men engaged in recovery, the staff tried to lodge the drafted volunteers' often shaky moral selving in support groups before their eventual termination from the institutional network at The

Salvation Army. Yet some staff resisted moving off-site. For example, Hank, a white cook in his fifties, formerly In-house, maintained his sobriety by living on-site. "I could be operating heavy equipment and making good money, but I'm just no good out there," he told me. Hank's fear of relapse played out when the Salvationists decided six months after his arrival that all staff would have to live off property. After news of this decision, Hank went off property, drank, got in a fight, and landed in jail. Kevin, a close friend of Hank's, explained that although the staff tried to help Hank find a place to live, he had been "grumpy, stubborn, and uncooperative."

> Kevin was clearly sad. He said that Hank was like a father to him. And he was just one of his real good buddies. I asked Kevin what would happen to Hank, and he said that he imagined that Hank would "move on." Kevin said that Hank couldn't come back as a cook but that he could come back and line up to be In-house and hang around the kitchen. Kevin said he supposed that if Hank talked with Howard [a Salvationist] and Dave and showed himself to be sincere, he would be moved back in as a chef but that Hank had too much pride for that. Hank had a really difficult time working the Eighth Step of the program: Making amends for the past. Hank just hadn't been able to do that. He had too much pride, which got in the way of doing that step. (Fieldnotes)

Hank stayed in touch with Kevin, who in turn wrote to him in care of general delivery on his way to either Montana or Oregon. Kevin said that Hank would return to the life of the "hobo."

Although Kevin's moral selving involved a commitment to "our common welfare," he could not help Hank to build the self-esteem and self-efficacy necessary to maintain his sobriety outside the support of In-house living. Although Kevin agreed with A.A. literature that The Salvation Army could not "furnish initial motivation for alcoholics to recover" (Alcoholics Anonymous n.d.a), he and other staff believed that the Shelter Services Center should buttress such a commitment with long-term residential stability. Kevin felt able to live alone for the first time in seven years only after he had spent two and a half years at The Salvation Army.

Hank's fear of losing In-house status revealed the tenuous linkages among moral selving and roles and relationships at The Salvation Army. Hank's role as a cook, coupled with the camaraderie of the In-house residents, supported his striving toward a disciplined sobriety. Hank, however, could not take the conceptual tools of moral selving offered him at The Salvation Army and adhere to the A.A. program off-site. The civilian counselors argued that for the transition from In-house to permanent housing to be successful, the recovering addict needed to live on-site for several years and then be immersed in an A.A. or N.A. group to provide, in sociological terms, a reference group for continued moral selving.

Some of the staff believed that The Salvation Army also failed to meet women's needs for long-term stability. Kevin told me, "It's a lot harder for women." Celia felt that the institution should offer women more support.

> For battered woman, who should have counselors for *all* of this [transition]. *Salvation*, you's suppose to be *saved* and *saved* from whaaatevver. Don't just limit it to alcoholism. From what I have known from down through the years, The Salvation Army has been mostly for the alcoholics, but honey, there are much more, larger crowd out there suffering from diseases such as incest, rape, spousal abuse, they're misfits, don't know where they fit in. And they need a little bit more counseling. Services. And housing.

These evaluations of The Salvation Army revealed that whereas the drafted volunteers placed great responsibility on the individual to build self-esteem and self-efficacy, they also understood that material resources and institutional support were crucial to lasting rehabilitation.

The commitment to sobriety linked institutionally inspired moral selving with work for "our common welfare." The volunteers and staff found in A.A. a recipe for sobriety that motivated their desires for feelings of increased self-esteem and self-efficacy. These A.A. regulars monitored the demeanor of the new recruits for anger and resentment. They accompanied each other to meetings and made regular telephone calls to check up on each other. They understood that self-esteem arose from mutually supportive relationships and that self-efficacy was established through a supportive transition to living off-site coupled with work.

## WORK: "SELF-RESPECT IN THE MAN"

> I do not wish to have any hand in establishing a new centre of demoralisation. I do not want my customers to be pauperised by being treated to anything which they do not earn. To develop self-respect in the man, to make him feel that at last he has got his foot planted on the first rung of the ladder which leads upwards, is vitally important, and this cannot be done unless the bargain between him and me is strictly carried out. So much coffee, so much bread, so much shelter, so much warmth and light from me, but so much labour in return from him.
>
> *Booth*, In Darkest England
> and the Way Out

The drafted volunteers struggled to find work, either at The Salvation Army or through the Salvationist job referral program. Organizational rhetoric reinforced the stigmatizing of laziness and welfare in favor of a self-sufficient work ethic. Some of the In-house residents chose to volunteer in the kitchen, and thereby feel self-respect, rather than take charity. The volunteers felt, in keeping with Booth's worldview, that self-respect inhered in work. The paid staff, almost entirely composed of former volunteers, became role models for the drafted volunteers. As a reference group, however, the staff created obstacles in the moral selving of the drafted volunteers by complaining about their low wages.

This section explores how the predominantly male drafted volunteers demonstrated their self-disciplining to *work* through the adoption of the "good-provider role." The ability to provide materially for a family underscored the successful adoption of the role. Self-disciplining entailed learning both how to extend appropriate deference to others within the Salvationist hierarchy and how to express self-esteem through one's demeanor. The good-provider role received affirmation not only from the staff but also through the adoption of surrogate gendered kin relationships among the volunteers and staff. In sum, the drafted volunteers spoke of the themes of the Salvationist work ethic, the interplay of deference and demeanor, and kinship relations and sociability when describing the importance of work.

### The Work Ethic

All volunteers in The Salvation Army kitchen signed a release form to forfeit any claim to Worker's Compensation or accident benefits each time they came to work there. ASP workers filled out additional paperwork to verify their hours. With few exceptions, those who stayed in the overflow shelter at Cal Expo could not volunteer in the kitchen, unless they were formerly In-house. In-house residents, however, received encouragement to volunteer from the staff.

> On the wall between the plastic glasses and the salad bar was taped a computer printout with a drawing of an older, bearded, street-looking man, who appeared white. Above the picture the caption read, "Wanted Faithful L. Volunteer," and below, "The Salvation Army Kitchen Is Looking for Volunteers. Please contact [the resident manager] for more information." (Fieldnotes)

The In-house residents could become drafted volunteers by remaining on-site to work in the kitchen.

In-house residents could live at the Shelter Services Center for one month. The staff required the In-house residents, except the ill or nonmobile, to leave the site from 8:00 to 4:00 Monday through Friday to look for employment. In-house residents who came on-site during the day faced suspicion that a nonresident volunteer, such as myself, escaped.

> As I left for the day a white woman, perhaps in her thirties, came from the dorms past the front desk. The African-American man at

the front desk, who had just teased me that normally he rented his
pen out, hailed her repeatedly and asked why she was inside. She
said something about needing her jacket. He replied, "You know
that you are not supposed to be inside during the day." She concurred. As I followed her out of the lobby, I noticed that she did not
have a jacket with her. She headed up 12th, toward Friendship Park.
(Fieldnotes)

A few In-house residents could remain on-site during the day if they volunteered in the kitchen. These rules illustrate how the staff attempted to
instill self-discipline in the In-house residents. Kevin explained that the requirements of In-house residency facilitated a transition to the work ethic:
"There are just two simple things the first-week In-house must do here.
You go to the housing workshop and you go to the jobs workshop. That's
all they have to do, and you would be surprised how many people just
don't get it." The In-house volunteers who demonstrated to the staff their
steadfast commitment to the job program, the housing program, and the
substance abuse programs sometimes earned another thirty days In-house.

Frequent checks on the cleanliness of the kitchen by Dave, the resident manager, underscored the importance of a disciplined work ethic
among the kitchen crew. The staff and volunteers formed a kitchen
crew for any particular meal.

Dave entered in a rush with an attitude of authority. He swept into
the kitchen and said, glancing toward the dishwashing area, "I see
two strikes against you already." Neither Speed nor Downtown [two
black In-house volunteers] had on hairnets, and Downtown tried to
explain that he took his off when we went outside for a break. But
Dave wasn't slowing down to hear this. It was also clear that Dave
was disgruntled at the condition of the kitchen. Dave left quickly.
Raul appeared to be especially frustrated and annoyed after his de-
parture. (Fieldnotes)

The crew was admonished for not helping to clean up after breakfast. In
this case, Greg, a white, formerly In-house staff cook, passed such or-

ders from Raul, then head kitchen supervisor, to the predominantly black lunch crew.

> Greg told us that Raul had asked him to hold a meeting to talk with us about cleaning the kitchen. Recently a man stayed to clean until 1:30 A.M. because the kitchen had been left a mess. Raul wanted the lunch workers to stay until 1:30 P.M. to help finish cleaning the kitchen and dining room after lunch. Apparently many of the kitchen workers leave by 1:00 and the dining room isn't even swept. Speed looked away and appeared annoyed. Downtown pointed out, agreeably, that if we continue to clean the kitchen as we go, as we have been doing, that this won't be so difficult. Greg agreed but made clear that this was would still not be enough. Although Speed looked annoyed, the men seemed okay with these new rules. (Fieldnotes)

My fieldnotes indicate that the staff encouraged "steady" work with breaks.

> Raul joked with Mikey [a white cook] about how we work hard and steady, but there is no need to rush. If any of us break a sweat, we are to take a ten-minute break. Jack [a white In-house volunteer] teased that he was breaking out in a sweat. Raul replied quite seriously that he could take a break. Jack kept working. Raul suggested that we work and get lunch ready so that we could take a five-minute break before lunch.

Disciplining to the work ethic also included threats of "being written up," which could lead to expulsion from The Salvation Army.[3]

The Salvationist hierarchy sometimes threatened the dignity of the kitchen workers. For example, Raul, before his promotion to head cook, proclaimed to a group of volunteers disgruntled by a surprise check on the kitchen, "It's a dog-eat-dog world." The volunteers expressed frustration with the incessant ringing of the telephone, for only the kitchen staff could answer it. Occasionally an annoyed front desk worker poked his or her head into the kitchen as the telephone rang unanswered to query, "Did your bosses leave you unsupervised?"

The staff most closely regulated the behavior of the new In-house and ASP volunteers and challenged the moral authority of any volunteers who appeared to stray from honesty. For example, Raul chastised a young white ASP worker accompanied by his hardworking non-court-ordered pregnant sweetheart for fudging their hours on the sign-in sheet.

> Raul checked the paperwork and then came back and challenged them. Raul marched them to the sign-in sheet and then to check the clocks. Interestingly, Raul addressed Joe, not Rosy, and explained in a strict, but not mean, voice, "You are not to fudge your hours. Three or four minutes here or there are okay, but if we find you off by one-half hour here or there, we will have to send you back to the ASP people." He told Joe that it was okay with them if Rosy came along but that Joe had to abide by the rules. (Fieldnotes)

Apparently Joe redeemed himself. On another day I noticed that some of the staff good-naturedly patted him on the back as he enthusiastically helped to unload a truckload of heavy kitchen supplies.

Male volunteers who joked around instead of working often received the dirtiest, most difficult assignments. For example, the staff penalized a new ASP volunteer who spent his time joking in the dining room.

> [The cook] asked another worker if there were any "disgusting" or "hard" jobs that needed doing and consequently enlisted [the ASP volunteer] to clean meat franks out of the freezer. I later joked that I would be careful not to sit around. [The cook] replied that he didn't like to see someone sitting around when there was work to do. (Fieldnotes)

In another case, Kevin explained to me that he turned away an ASP volunteer he believed used a medical slip (prohibiting him from lifting more than ten pounds) to escape work.

> Every time we came in he was setting on his rear end or he was talking with the clients, so we, he wasn't working, and all the other vol-

unteers were getting mad, because why was that guy? So we moved him back to the kitchen doing dishes, and, well, he wouldn't do dishes. So I lifted a plate and said, "Is this ten pounds?" What happened was we got in a big argument and kicked him out. But he wasn't here to work in the first place, he came here looking to get kicked out so he could go back to his probation officer and say I can't do volunteer hours. (Fieldnotes)

The volunteer's apparent laziness led Kevin to judge him as irredeemable.

Although the staff also expected the female volunteers to abide by the work ethic, work assignments revealed gender distinctions. Whereas male volunteers received work orders to help unload the delivery truck and move heavy items in and out of the coolers, female volunteers often prepared bag lunches, baked cookies, or served food. I frequently made batches of cookies with other female volunteers. Often female volunteers resented being told how to cook.

> We sprayed the sheets with "Food Release" first. As Greg instructed us about how to flatten the cookies, Molly [a white ASP volunteer] told me that she sometimes felt like we were treated like imbeciles, and she said, a bit sarcastically, but with wonderment, "Don't they think that we have done this type of work before?"

Women also often set the tables and helped to arrange food platters for visiting Salvationists. They did not, however, work as paid cooks.

> Greg [a white cook] explained to me, quite seriously, that they had had a woman cook several years ago and that she had difficulty carrying things, so that one of the men would have to stop what he was were doing to help her. She hurt her back on the job and then sued The Salvation Army. They had not had a female cook since. (Fieldnotes)

The job of kitchen cook remained a man's province. But, if I arrived just before serving, a cook would often remove one of the male volunteers from the serving line to make room for me.

> I took myself to the back room to leave my coat and wash my hands, as people seemed busy. When I came back, I put on my disposable hairnet and Raul moved a male ASP worker off of the food line and put me near the end, serving garlic bread and chocolate chip cookies. The ASP worker seemed displeased, as if he wished to retain his place on the food line; he was directed toward the dishwashing. (Fieldnotes)

Although the work ethic imposed a gendered division of labor, the organizational model of moral selving for both women and men entailed self-disciplining without complaint.

The hope of paid employment at The Salvation Army gave incentive to the moral selving of both the In-house and the rare volunteer from The Salvation Army–run overflow shelter at Cal Expo. An encounter from my fieldnotes illustrates this incentive.

> Eddie [an older black] responded quietly that he volunteered as an overflow person with the intention of showing those in charge that he was a hard worker. He explained that if an overflow volunteer works hard, then he is noticed and may get moved In-house. Eventually, there is even the possibility of being hired as staff.

Although the staff discouraged the volunteers from counting on employment at The Salvation Army, Dave explained, "Most of the staff were, I would say, gosh, probably better than 50 percent were volunteers, you know, at one time. Out of ninety people, that's quite a few."

ASP volunteers who completed lengthy volunteer sentences and demonstrated successful moral selving sometimes were recruited for staff positions. Randy, the Mexican-American butcher, explained to me that he received a job offer when he finished his ASP hours and neared early retirement from his paid job: "They wanted to know if I wanted to come to work for them part-time. 'Cause they wanted me to show these guys what I knew, you know, and everything, and I said I didn't know, really." Randy decided against a paid position, but, like Celia, he planned to stay involved at the Shelter Services Center to maintain his commitment to the men there. Celia happily anticipated the day when she could "choose" to volunteer: "But now *I* have the choice of wanting to do it on my own. Without having been *regulated* to do so."

Other volunteers chose not to become paid staff members because they welcomed opportunities to earn more money elsewhere. For example, Newell, a young, white, ASP worker with head cook experience at a nearby college, declined a position at The Salvation Army. As the employment director left the kitchen, he said to me and a Latino man that he would not want a job there. At first he said that he wanted to earn $25 an hour, but then, more seriously, that he would not work for less $15 an hour. Those who chose to work elsewhere did not necessarily reject the institutional moral selving of The Salvation Army. For example, Jerome, a young, black, In-house volunteer, told the employment director that he planned to use his previous experience as a prep cook in an expensive restaurant to find other work. Nonetheless, he abided by the rules of the work ethic. On one occasion, as we sat together at a table, Jerome told one of the men that he loves The Salvation Army. When a young woman approached asking for help because she did not want to break a rule by going into the kitchen, he refused to do it for her, saying that you have got to play by the rules. I never heard of an ASP volunteer who accepted a paid position at The Salvation Army; yet many of the In-house volunteers forsook better pay to work there.[4]

Many staff members demonstrated their commitment to the worker role at The Salvation Army by resistance to leaving, despite the low wages, which started at $4.25 an hour. The fragility of moral selving became apparent as they struggled with the blows to their self-efficacy and self-esteem that the low wages brought. Raul, who worked his way from In-house volunteer to head cook, shared sentiments with Dave and Kevin, also both formerly In-house, when he told me several times, "I love my job. Something new and different happens every day." Other workers told Raul about higher-paid jobs ranging from restaurant to warehouse work.

Raul told me that he was to work from 4:00 A.M. to 12:30 P.M. but often stayed later to finish things. As we talked, Raul teased Mikey about his dislike of chili powder (which the soup contained) because Mikey was probably going to manage a Taco Bell in Del Paso Heights. Raul, though, was clearly proud of Mikey and told me that he was one of the best managers. Mikey asked Raul why he stayed at The Salvation Army when he could earn three times as much at Taco Bell. Raul replied that he would not be happy at Taco Bell. He said that he loved it at The Salvation Army. (Fieldnotes)

When told some months later by Randy of a job opening for a forklift operator elsewhere, at $12 an hour, Raul responded that maybe he should move beyond just making ends meet.

Greg worked his way up the ranks from In-house to cook, went on a drinking binge, and then came back to work his way up to cook again. Greg told me that he would be "grumpy and mad" if he had to work anywhere else. A few months later, however, Greg told me that he hoped to open his own restaurant. He demonstrated the tension between the good-provider role and loyalty to The Salvation Army that I saw repeated again and again.

I sat outside with Greg and some other man on a break, and the two talked about Greg's desire to make more than $4.25 an hour and the possibility of working on the oil rigs again. Greg said that his girlfriend now makes more than he does and that unless he does something else they will never have anything else. Greg wants a motorcycle. Greg said to me, "I like my job. Do you know I like my job?" And I said I knew that. (Fieldnotes)

The low wages complicated Greg's struggle for self-esteem as well as for self-efficacy, yet he valued the Salvationist community and the affirmation that he was a good cook. About a year later, Greg left Sacramento to work in a kitchen at America Live, an entertainment bar complex in a nearby city.

The men employed by The Salvation Army grounded their moral

selving in being responsible, disciplined members of society through work. Wilson worked in the kitchen as a cook, a skill learned during his seven years as a drinker and gambler in Las Vegas. He earned $4.25 an hour plus room and board. He also enrolled in a nursing program at Sacramento City College. The Salvation Army selected him to join NABORS, a joint venture between The Salvation Army and the Sacramento Housing Redevelopment Agency.

> I was dealing a $5,000 a hand (blackjack). I was a good dealer. It was something to be. I handled more money than some bankers. But what was I putting back into life? That wasn't what I wanted to be. I've changed. I had to humble myself. (Wilson, cited in Sylva 1993: C1)

Wilson mixed A.A. talk about the importance of "showing up" and "taking care of business" with Salvationist moral rhetoric about humility in his moral selving. He believed in the importance of working as "a team," and he built his moral self through discipline in the NABORS program.

> The whole message of this project is not to give you a job. . . . But to get you up everyday and get you into a routine. I'm building a good, strong foundation. When August comes, and this program ends, if I keep doing the things I'm doing, I'm going to be all right. (Wilson, cited in Sylva 1993: C5)

Adherence to a disciplined work ethic enhanced both Wilson's self-esteem and his sense of self-efficacy.

Minimum-wage work provided men with the satisfaction of work but troubled their feelings of self-efficacy. Shorey, a former construction worker with a back injury, rented a room in a friend's mobile home and rode a used ten-speed bike six miles to The Salvation Army shelter where he worked as a janitor to stay off welfare.

> I don't like living off other people. A person has to learn how to handle himself. It's just part of life. . . . I really like the job. But the pay is lousy. . . . At least it's a job. It's a competitive world out there. It's better to have something. There are a lot of people worse off than I am. (Shorey, cited in Zaldivar 1995: A28)

The pride of practicing the work ethic, even at the minimum wage, contrasted dramatically with the loss of dignity experienced by men who were unable to work. Stuart Landers, known as Pork Chop, went from working in the kitchen to living in overflow housing at Cal Expo.

> It puts wear and tear on the mind. But it's better than being on the street. And it's better than paying $400 a month for some hotel room where you can't even cook in your room and you have to walk down the hall just to use the bathroom. People look at that and figure you might as well stay in the overflow. (Cited in Guyette 1994: 15)

An unidentified man spoke of the wearing down of self-esteem at the overflow.

> It's good, it's free and it's better than the streets. But there's a cost, too. It costs you your dignity. . . . After a while things begin to deteriorate to the point where you don't give a damn. (Cited in Guyette 1994: 1)

The worker role in the kitchen appeared to initially provide an opportunity to build self-esteem and worthiness, but over time the low wage ultimately undercut the value of the work for many of these men.

The low wages made some of the workers distrustful of The Salvation Army. These workers acquired cynical knowledge of the organization (Goldner, Ritti, and Ference 1977) that undermined easy acceptance of the altruistic goals of helping all espoused by the staff. Sonny, an African-American man, organized the supplies for the kitchen. My fieldnotes detail Sonny's suspicions.

> I said hello to Sonny on my way in and we ended up talking. Sonny complained about the workings of The Salvation Army. He was unhappy and angry about the pay, $4.25 an hour to start, and he claims that The Salvation Army lets men go who have been there a while, in order to reduce expenses. He told me that some men work for up to $7 or $8 an hour, but these are few. He told me that he has been having financial troubles.

A former construction worker, a black man in his mid-fifties whom I met briefly at lunch one day, was typical of In-house volunteers who did not want to be employees of The Salvation Army because of the low wages. He told me that he believes that people should be trained on the job and that 85 to 90 percent of the people at The Salvation Army would rather work elsewhere for $8 to $11 an hour. One simply cannot get by on a minimum wage.

On another occasion a Mexican-American cook, Danny, complained to me about earning only $4.25 an hour. He had hoped to save enough money to rent a small house. But Danny was unhappy with more than the low wages. He also resented the close supervision he was subject to in his work as a cook. On one occasion Raul had come in to check on the spaghetti Danny was making. When he asked Danny about it, I could see Danny bristling at what he considered interference. Raul tasted the spaghetti sauce and said that it was thin. Nor did Danny supervise the other kitchen workers. One day I felt that preparation of the lunch was scattered. As the meal was easy to prepare, the food was ready on time, but Danny's management of the kitchen staff was lax. The other cooks were the ones who kept the joking and crudeness in check. Finally Danny was fired for not being a team player.

Danny's casual management revealed how the close supervision of the other cooks regulated the production of the meal, and the moral order, in the kitchen. Danny, the only openly gay kitchen worker I encountered, complained about the wages and did not adhere to the disciplined worker role. This led to his dismissal. Danny's experience illustrated the injury to self-esteem some of the kitchen workers experienced in adhering to the worker role at The Salvation Army.

Male workers at The Salvation Army, whether volunteers or staff, could be understood in Joanne Passaro's (1996: 37) terms as in "an excruciating gender crisis." Yet, although the committed volunteers had not shed their allegiance to the merits of disciplined work, this alone did not promise their salvation. Many of the drafted volunteers mirrored the beliefs of the poor blacks analyzed by Jennifer L. Hochschild

(1995) who believed that the American Dream was attainable but all too often unrealized because of their problematic individual lives. Richard Sennett and Jonathan Cobbs's *The Hidden Injuries of Class* (1973) sheds light on this paradox. In their study of the self-worth of working-class men in Boston, Sennett and Cobb argued that "what needs to understood is how the class structure in America is organized so that *the tools of freedom become sources of indignity*" (1973: 30; emphasis in original). For some of the kitchen workers who originally experienced the Salvationist work ethic as a source of freedom and dignity, this undoubtedly came to ring true as low wages caused them to feel a loss of dignity that limited their mobility and self-sufficiency. Nonetheless, mastery of the work ethic taught them the rules of deference and demeanor.

### Learning Deference and Demeanor

Appropriate deference and demeanor demonstrated successful enactment of the disciplined worker role. The appropriate display of deference signaled regard for superiors and knowledge of the local Salvationist hierarchy. An understanding of the requirements of the worker role was manifested in one's mannerisms, clothing, and attitude. The volunteers thus tried to shed their stigmatized status through successful role enactment.

Rules governing appearance marked status and regard for one's work role. Workers had to abide by strict kitchen rules. They wore the required hair net or paper chef's hats, and most donned white kitchen aprons, often already dirty and damp. In the summer a computer-generated notice directed, "The Salvation Army Dress Code for Staff and In-house Clients: Tank tops and hats not permitted in the Kitchen or Dining Room." The cooks wore professionally laundered white chef's pants and shirts. Volunteers could not wear shorts. Respectability involved adhering to these guidelines.

Attention to manners figured prominently in the attention to deference and demeanor. Kitchen workers used "thank you," "excuse me," and "please" often.

Raul offered to get me soup when I told him I had none because no one had been serving when I went through the line. He acknowledged my thanks with great warmth. Earlier Raul had told Mikey [another cook] that he shouldn't work too hard and that he could ask me for help with carrying. At another point, as he passed me he said, "Excuse me," in a way that made me think maybe I should have said excuse me. When he carried plates out to me, I made myself say with greater than usual enthusiasm and a smile, "Thanks." He gave me an okay with his hand and smiled and seemed pleased. (Fieldnotes)

The kitchen workers paid particular attention to manners around the Salvationist staff.

The local Salvationist hierarchy demanded precise knowledge of others' status so as to extend appropriate deference. As discussed in chapter 2, the hierarchical organization of The Salvation Army extended from the Salvationists to the front desk staff and kitchen managers to the cooks and then the volunteers. Among the volunteers, In-house and ASP volunteers earned status through the demonstration of their adherence to the work ethic. The In-house residents acquired status in the kitchen if they were chosen as a dorm representative, with responsibilities for monitoring other In-house residents.

Awkward violations of the hierarchy revealed the importance of social location most dramatically. Raul, the head cook, frequently complained that the front desk workers failed to notify him of a change in someone's status. He once told me that he had not been told there was a new dorm rep and had told this individual that he could not come in for coffee one morning. He was very defensive about having done it. Another instance of confusion over placement in the local hierarchy exposed the deference extended to those who take on positions of authority among the In-house residents.

Raul returned around 2:00 and asked about the new young man and an older man drinking coffee. The latter told him he was staff and Raul kind of apologized. The younger man responded he was ASP and was put back to work. (Fieldnotes)

The staff extended deference, often in the form of dining room and kitchen privileges, to those rewarded for their moral striving with positions of authority. Those with higher status could enter the kitchen during the daytime hours and even get extra food.

These examples illustrate how the kitchen workers used deference and demeanor to create and maintain the local hierarchy. Michèle Lamont (1992: 9) provides a useful interpretation of how actors do "boundary work" to maintain "the subjective boundaries that we draw between ourselves and others." Boundary work operates at the microsociological level as individuals generate distinctions between themselves and others; boundary work also operates at the macrosociological level to organize communities (Lamont 1992: 11).

The successful enactment of the worker role included attention to the local Salvationist hierarchy through the use of deference and demeanor. This attention drew the volunteers, and other kitchen workers, to participate in boundary work. This generating of distinctions, as we shall see, contained emotional underpinnings, in what Clark (1990) calls the micropolitics of social place. Within the micropolitics of place, the kitchen workers, staff, and volunteers alike used emotions to mark and claim a place for themselves and others within the local hierarchy. For example, the ASP status indicated previous lapses in moral selving and consequent stigmatization. To miscategorize a worker as ASP necessitated boundary work, in the form of an apology, and a redefinition of their status.

> As I signed in at the desk, the woman at the desk began to hand me the three-inch or so slip of paper for ASP, and I said, "Thank you, but I'm not ASP." She said, "You're not? I'm sorry," with sincerity, as though she might have offended me. (Fieldnotes)

The staff's close supervision of ASP volunteers also operated as boundary work.

> Raul introduced me as Becky and a new cook asked carefully if I had signed out. I said that I wasn't ASP, and Raul interjected, saying that

I was "normal." I hit him on the arm and laughed, and the cook apologized. I said that it was okay. (Fieldnotes)

Although the ASP volunteers' hours were closely monitored, many of them appreciated the respect with which they were treated by the staff.

The Salvationist moral rhetoric demanded that its workers treat each other with respect. Staff often lectured the kitchen workers on the need to act with deference to all of the volunteers, as the following examples illustrate.

> Greg talked about the kitchen crews. He didn't like how some of the kitchen supervisors yelled at their volunteers and said that there would be none of this in his kitchen. He told us that volunteers were giving their time, so please and thank you should be used. (Fieldnotes)

> You just can't do that with people. You have to treat people like you want to be treated. We are real *thankful* to have volunteers come in, ASP or not, and so that is why we always try to ask them what they would like to do. (Interview with resident manager)

> The two women [ASP volunteers] talked about how at The Salvation Army you aren't judged for doing community service hours and how this is part of its appeal. (I thought about how the ASP volunteers receive a careful thank you after every shift.) They discussed their desire to avoid "work projects." One of the women noted that once when she did community service hours at another place she was judged poorly. Both seemed to regard this other work as more humiliating, and perhaps, I thought, more punitive. They both repeated how nice the people at The Salvation Army are and how they don't judge their volunteers. (Fieldnotes)

These two women talked about their desire to volunteer at The Salvation Army after they completed their ASP hours. The deference they received relieved the stigma of punishment. They accepted the hard work in the service of moral self-betterment. Whereas some forms of court-ordered volunteer work challenged their self-esteem, volunteer work at The Salvation Army increased their self-esteem and led to the desire to help others.

The intricacies of deference and demeanor at The Salvation Army revealed the local hierarchy to be highly gendered. As previously discussed, the male kitchen staff frequently asked the female volunteers to decorate the tables for visiting Salvationists, to arrange platters of cheese and cold cuts, or to cut cakes. For example, Raul once asked me to help with the "pretty stuff" when arranging colored paper tablecloths for the Salvationists. In a particularly poignant case, I waxed the Formica tables with Lemon Pledge wood polish.

> Several men commented how nice it was that I was polishing the tables. I found the chore absurd and a bit puzzling because the Lemon Pledge simply beaded up and grew waxy on the Formica. I sprayed it on and then wiped it off on the apron with no visible change, not even a residual lemon scent. (Fieldnotes)

On another occasion Raul told another cook to put me on the serving line because, he said, I was "a delight." Dave told me once that I gave the place a "woman's touch."

An appropriately gendered demeanor for women ranged from doing women's work to treating men with deference through a smiling presentation of self. Women sometimes resisted the requests to smile for the men.

> When a heavy-set blond man came through the line and demanded that all the kitchen staff [the servers were all women] smile, Linda [a white ASP worker] was visibly annoyed and gave him a disgusted look. She didn't respond to his request/order and gave him his tray with no warmth. He seemed a bit put off by her response. Cathy [another white ASP worker] smiled and looked a bit confused by this exchange. (Fieldnotes)

I too often found these requests patronizing. As I wrote in my fieldnotes, "I was trying to maintain a friendly and smiling demeanor. Shortly after I came in, one of the men, I couldn't identify which one, told me in a friendly way to smile. This smiling comes with difficulty to me." I received many compliments for my smile, and in time I learned to smile more.[5]

When I returned to The Salvation Army in 1993, after an absence of almost a year and a half, I noticed that the In-house residents and the staff were sensitive to any behavior that might be construed as sexual harassment. The male kitchen workers endeavored to be sensitive to this issue in their interactions with female workers. One of the white custodial workers saw me and said, "Hi, cutie," then immediately retracted it, telling me that he knew he could get in trouble for saying that. I was a bit unsettled but smiled at him. A minute later he said, "After all, I have children your age." The male workers struggled to make sense of appropriate behavior toward women.

> As I approached the door to the dining room carrying two leftover jello trays, Raul materialized as I realized I couldn't open the door with trays in my hands. He told me later that he had hesitated to offer to open the door as "these days" you never know about opening the door for a woman. He said that sometimes he offered and found it was a mistake. (Fieldnotes)

Women gained power in managing men's deference with the threat of sexual harassment charges. For example, a staff member teased me about not deserving a break. Although I felt quite comfortable with this exchange, Raul took the man aside and quietly lectured him. This man told me later I had "clout" as a woman. The threat of writing up a report on "the incident" maintained women's status in monitoring sexual harassment.

After his promotion to head cook, Raul enforced the ban on sexually offensive language.

> As we talked Raul approached and Danny complained to him, using the word *bitch*. Raul stood back a little and became very serious. He told Danny that there were three reasons not to use that word: first, it is not permitted to be used at The Salvation Army; second, he could be written up for using it; and third, it is offensive to women.

Danny did not appear to be put off and continued joking, telling
Raul that he did not find this word, or words such as *ass*, offensive.
Raul cut him off, saying that he was not going to enter into a discus-
sion of this with him. (Fieldnotes)

In another instance, Raul stopped a female ASP volunteer when she
talked about Joe Montana's "tush."

As these examples illustrate, rather than engage in talk about the inap-
propriateness of sexual harassment or sexually offensive language, the
staff simply told the offending party to quit the talk and then underscored
the seriousness of this rule with the threat that they might be written up.

> One of the men [a white ASP volunteer], who stood farthest from
> me, serving the dessert, told me that he would hire me in his restau-
> rant, that I could stand at the cash register taking money and
> wouldn't have to move, I would just have to look pretty. He added
> that all the waitresses would have to wear short skirts, and I replied
> sarcastically, "Thanks." Then Chris [a white staff cook] interjected,
> calling the man back to talk and telling him, "There isn't any talk
> like that in our organization." I think the man tried to defend him-
> self a bit, but Chris wouldn't let him. (Field notes)

The above illustrates how learning proper deference and demeanor entailed following nonsexist interactional guidelines without challenging
authority.

The staff banned pornography as well as sexual harassment. One
week the paid kitchen workers received a pamphlet titled "About
Pornography" with their paychecks. Dave explained to me that ASP volunteers who harassed women could not remain at The Salvation Army.

> Another time when ASP volunteers don't work out is when we get
> our young studs in here, twenty-one, twenty-two years old, and they
> are here to try to make dates with girls like you and other ladies who
> come in here. And we have to watch that. That is really the only
> time we have to get on people.

Boundary work ideally involved adhering to codes of sexual conduct so as to grant women freedom from harassment.

The emphasis on deference and demeanor at The Salvation revealed how the struggle to play the worker role differed from the attempt at Loaves & Fishes to align deeply held emotions with the feeling rules of personalist hospitality. At Loaves & Fishes the volunteers struggled most dramatically in their attempt to treat all of the guests as Ambassadors of God. Their moral selving involved emotion work to bring their feelings in line with this understanding of personalist hospitality. At The Salvation Army the kitchen workers learned how to play the worker role in which deference and demeanor functioned as boundary work to maintain what Everett Cherrington Hughes (1958: 71) has called "the moral division of labor." For example, at The Salvation Army the staff worked to present a "tight ship" to the higher-ups, without financial waste, whereas at Loaves & Fishes the volunteers expressed concern about being environmentally wasteful. Boundary work at The Salvation Army directed attention outward to the civility of interaction within the local stratification rather than inward to emotion alignment.

Learning appropriate demeanor demonstrated that one had moved toward self-efficacy within the worker role. The extension of deference acknowledged another's status and may have built self-esteem. The role competency that accompanied the appropriate use of deference and demeanor was also assumed to build self-esteem. Building self-esteem flowed not from emotion work but from attention to the careful playing of the worker role.

Similar to the men whom Duneier encountered at the Valois Diner, the male kitchen workers' concern for what Duneier called respectability entailed "a strong belief in deference to authority" (Duneier 1992: 74). In both cases the men were cynical about powerful institutions. Low wages led some at The Salvation Army to feel cynical about the motives of those in charge, despite their fundamental affinity with the

moral selving into the etiquette of the gendered worker role. This cynicism troubled the moral selving of the men who worked their way from
the volunteer role to the worker role. We will see that those most embedded in sociability and adoptive kinship relations felt the least cynical
about The Salvation Army.

### Camaraderie, Kinship Relations, and Sociability

Although the worker role required attention to self-discipline and
personal responsibility, sociability at The Salvation Army provided
camaraderie and great emotional warmth. The moral self developed
in support of the work ethic enforced only marginally what Schwalbe
(1992) identified as a narrowly masculinist self with its attention to
control, production, and competition. Talk of family[6] and concern for
other workers encouraged a more empathetic moral self among those
who spent considerable time in the kitchen. A.A. and Salvationist ideology as practiced at the Shelter Services Center fostered self-control
and production but discouraged competition in favor of an empathetic fraternity.

This camaraderie evidenced itself in the concern the men gave to
their friendships. Men often accompanied each other to pick up paychecks earned off-site. Randy, a truck driver sentenced to 240 hours of
volunteer service for driving a company semi that was over the weight
limit, told me that he volunteered at The Salvation Army because he
likes being around people. Randy remained committed to volunteering
after finishing his ASP hours.

> That's like me, I go to back to my regular life, and you miss the
> guys, like, I made a lot of friends here, just by the time I've been
> here. Oh yeah, it like, grows on you really. You know, you get people
> that go through that program. You could tell I met a lot of friends
> here, just by being here, you know. It's a different atmosphere.

Randy invited "the guys" to visit Cal Expo where he kept his racehorse
and to come to his home to watch television. He videotaped news cov-

erage of the kitchen for the men to watch. Fred, a white cook, arrived in the kitchen for one of his shifts and announced, "You folks are the reason I keep coming in."

These men's friendships with each other, forged in the dormitory, in their shared work in the kitchen, and in mutual support, exemplified relational selves. Clyde W. Franklin II found that friendships among black working-class men contained caring and intimacy not found in friendships among men of higher economic status: "Because working-class black males experience greater isolation from mainstream society than upwardly mobile black men, they may not internalize the same taboos against male same-sex friendships, which result in non-self disclosure, competitiveness, and nonvulnerability" (1992: 203). Patricia Hill Collins's (1991) work suggests that this intimacy may resonate with an Afrocentric ethic of caring. Respect for individual expressiveness, importance of emotions, and the capacity for empathy compose this ethic.[7]

At The Salvation Army men of diverse ethnicities shared caring friendships based on mutual support and expressiveness. The moral code of sociability at The Salvation Army fostered solidarity and, to a lesser extent, generosity as moral ideals among all the kitchen workers. In contrast, Lamont (1995) found in her study of Euro-American and African-American male morality that Euro-Americans emphasized the work ethic and responsibility whereas African Americans highlighted solidarity and generosity in their morality. If we understand culture in the Durkheimian tradition, as "institutionalized repertoires that have as powerful an effect on the structurations of everyday life as do economic forces" (Lamont 1995: 4), then the moral convergence of the kitchen workers around solidarity and generosity makes sense. That is, Salvation Army kitchen workers organized their self work around the solidarity and generosity so central to Salvationism and A.A. practice.

The staff talked of family relations frequently. For example, Raul shared stories of visits from his four children from a previous marriage.

He helped to support the four children and spent most of his days off with them, often taking them to stay at his mother's home.

> Raul talked to me by the serving line about how his children's mother had come by. Their mother called yesterday to ask if he had any extra money and he said yes, and she asked for some for doing something with the kids. He told her to come by today and he would give it to her. (Fieldnotes)

As the kitchen crew sat outside, many smoking, during breaks, I often learned of special celebrations or visits with family, as illustrated in the following excerpt from my fieldnotes.

> I joined this group, taking a break, pulling up an overturned milk cart, next to Raul on a chair, on the sidewalk, facing Sonny, Danny, and Deborah, also on a milk cart. Sonny rejoined us quickly and continued his story. He told us about his previous night and his up-coming plans for his "old lady's" birthday tonight. He told us that she was spending the day getting ready, having her hair and nails done. Deborah said, "Nice." He explained that his wife had told him that she wouldn't bring her wallet tonight. Sonny imagined that he would take her to the Sizzler. He explained that by the time he paid rent out of his paycheck (about $380), he had little more than $50 left for the month.

Men often told me nostalgic stories of their dreams for homes and family. The telling of these stories as a way to personalize the helping re-lationship between staff and drafted volunteers resembles the mediator style of mentoring Ruth Horowitz (1995) found among a group of social workers in a high school equivalency degree program for teen mothers. Horowitz contrasts the mediator style, with its concern for establishing commonality and encouraging responsibility through according respect to the young women, with that of the arbitrator style, with its attention to strict rule enforcement and maintenance of hierarchy. Horowitz's sympathies clearly lie with the mediators who frame welfare as "scholar-ship" and offer the program participants citizenship rights rather than the dependency status of the wronged offered by the arbitrators. Staff at the Shelter Services Center office—in keeping with A.A. practice—tell their stories of personal failure to hold out hope for redemption and to gain legitimacy in their role as rule enforcers. While certainly hierarchical in orientation, they clearly favor the relational mentoring role Horowitz observed among those she called the mediators.

Some men without relatives in the area adopted surrogate kin relationships with other workers, which further embedded moral selving in locally established roles. Kevin, the white cook promoted to intake and counseling, called Hank, the white cook who left after the kitchen after a drinking binge, his father. One morning as Hank and I served lunch, Hank told me that he would like to have a daughter like me. He said that he was going to adopt me, and then he joked that he would marry Celia and they would be my parents. He teased me about how my new parents would look. Later that day Kevin asked if he could marry me.

> Kevin asked Hank the second time if he could marry me, and Hank joked that he couldn't afford to support Kevin as well as me. I teased Hank that I could use help with school. Later Hank told Kevin that his daughter was displeased with him because he didn't have any money. (Fieldnotes)

After this exchange, Hank supervised my interactions with Kevin. When Kevin accompanied me to the outside cooler to look for parsley, Hank followed us into the cooler and told me, "Don't you go in there with him, you hear me?" These exchanges suggested that the responsibility to oversee women's sexuality was one of the various manifestations of the good-provider role.

Kevin was not the only one who asked me to marry him or be his girlfriend. These requests almost always occurred in the presence of others.

> As Greg and Matt [both white cooks] and I worked on the potatoes, Matt told me for a second time not to be put off by these men. He explained that they are lonely for female companionship and don't mean to be overly friendly with me. He said, "You're not married,

are you?" and leaned his head on the counter with a sigh of discouragement when I told him that I was engaged. Greg told him that he had to get a "real job" before he could have a "real woman" like me. (Fieldnotes)

These moments elucidated the requirements of the good-provider role. I rarely heard direct talk about sex.

The staff took responsibility for shielding me from the advances of men who advanced beyond the parameters of teasing.

> After lunch Raul came looking for me. He asked if I had seen the guy with the long, full hair looking for me. I told him no, without much concern. He responded more seriously, telling me that if this guy bothered me, or didn't go away, to let him know. Then as I sat with two female ASP volunteers a white guy in his twenties came in and sat down next to me, asking if he could take me out for coffee. Firmly, I told him no, I wouldn't do this.

I learned to use my fictive kin position to protect myself from men who would not leave me alone. In the most uncomfortable situation I experienced, I was followed around the kitchen by a middle-aged African-American ASP worker who watched me as I baked one thousand cookies. At one point he clasped my face in his hands and told me how good I looked. He supervised me as I scooped the cookies onto the baking sheets.

> Then the song "Disco Lady" came on and I found myself working to the leaning presence of this man, with one hand on the counter, hip to side, crooning, "Move it in, move it out . . . shove it in, shove it out . . . Disco Lady." I remembered how increasingly I thought of The Salvation Army as governed by kin relations and I resolved to try and call on this network. I told Kevin, after perhaps twenty more minutes of this and feeling increasingly resentful, that I felt uncomfortable and asked if he could find something for this man to do. Without blinking an eye, Kevin told the man to leave me alone, but he kept reappearing. Clearly word got out, for later the ASP woman, who I know didn't overhear this, asked me if "that man" was leaving

me alone. When I looked a little puzzled, she said, "The one who
was bugging you," and I said, "Yes," a bit surprised that she knew
about this conflict. (Fieldnotes)

In another instance a cook asked a male volunteer who kept following
me, "Don't you have anything better to do than watch her?" When I
went to the overflow shelter with some men from the NABORS program, Raul gave Jerome, the African-American coordinator whom I did
not know, a lecture about his duty to watch out for me and keep his language clean. These examples illustrate how kin relations gave men, in
the role of the good provider, as father, brother, or suitor, the duty to
guard a woman's honor.

Generosity with special food treats also revealed camaraderie among
male workers. For example, Wilson, at a lunch where he ate three large
meatballs rather than the one allotted to nonkitchen workers, pro-
nounced, "We may be poor, but we don't go hungry." Every few weeks
the staff would pool dollar bills and buy soda for the workers. I noted on
one such day, "People's spirits picked up." When the kitchen crew made
several casseroles or trays of food for lunch, the kitchen workers got the
best one. Randy frequently made special dishes with meat for the other
kitchen workers.

Randy made pot roast sandwiches for us. I trusted his claim that he
found some really good meat for lunch. I ate this sandwich on two
pieces of toast fried in butter. Another volunteer made a roux and
then gravy to put over this lunch. The sandwich tasted good, and I
was glad not to eat sloppy joes, especially after having cleaned the
pan. (Fieldnotes)

Hank also frequently cooked for the volunteers and staff. On one such
occasion I wrote in my fieldnotes, "As I had almost finished the salads
for lunch, Hank asked me if I would like some steak. I quickly said yes,
having not eaten yet and knowing that these snacks often tasted better
than the official lunch." And Raul prided himself on his "high dollar"
cold cut plates, which he shared with the staff and volunteers.

The kitchen workers at The Salvation Army worked at sociability, similar to the men Elijah Anderson ([1976] 1981) observed at Jelly's bar and liquor store on Chicago's South Side. Sociability in both places required careful attention to "rules," and infractions were "reprimanded" (23). Men in both settings suffered from being stigmatized by the larger community as "lacking in moral responsibility" (31). Perhaps most critically, the comparison illuminates the vulnerability of moral selves wherein "status, as achieved in the hierarchies at Jelly's [or The Salvation Army], is not transferable to just any street corner" (180).

Sociability and the adoption of kin relations at The Salvation Army fostered the entrenchment of the self in the institution. As one African-American In-house volunteer explained, "This is my home." In a participant-observation study of personal relations among New York's homeless, Dordick describes how homelessness creates

> a process in which personal relationships are mobilized in the production of what the physical environment fails to provide: a safe and secure place to live. The beliefs, values, and understandings that emerge from this process are situationally specific and local in nature. (1997: 193)

In a poignant example, Hank acquired kin relations, the warmth of sociability, and stability at The Salvation Army; when asked to move offsite, he became depressed and returned to drinking.

Michael Hughes and David H. Demo's (1989) study of self-esteem and personal efficacy, a concept similar to self-efficacy, helps us to understand the fragility of self-esteem among the kitchen workers at The Salvation Army, where even microsocial relations lacked stability. Hughes and Demo attempt to explain why black Americans' self-esteem does not lag behind that of white Americans, while personal efficacy is significantly lower. Using survey data on black Americans, they argue that self-esteem arises within microsocial relations, thus protecting self-esteem from institutional inequality, whereas low personal efficacy reflects a history of racial discrimination. Kitchen workers such as Hank may have feared that without the sociability and kin relations of The Salvation Army they could not maintain the personal relationships that buttressed their self-esteem "out there." These workers might not have been confident in their self-efficacy without their entrenchment in the social relations of moral selving at The Salvation Army.

### REDEMPTION: "THE SAME DIVINE GRACE"

> If we ourselves, for want of a better way of speaking, re-
> fer to our evangelical work and also to our social work, it
> is not that these are two distinct entities which could op-
> erate the one without the other. They are but two activi-
> ties of the one and the same salvation which is con-
> cerned with the total redemption of man. Both rely on
> the same divine grace. Both are inspired by the same
> motive. Both have the same end in mind. And as the
> gospel has joined them together we do not propose to
> put them asunder.
>
> *General Frederick Coutts, C.B.E*

Salvationists advocate physical salvation as an avenue to spiritual salvation and redemption. For many, administering Salvationism involved both evangelical and social work.

After supervising the Sacramento Salvation Army's fund-raising for sixteen years, the third-generation Salvationist Trevor Washington told Dan McGrath, a local reporter, "We have successes. They're not vast, they're not great, but we do have them. I'm proud of them" (McGrath 1994: A2). Washington called on The Salvation Army's motto, "Heart to God and Hand to Man," to explain the mission.

> I want to help people become self-sufficient, not just help them with
> a handout. I've seen the other side of America—the poor and the
> destitute, those without hope, so to speak. Nobody should have to
> live like that. The Salvation Army was started to raise people out of
> those circumstances, to get them back on their feet and into society.

Our goal is not to see them again unless they come back to volunteer after they've straightened themselves out. (Washington, cited in McGrath 1994: A2)

Some workers felt their redemption was profoundly religious. Celia thanked God for her recovery from drugs.

I thank God that the Judge sentenced me to, *gave* me the opportunity to go, to Alternative Sentencing, because it's even helped me as a better human being to understand that everybody is not fortunate and some people's minds are gone, from dope and whatever. And for me to be able to wake up in the morning and have some control of my faculties, I am blessed. I thank God, and I am going to do what I *have* to do to make my self worthy of His sight. And that means that I got to look at the next person I see as my brother or sister 'cause he is. Do what I can to help.

Celia felt she was blessed. Her self-esteem and self-efficacy grew through her involvement in her church and spiritual transformation.

Many of the In-house attended The Salvation Army core church as well as the morning chapel service, which was offered every day but Saturday at the Shelter Services Center. Raul often played his guitar and the men sang. Wilson understood his good experience with the NABORS project to be based in his attendance at Bible study groups. Randy encouraged folks from his Baptist church to join him at The Salvation Army. He told me, "Yup, this church I belong to, I have talked some people into coming down to volunteer, I know some other friends coming down to volunteer. They come on the holidays, a lot of them."

Yet redemption based on recovering respectability in society, beyond The Salvation Army, seemed of utmost importance to many of the men. Moral redemption involved the transition to self-sufficiency of which Trevor Washington spoke. While men could earn honor within the social world of the kitchen, they felt discredited in the outside world.

Kevin said that I was "betrothed" before I came to The Salvation
Army. Hank said I had not picked a "Sally tramp," referring to the
men at The Salvation Army. Raul said something about the wedding
and all of the Sally guys being there and that my family would wonder who Rebecca's friends were. As he said this, he walked along,
with his head down and a slight swagger from side to side as if to
demonstrate their disreputable presence at my wedding. (Fieldnotes)

Hank told me that I would have to go to church a long time to save his
soul, but he joined Raul and the other men in laughing at the image of
the Sally tramps at my wedding.

These men understood charity to be good for women and children
and older people but not for themselves.

Raul said I should come for breakfast or dinner to see the children
and older folks. Raul said that he finds the older folks, and older
men, as well as the bussed children sad, but not the men his age and
younger. It doesn't bother him to see them. (Fieldnotes)

Some men thought that Loaves & Fishes was for "women and children," noting that they felt more comfortable at The Salvation Army.

A white In-house volunteer told me that he had been to Loaves &
Fishes to eat and that he liked The Salvation Army better. He said
that at Loaves & Fishes they have all sorts of rules about not swear-
ing and what you can and cannot say. Later, when I added that
Loaves & Fishes looked fancier with flowers on the tables and
wooden chairs, he chipped in that those chairs wouldn't last here,
that they would be marked up in no time.

The men often spoke of "the strict rules" at Loaves & Fishes, although
a white In-house volunteer who worked at Loaves & Fishes' Friendship
Park told me that, although the "environment" felt different, he found
it "calmer" and "a pleasant environment." While the men spoke fondly
of Friendship Park, where they hung out and played basketball, they
less frequently mentioned Loaves & Fishes' meals and social services.

Yet most respected Loaves & Fishes. For example, Brian, a black In-house volunteer, asked about what I was doing. When I told him that I volunteered at The Salvation Army and at Loaves & Fishes, he said that Loaves & Fishes is the place to see "homelessness at its best" and that I should speak with the people there. Most of the men and a few of the women did not, however, want to understand themselves as in need of Loaves & Fishes' charity.

The kitchen workers sought to carry their message of redemption through self-sufficiency to others beyond the Shelter Services Center. A.A. "stepwork" encouraged this practice: "Having had a spiritual awakening as the result of these steps, we tried to carry this message to alcoholics, and to practice these principles in all our affairs" (Twelfth Step of Alcoholics Anonymous, cited in Alcoholics Anonymous 1965: 54). While they might earn respect within the reference group of the other kitchen workers, they worked toward moral redemption in the larger social world.

## SOCIAL CONTROL OR PERSONAL REDEMPTION: THE POLITICS OF ETHNOGRAPHIC REPRESENTATION

The drafted volunteers' stories of their experiences at The Salvation Army contrasted sharply with most portrayals of The Salvation Army in sociological literature. In these ethnographic accounts The Salvation Army is commonly described as a site of social control for already marginalized populations. My research pointed to a disjuncture between this representation of The Salvation Army in the literature on skid row and the homeless and the experiences of the men at The Salvation Army who chose to commit themselves to the organization as civilian employees.

Most sociologists have addressed The Salvation Army as an institution of oppressive social control, as in Nels Anderson's *The Hobo* (1923), Samuel Wallace's *Skid Row as a Way of Life* (1965), James Spradley's *You*

*Owe Yourself a Drunk* (1970), and with greater detail, albeit under a pseudonym, Jacqueline Wiseman's *Stations of the Lost* ([1970] 1979). The Salvation Army emerges in Anderson's portrait as "not popular," in Spradley's as a "sinecure" with "clannish" staff who further the exploitation of skid row men, and in Wiseman's as a place of "last resort" staffed, once again, by zealous converts. More recently, David Snow and Leon Anderson's *Down on Their Luck* (1993) describes The Salvation Army as an inadequate "accommodative" organization.

I do not suggest that these accounts ring false but rather that, when taken together with my account of The Salvation Army, a richer, more complicated story emerges. This story is closer to the complex historical portrait offered by Gertrude Himmelfarb in *Poverty and Compassion* (1991), in which she characterizes The Salvation Army as both a site of oppressive social control and a site of radical inspiration.[8] Many of the volunteers whom I interviewed (both In-house and court-ordered volunteers) found stability in the working arrangements of charity at The Salvation Army. Staff at The Salvation Army, although they did not use that language, prided themselves on being a haven of last resort for street people plagued by drug and alcohol dependency. Many of the staff and volunteers mediated a relationship between The Salvation Army and A.A.[9] This finding contrasts with other work on The Salvation Army. I focus here on the recent ethnography, *Down on Their Luck*, and its portrayal of the relationship between street people and The Salvation Army in Austin, Texas.

Snow and Anderson used Salvation Army data to track homeless street people through Austin and spent many hours doing fieldwork at The Salvation Army. The Salvation Army emerged as one of the "remedial caretaker agencies" (Snow and Anderson 1993: 87). Following Wiseman, Snow and Anderson assigned The Salvation Army to the "institutional margins" where homeless people "make do" (282). In their account, instead of relegating resources to rehabilitation, The Salvation Army extended mostly "accommodative services." The homeless received services rather than rehabilitation and support to become self-sufficient (283).

Snow and Anderson found that The Salvation Army staff encouraged their residents and employees to disengage themselves from those still on the streets. Although they do not note this, such a directive is a contradiction of A.A. principles. More specifically, they reported the social services director as explaining to them:

> We just can't have the workers or the women who are staying in the shelter associating with the guys on the streets. They start doing favors for their friends, or wanting favors, and that just means trouble. So that's why we have the policy. That way I don't have to chew people out all the time and things go smoother. We just don't need the friction. (181)

In accordance with this policy, the recently dislocated (newly homeless) made good employees for the Austin Salvation Army because of their reputed "antipathy" toward the other homeless (181). In this account the Austin Salvation Army emerged as a "greedy corporation" (218), controlling the behavior of its underpaid and exploited employees.

Although The Salvation Army staff in Sacramento encouraged clients and volunteers to stay away from certain places, they did not encourage clients and volunteers to stay away from all homeless people. For example, the staff in Sacramento cautioned their clients and volunteers to stay away from a nearby railroad underpass, reputed for drug selling, and homeless encampments on the nearby river. This vigilance reflected the intolerance of drinking and drug use that reportedly occurred at both places, as well as moral condemnation for straying from a disciplined work ethic. The Salvation Army resident manager's judgment about Loaves & Fishes' support of the encampment illustrated this attitude: "Loaves & Fishes, some of their policies are totally contrary to what we believe. For instance, they were fighting to let the people on the river stay there, and we don't agree with it. For their sake. There was some sanitation issues and some other stuff." Nonetheless, both Dave and Kevin, in their work as intake counselors, spent hours talking with homeless people, mostly men whom they knew, and expended a great deal of effort searching for friends they were concerned about. Nor could either man, on arrival at The Salvation Army, be categorized, in Snow and Anderson's typology, as "recently dislocated."

For some, the politics of moral selving involved subscribing to the Golden Rule. Kevin maintained, "You have to treat people like you want to be treated." Wilson believed he found redemption at The Salvation Army through his work with the NABORS project. He said, "I think the government could learn a few lessons from these guys" (cited in Sylva 1993: C5).

The men I encountered expressed positive feelings about their work and consequent friendships at The Salvation Army. In contrast to the ethnographic tradition that argues that The Salvation Army, at best, is a beleaguered, accommodative charity, or, at worst, a repressive, demeaning institution, my fieldwork suggests that some of the drafted volunteers welcomed the mental health and material benefits offered by The Salvation Army. Similarly, David Wagner (1993), in a brief but sympathetic account of self-help groups among a homeless population, notes that some street people merge self-help, charity, and politics into a strategy to help other street people. Perhaps the volunteers I observed did not experience the demands of The Salvation Army as social control, because their moral selving involved the acceptance of self-control. For example, Nicole Woolsey Biggart explains of the entrepreneurs she studied:

> Self-control does not *feel* controlling. If an individual accepts the standards that attach to the social ideal—and this is a critical hurdle—then there is the perception of self-determination. There is an experience of autonomous competence. (1989: 164; emphasis in original)

Like the entrepreneurs studied by Biggart, the kitchen workers accepted a social ideal in which they welcomed strategies for disciplining the self.

One important aspect of the drafted volunteers' embracing of self-discipline involved their participation in drug and alcohol treatment programs. The sociologists James D. Wright and Peter H. Rossi, in reviewing Alice S. Baum and Donald W. Burnes's *A Nation in Denial* (1993), argue that the needs of homeless people for rehabilitative programs should not be mistaken for the cause of their homelessness. Nonetheless, they offer a tempered critique of the ignorance of those needs: "Homeless advocates and, to a lesser extent, social researchers have tended to downplay the importance of mental illness and substance abuse among the homeless. Leaning over backward to avoid blaming the victim, it is easy to lose one's balance" (1994: 42). The voices of those who find respectability, stability, and release from troubling alcohol and drug use in the charitable action practiced at the Shelter Services Center enlarge this limited representation of The Salvation Army in ethnographic writing.

Perhaps researchers of The Salvation Army have too easily affirmed cynicism over idealism. Reflecting on the problems of studying the social psychological development of medical students, Howard Becker ([1956] 1970) considered how academics often give more credence to cynical, rather than idealistic, values. In his consideration of how an interviewer may pursue problems as the underlying truth, Becker explained:

> Important and justified as is the interviewer's preoccupation with the problem, it creates the possibility that he will either misinterpret idealism sincerely presented to him or, by his manner of questioning, fashion a role for himself in the interview that encourages cynicism while discouraging idealism. For the interviewer's manner and role can strongly affect what the interviewee chooses to tell him, as can the situation in which the interview is conducted. (104)

Those who gain admittance to The Salvation Army rehabilitation programs may find personal redemption in an atmosphere of social control. In the words of Steven Worden, in a review of two qualitative studies of the homeless, "It is unfortunate that the same compassion, complexity, and depth of understanding that researchers routinely grant the homeless cannot be extended more often by those who, day in and day out, stay to work with them" (1998: 250). Thus, as we study welfare organizations, we must attend to expressions of personal redemption, as well as unbearable social control, lest fieldwork simply reproduce allegorical tales of oppression (Warren 1988) in settings such as The Salvation Army.

## COMPARING MORAL SELVING AT TWO SOUP KITCHENS: THE AMBASSADORS OF GOD AND THE SINKING CLASSES

Moral selving at both Loaves & Fishes and The Salvation Army challenged participants to construct moral selves grounded in charitable action. At Loaves & Fishes the volunteers wrestled with their deep emotions as they worked to extend to all of the guests the nonjudgmental welcoming due Ambassadors of God. The kitchen workers at The Salvation Army struggled to attain a disciplined worker ethic to rescue themselves from the sinking classes. In contrast to the mostly white, middle-class volunteers of Loaves & Fishes, the more predominantly nonwhite, working-class men of The Salvation Army worked to attain the good-provider role.

Moral anxieties at Loaves & Fishes and The Salvation Army revealed contrasting understandings of the moral self. The routine volunteers confronted their emotions, driven by the desire to wed authenticity and self-efficacy. They worked to participate in meaningful charitable action. Their greatest moral anxiety lay in the struggle to accord all the guests dignity as Ambassadors of God. Gender faded in salience in relation to their anxieties about bridging the gap between themselves and the guests created by class. The drafted volunteers wrestled with boundary work as they worked to attain the disciplined worker role, driven by a desire to increase both self-efficacy and self-esteem. The Salvation

Army prescribed a moral division of labor that demanded that the kitchen workers rescue themselves from the sinking classes. Anxieties about gender, and the capacity of men to play the good-provider role, overshadowed concerns found among the Loaves & Fishes volunteers about class divisions between themselves and the clients. The drafted volunteers worked on becoming more autonomous,[10] yet for some, the low wages they earned eventually caused despair and resentment.

Moral selving among the drafted volunteers was messier than among the routine volunteers. The routine volunteers lodged less of their moral selves within the organizational context. For some, Loaves & Fishes was one of several volunteer commitments. They more freely chose to volunteer at Loaves & Fishes. The working arrangements made fewer demands on them. In contrast, the drafted volunteers came to The Salvation Army to escape homelessness or fulfill a court sentence. The In-house volunteers lived at The Salvation Army and had to abide by its strict rules. Even the ASP volunteers were subject to close monitoring by the staff. The drafted volunteers clearly had less power to freely choose volunteering. Moral selving was easier among the routine volunteers, who chose fairly freely whether or not to wrestle with feeling charitable love for the guests. Many of the drafted volunteers, because of a paucity of financial and personal support, viewed the low wages found at The Salvation Army as a barrier to their struggle to achieve autonomy. The drafted volunteers adhered to a conservative vision of the importance of hard work and self-discipline among the poor.

This study of moral selving reveals how concerns with moral self-betterment take different forms among mostly white, middle-class volunteers and mostly working-class, and predominantly male, volunteers, many of color. As Mead ([1934] 1962: 385) told us many years ago, a theory of ethics must reflect the social context of the self: "It is as social beings that we are moral beings."

## PART THREE

# Moral Visions of the Welfare State

This study illuminates the construction of caring selves in the work of feeding the urban poor. Although much scholarly work has explored caring, and especially its gendered nature, fewer studies have considered the implications for moral selving in the realm of welfare politics. This work develops the idea of moral selving in the context of charitable action and makes clear how structural arrangements guide self-betterment while concurrently individual actions make possible particular structural arrangements.

Situated in the fundamental symbolic interactionist belief in the mutually constitutive nature of self and society, this work shows how the work of self-betterment implicates caring individuals in the local politics of welfare and in national debates about service provision to the poor. By looking at moral selving in the context of volunteers feeding the homeless, this study provides an opportunity to consider how volunteerism, charity, rehabilitation, social movement activism, and welfare provision are not mutually exclusive practices but rather are configured in complicated and often contradictory ways in the context of both the actions of different individuals and the work of different organizations.

# CHAPTER 5

# The Politics of Charity

*Constructing Moral Selves
in Religion and Conflict*

I did not embark on this fieldwork intending to describe moral selving.
And I could have focused my interviews and observations so as to have
told a story of economic, political, social, cultural, religious, ethnic,
racial, or gender selving. That pieces of those stories emerge in this
ethnography suggests that we are all engaged in many different simultaneous projects of selving.[1] While the language of selving I have adopted
may not be widely used, many different studies offer insights into the
often contradictory and complicated self work of striving at times to
conform and at other times to challenge economic, political, social, cultural, religious, gender, ethnic-racial, and sexual ideals.[2] This study illuminates the work of individuals to be better people at a time when many
berate the moral bankruptcy of our national culture and herald voluntary action and charity as important solutions to our poverty crisis. The
second half of this conclusion speaks more directly to the political implications of this study. The first half addresses how my formulation of
moral selving and its particular manifestations at Loaves & Fishes and
The Salvation Army fits into social psychological understandings of the
emotional self and orientation of the self, as well as the feminist literature on the caring self.

## THE CARING SELF WITHIN CULTURES OF
## DIGNITY AND HONOR

That moral anxieties revealed tensions in emotion expression and experience at Loaves & Fishes, in contrast to role attainment, or what the social psychologist Ralph H. Turner (1978) called the role-person merger, at The Salvation Army suggested two quite different constructions of the self. These constructions corresponded, although not perfectly, to Turner's (1976) formulation of institutional and impulsive selves. Turner maintains that Americans' interpretive location of their true selves has undergone a transition from an institutionally located self to an impulsively located self. In the former, "the self is something attained, created, achieved, not something discovered," whereas in the latter, "the true self is revealed only when inhibitions are lowered or abandoned" (Turner 1976: 992, 993). Moral anxieties at The Salvation Army corresponded to the goals of the institutional selves, while those at Loaves & Fishes corresponded to the goals of the impulsive selves: "The institutional goal is correspondence between *prescription and behavior*; the goal of impulsives is correspondence between *impulse and behavior*: hypocrisy in either instance is a lack of appropriate correspondence" (Turner 1976: 994; emphasis in original). That is, the drafted volunteers at The Salvation Army experienced moral anxieties about an inadequate performance of the good-provider role, whereas the routine volunteers at Loaves & Fishes felt challenged in their desire to feel charitable love for the guests.

The fit between institutional selves as an ideal type and the drafted volunteers seems to be tighter, however, than that between the impulsive selves as an ideal type and the routine volunteers. The drafted volunteers worked to match role and behavior to the worldview of Salvationism. The routine volunteers strained to feel charitable love for the guests, yet the institutional context of the volunteer role was not without importance to them. Perhaps institutional and impulsive selves should be understood, as John P. Hewitt suggests, not as empirically variable but rather as a reflection of two different discourses that people use for anchoring self-concept. In Hewitt's (1989: 31) words, "The distinction between institutional and impulsive selves . . . is a cultural interpretation of importance and use to cultural members."

As theaters of caring, Loaves & Fishes and The Salvation Army provided scripts for doing good. Thus, in Hewitt's terms, these two discourses may provide resources for anchoring the self, or, as Sidonie Smith and Julia Watson (1996: 9) elaborate in their work on autobiographical storytelling and identity construction, "ready-made narrative templates" that organized experience by providing "culturally designated subjectivities." These narrative templates corresponded with gender socialization in American culture about the meaning of caring for others. In his research among young people on the meaning of caring, Wuthnow (1995) found, as I did at Loaves & Fishes and The Salvation Army, that volunteers mixed the language of relationality with that of rights. However, Wuthnow also found evidence to suggest that women invested the meaning of caring in selfhood while men invested the meaning in roles with implications for how they understood caring:

> If women associate caring with their sense of selfhood, then it makes sense that they should regard caring as an intrinsic value. If in contrast, men associate caring with the specific roles they play, it makes sense that their view of caring would depend more on the instrumental logic that generally governs such roles. (1995: 169)

In an earlier study of a volunteer logbook in a night shelter, Ralph Anderson and Kyra Jones Osmus (1988) arrived at similar findings: they concluded that female volunteers attended to personal development in their volunteer work, whereas male volunteers focused on the goals of the shelter.

These gendered distinctions correspond, although not perfectly, to what I found at The Salvation Army and Loaves & Fishes. Drafted volunteers committed to the good-provider role appeared to anchor their moral selving in the roles offered them at The Salvation Army. Leaving the site wrenched their self out of this context. Steven L. Gordon (1989) has argued that emotional attachments may provide important indicators of interpretive orientation of the self. Loyalty to roles played at The Salvation Army as well as deeply held needs to meet institutionally determined guidelines for deference and demeanor suggest that the drafted volunteers at The Salvation Army experienced an institutional orientation to the moral self.

The routine volunteers practiced moral selving at Loaves & Fishes through the challenge to feel charitable love for the guests. Some volunteers failed, for these feelings did not come naturally or spontaneously. They did emotion work to bring their deeply held feelings in line with this feeling rule. Turner and Gordon (1981) maintain that questions of authenticity reveal the boundaries of the true self. Thus the routine volunteers' emotion work, with its attendant concerns about authentic emotions, corresponded to the impulsive orientation to the self. The routine volunteers, however, did not emphasize the expression of emotions without concern for morality, institutional standards, and role performance. Although there was resonance between the moral culture of Loaves & Fishes and "the impulsive emotions," the attention paid to institutional standards, sympathy, and principles (Gordon 1989: 118) illustrates how the interpretive orientation of the self at Loaves & Fishes evaded easy categorization as merely impulsive.

Turner and Gordon (1981) suggest that the practice of morality through feelings and action lodges experience in institutional contexts. Yet the example of the routine volunteers troubles this easy dichotomy. Although seemingly impulsively oriented, they revealed concern with altruism, contrary to Turner and Gordon's (1989) assertion that this concern is the social form of the institutional anchorage. They strove for moral betterment and to uphold institutional standards, as well as worked to express charitable love as an uninhibited, authentic emotional response to the guests.

The drafted volunteers, however, were more firmly lodged in the institutional relations established at The Salvation Army than were the routine volunteers at Loaves & Fishes. For example, the drafted volunteers, especially the In-house residents, and the staff spent much of their time together outside of the kitchen and appeared to define themselves in terms of roles offered at The Salvation Army. The power of the Loaves & Fishes culture to shape the moral experience of the routine volunteers across contexts outside of the organization remained more of an empirical question. In his consideration of emotional cultures and orientations to the self, Gordon (1989: 126) suggests that "impulsive culture may serve more often as an interpretative resource for emotions confined to transient *situations*, while institutional culture tends to define emotions over enduring *relationships*" (emphasis in original).

Perhaps Loaves & Fishes' culture can best be understood as a regulated impulsivity that highlighted the giving of dignity to the guests and volunteers, whereas the more institutional culture of The Salvation Army emphasized the attainment of honor for the In-house volunteers and staff. Berger's (1973) work on the changing character of Americans given the pluralization of the social lifeworld, or everyday taken-for-granted experience, provides an important means to analyze further regulated impulsivity and institutional culture. Berger has argued that both dignity and honor link self and society. Honor, however, weds identity to institutional roles, whereas dignity inheres in the individual, outside of social structure.

At The Salvation Army the drafted volunteers adhered to General Booth's Scheme of Social Selection and Salvation as they attained moral betterment through the disciplined work ethic:

> In industrial affairs we are very much like the French Republic before it tempered its doctrine of the rights of man by the duty of obedience on the part of the soldier. We have got to introduce discipline into the industrial army, we have to superadd the principle of authority to the principle of co-operation, and so enable the worker to profit to the full by the increased productiveness of the willing labour of men who are employed in their workshops and on their own property. (1890: 231)

We saw in chapter 4 how the drafted volunteers found honor in the good-provider role. Men who lost this respectability, such as Hank, often avoided volunteers and staff who continued to adhere to the tenets of Salvationism.

For the routine volunteers, dignity inhered not in an accumulated performance of a role but rather in present concern for others. The following statement by the New York State Catholic Bishops illuminates the religious philosophy informing this orientation to respect for self and others.

> We are called to proclaim a set of moral principles known as Catholic social teaching. At the heart of this teaching is the knowledge that the human person is central, the clearest reflection of God among us. Every person possesses a basic dignity that comes from God, not from any human quality or accomplishment, not from race or gender or age or economic status. Human life is inherently precious.
> (1995: 1)

The routine volunteers' practice of personalist hospitality challenged them to pursue self-betterment in caring for the less fortunate. Some routine volunteers struggled, however, to acknowledge the dignity of the guests; many of these volunteers did emotion work to feel charitable love for the guests as Ambassadors of God.

Within both cultures the volunteers strove toward moral betterment; however, at The Salvation Army honor had to be earned. In his attempt to map the historical transformation from an honor culture to one of dignity,[3] Berger suggested the precariousness of moral selving in a way relevant to understanding The Salvation Army: "The social world of honor lies in a world of relatively intact, stable institutions, a world in which individuals can with subjective certainty attach their identities to the institutional roles that society assigns them" (1973: 93). As Peter L. Berger, Brigitte Berger, and Hansfried Kellner (1973) argue, modernity reputably brought with it the pluralization of social lifeworlds. Consequently, those who inhered their moral selving in an institutionally based world of honor, as did the drafted volunteers, faced particularly great threats to their moral selves when they left that world.

This study suggests an intriguing correlation between the moral rhetoric and institutional structure at The Salvation Army, its emphasis on honor, and the predominantly male nature of the volunteer force and their predominantly working-class roots. The Salvation Army, with its resemblance to muscular Christianity, promised reclaimed manhood through hard work and battle with the evils of the body.

By the same token, similarly intriguing correlations were apparent in the predominantly middle-class Loaves & Fishes setting. Loaves & Fishes moral rhetoric and practice resembled the feminine symbolism and behavior Phyllis Mack (1987) studied in the radical religious movements of the Franscicans, the Quakers, and the followers of Gandhi. Loaves & Fishes and these religious movements shared an emphasis on the power of persuasion and the importance of nonviolent protest. Ronnie J. Steinberg and Jerry A. Jacobs's analysis of nonprofit organizations shows that they have a "feminine cast":

> The missions of nonprofit organizations are "soft"—encompassing the provision of services, a preoccupation with moral and ethical concerns, producing beauty, helping people. They must, at the very least, give the appearance that such hard-nosed concerns as making money are secondary to service provision or to the maintenance of cultural and moral standards. (1994: 100)

At Loaves & Fishes the moral rhetoric and institutional structure highlighted human dignity and a kind of caring and relational atmosphere characterized by Carol Gilligan (1982) as predominantly female, although the workforce is almost evenly mixed. Interviews by Lene Arnett Jensen (1995) on the moral language of younger and midlife, predominantly white, middle-class Americans helps us to understand why the midlife and older white, middle-class routine volunteers, both female and male, may have felt comfortable with the Catholic Worker vision of doing charity. Jensen found that whereas young Americans spoke a moral language characterized by individualism, midlife and older Americans used a language of community and divinity concerns as frequently as individualistic considerations in their moral reasoning.

Loaves & Fishes and The Salvation Army may be thought of as "gendered institutions" wherein "gender is present in the processes, practices, images and ideologies, and distributions of power in the various sectors of social life" (Acker 1992: 567). The moral rhetorics at each institution provided space for elective affinities among a constellations of factors, including religion, class, gender, and perhaps even race. In an analysis of race and schooling, Cameron McCarthy argued that intersections of race, class, and gender should be understood as "nonsynchronous interactions" in which either race, class, or gender may compose an "articulating principle," or "dominant character," in any given setting:

> Such a "dominant" character refers to the relations along which "endogenous" differences in the school are principally articulated. These dominant relations thus constitute an "articulating principle" . . . , pulling the entire ensemble of relations in the school setting into a "unity" or focus for conflict. Such an articulating principle may be race, class or gender. (1990: 86)

At The Salvation Army anxieties about gender performance showed gender to operate as the articulating principle of moral tensions for the volunteers and kitchen staff, whereas at Loaves & Fishes anxieties about class relations revealed class to operate as the articulating principle of charitable tensions for volunteers.

Yet this study discredits simple gender dichotomies about caring behavior. In a more abstract argument, the philosopher Joan C. Tronto (1993) argues that we should formulate a political ethic of care that would include values traditionally associated with women rather than talk about "women's morality." The anthropologist Carol B. Stack (1994), in a more empirical vein, studied how African Americans talked about the moral dimension of return migration to the South. She found that shared experiences in the construction of self among women and men produced "a convergence in the vocabulary of rights, morality, and the social good" (297). Stack's research, however, also indicated a disjuncture between how men and women talked about morality and the strategies they adopted for action, particularly in the political realm.

This work illustrates the power of the organizational context and its attendant emotion culture to shape morality and the politics of compassion. These visions provide moral rhetorics of charitable action that operated, in David A. Snow and Robert Benford's terms (1992), as "master frames" to construct relations of charity and political action. While Loaves & Fishes and The Salvation Army may be characterized as gendered institutions, they defy simple categorization in terms of an "ethic of care and responsibility" based in attachment or an "ethic of justice and rights" rooted in detachment, to use Gilligan's (1982) schema. Like the subjects in Stack's research on gender, culture, and moral reasoning, the drafted and routine volunteers mixed care and responsibility with justice and rights in their provision of charity. Stack's attention to culture and Tronto's attention to moral boundaries point to the importance of studying morality in institutional contexts. Tronto (1993: 119) argues against the containment of theories of care in personal relations and for a political theory of care that examines care and community: "Unless we also understand care in its richer sense of practice, we run the risk of sentimentalizing and in other ways containing the scope of care in our thinking." Charitable work at Loaves & Fishes and The Salvation Army revealed how context shapes both the discourse and the practice of caring and moral selving.

As Tocqueville ([1838] 1899) pointed out a century and a half ago, individuals seek community associations to shape their own characters in relation to others. We have seen here that this holds true but that what it means to become a "better person" differs within the moral rhetorics of charitable action found in different organizations. And, of course, the politics of the day shape profoundly the climate in which community associations organize their work.

## CHARITABLE ORGANIZATIONS AND THE STATE

Volunteers at Loaves & Fishes and The Salvation Army stepped into traditions of doing charity with very different relations to state welfare funding and policies. As we have seen, Loaves & Fishes staff protested Sacramento's policies vis-à-vis the homeless. Through its monthly newsletter, spiritual retreats, and the work of feeding the poor, Loaves & Fishes' moral rhetoric of charitable action encouraged its adherents to protest social control measures instigated by the city council and the police and the inadequate resources for the homeless in Sacramento. The Salvation Army, in contrast, sought funding from the city to provide not only the overflow winter shelter but also basic social services. At the Shelter Services Center, the Salvationists and many of the civilian staff and drafted volunteers regarded Sacramento's social control measures with approval. The staff expected its recruits to abide by strict welfare provisions. While the staff favored increased city spending for help with rehabilitation and housing, they felt themselves less at odds with the city than did the Loaves & Fishes staff.

Only at Loaves & Fishes did moral selving among the volunteers ideally entail political action. Yet in this setting, where some volunteers felt uncomfortable in face-to-face interactions unmediated by the serving line counter and others struggled to accept all of the poor as deserving of charitable assistance, most remained divorced from the activist politics of caring for the poor. Just as the staff modified personalist hospitality to allow the volunteers the choice to engage in the interactive work of personalist hospitality, they provided opportunities for service rather than the obligation to participate in political action. Most volunteers at Loaves & Fishes limited their political involvement to the confines of the kitchen and the dining room. The staff in both settings, however, shaped the political discourse on and the outcome of public policy with regard to the poor in Sacramento.

As early as 1982 Lester M. Salamon (1987: 103) estimated that federal and state governments provided only 40 percent of social services, the for-profit sector 4 percent, and the voluntary sector 56 percent. Most of the voluntary sector, however, received subsidies from the government, thereby residing in what Wolch has called "the shadow state," defined as

> a para-state apparatus comprised of multiple voluntary sector organizations, administered outside of traditional democratic politics and charged with major collective service responsibilities previously shouldered by the public sector, yet remaining within the purview of state control. (1990: xvi)

In an examination of the fifteen largest U.S. metropolitan areas, Wolch shows how the uneven regional development of the voluntary sector reflects the importance of local politics to the formation of voluntary organizations. Wolch argues that voluntary organizations within the shadow state leave themselves particularly vulnerable to state regulation and withdrawal of funds. Yet, as I indicate below, reliance on private donations alone does not insulate charities from either the punitive reach of government regulation (in Loaves & Fishes' case, particularly zoning laws) or the downfalls of public controversy. Wolch's study provides a backdrop for beginning to think about the central role of staff from both Loaves & Fishes and The Salvation Army in providing charity for the poor in Sacramento. This analysis of local politics could not be complete without a consideration of how religious affiliation lent moral authority to the staff's claims on the local government.

At The Salvation Army, firmly within the shadow state, the In-house and drafted volunteers registered with the state in compliance with government bureaucratic requirements. Clearly a "nonprofit for hire" (Smith and Lipsky 1993), The Salvation Army professionalized charity with the goal of rehabilitation. Salvationist charity and rehabilitation contributed to the local and national social welfare policy. In contrast, Loaves & Fishes staff—with their rejection of most government funding and distance from most government programs—worked to remain

outside of even the shadow state.[4] Loaves & Fishes staff made significant efforts to retain freedom of political action.

In winter 1994–95, The Sacramento Salvation Army received approximately $70,000 a month from Sacramento County's Department
of Human Services to run the overflow shelter at Cal Expo (Guyette
1994: 13), in addition to other government funds for providing social
services. Although the national Salvation Army received more private
donations than any other single charity in the United States in 1993—
nearly $638 million (*Sacramento Bee* 1994: A18)—the New York City
Salvation Army, for example, reported in the same year that nearly half
of its $68 million budget came from government contracts (Norman
1994: 40).

The Salvation Army has a long history of working with the state to
"rescue" the sinking classes. In 1886 President Grover Cleveland began
the tradition of heartfelt endorsement of The Salvation Army. All pres-
idents since have continued this tradition (Fellows 1979: 19). The U.S.
National Commander in 1994, Kenneth L. Hodder, urged Salvationists
to "speak unashamedly and act in the marketplace of State policy" based
on their understanding of God. Furthermore, Commander Hodder encouraged Salvationists to use state funds to do this work:

> With measured word and legitimate action, we request and expect
> our share in government largess for portions of complete Salvation
> Army programs that do not involve us in a conflict with the estab-
> lishment or free exercise of religion. There is no reason at all why
> The Salvation Army should hold back from applying for govern-
> mental support of any program, if we are convinced that in so doing,
> we are not involving ourselves in a practice which could be inter-
> preted as the establishment of a religious or an abuse of free exer-
> cise. (1994b: 4)

The Salvationists and the civilian staff at the Social Services Center
called for more governmental funding for rehabilitation and housing.
Staff members could be understood, in Michael Lipsky's (1980) terms,

as "street-level bureaucrats" within the shadow state. That is, often the staff represented state policy in face-to-face interaction with their clients.[5] They lobbied the Salvationists to build more housing and to expand their treatment program. This plan resonated with the staff's concern, as expressed by Kevin, an intake counselor, to obtain more funding for social services.

> What I see is if we could get more social services involved, I think what [a Salvationist] is planning to do is to make a more concerned effort to reach out and then I think we would get better success rates with the people here if we were more thorough and helpful.

Dave, the resident manager, who served on the mayor's committee on homelessness, echoed Kevin's attitude:

> They are having a workshop next month on mental health issues in Sacramento. It's like a brainstorming meeting. All the decision makers will be there, the police department, the mental health, the shelters, and we are going to try to brainstorm, and come up with some answers.

Rehabilitation served as the primary focus within their vision of charity. The staff, as exemplified by Raul's irritation at The Salvation Army kitchen being labeled a "soup kitchen" with "quite good food" by the *Sacramento News and Review* (Guyette 1994: 13), valued rehabilitation over handouts. Kevin explained success as effective rehabilitation: "What I *feel* is, what I *see*, is probably out of all the people we see, maybe 10, 15 percent *really* latch on and go do something." State resources aided this rehabilitation focus.

The Salvation Army's concern with rehabilitation and the good-provider role dovetailed with state concerns about creating independent workers. A study of social service provision in a different realm provides useful insights into the potential costs of inclusion in the shadow state. In a study of the feminist antirape movement, Nancy A. Matthews (1994) argues that the professionalization of antirape centers, which included growing reliance on state funds, resulted in their closer resemblance to social service agencies than social movements. Matthews shows how the use of state funds resulted in the emphasis on therapeutic services rather than on progressive political challenges to the state and social relations.[6]

Although Salvation Army workers entered into partnership with local state politics in solving homelessness, they did not in their therapeutic practices endorse a simple victim blaming perspective of the homeless. Similar to the shelter service providers who worked with the homeless in Toledo, Ohio, studied by Elizabeth Tracy and Randy Stoecker (1993), the staff at The Salvation Army adhered to a more complex individual and systemic understanding of homelessness that defied simple characterization as victim blaming.[7]

The Catholic Workers, in contrast to the Salvationists, denounced participation even in the shadow state. In this sense they may have at least initially gained adherents among even the so-called civic conservatives (Starobin, cited in Skocpol and Fiorina 1999) who valorize private initiative to solve social problems. Yet, beginning with Dorothy Day, the Catholic Workers have understood themselves to be not merely a charity but also a social movement for change:

> Since The Catholic Worker is a movement rather than an accredited
> charitable organization, the widows even paid our taxes. The point
> we make of emphasizing personal responsibility, rather than state or
> organized responsibility, has cost us a good deal through the years.
> (Day 1963: 33)

The movement has traditionally attempted to spark the collective moral conscience. Day described this position in the following exchange between herself and Peter Maurin.

> "Is that what you meant, Peter?" I asked him once about an over-
> crowded house of hospitality.
> "Well," he hesitated. "At least it arouses the conscience."
> Which is something. (1963: 193)

Although Loaves & Fishes accepted government surplus food, they did not accept government funding. They operated almost solely on private donations. This stance allowed the organization greater freedom to function both as moral conscience and political actor in Sacramento. Loaves & Fishes offered a greater challenge to mainstream politics in Sacramento than did The Salvation Army.

Although Catholic Worker houses of hospitality have been repeatedly valorized by academics,[8] many academic considerations of charity implicitly deride charitable organizations for failing to work adequately for social change. For example, the historian Michael B. Katz (1986) argues that Catholic philanthropy brought charity, not social change. The social scientists Charles Hoch and Robert A. Slayton (1989: 215) maintain that the politics of compassion "reproduce the dependence in their clients they hope eventually to remove." And Joel Blau (1992: 5) claims unequivocally that "organized private charity espouses an ideology of individualism, self-reliance, and minimal government." Blau argues for replacing charity with social movement politics:

> The social movement to house the homeless sees homelessness as a social problem rather than as a private trouble. Politics replaces charity. Food, clothing, and shelter are no longer donations to the less fortunate. Instead, in this social movement, advocates see the necessities of life as a basic human right. (1992: 95)

Blau understands the advocates for the homeless in this social movement to best resemble what John McCarthy and Mayer Zald (1977) call "conscience constituencies." In McCarthy and Zald's terms, conscience constituencies, unlike beneficiary constituencies, do not stand to benefit directly from social movement gains.

Janet Poppendieck's *Sweet Charity?* (1998) advances Blau's argument with her contention that the work of administering and maintaining emergency food programs consumes the labor of many of those most dedicated to eradicating poverty. She provides compelling evidence that the work of food distribution effectively diverts much of the energy of those most likely to challenge the "distributional politics" that necessitate food assistance for the poor. In this important critique of the politics of emergency food aid, she credits the beleaguered food stamp program for its premise that the poor have an entitlement to food that should allow them to remain in the mainstream with rights to purchase food. Poppendieck's argument is, in brief, that charity functions not only as a symptom but also as a cause of the growth in poverty. She provides convincing evidence that many citizens give their time and money to charity rather than social change and, perhaps even more important, that charity cannot begin to meet the food needs of the poor in this country. Yet this account falls short in its appreciation of the complexity of how charitable organizations may be simultaneously active in distributional politics and social service provision.

Loaves & Fishes devoted organizational labor both to charitable good works and to social change, which suggests the false simplicity of an analysis that posits providing for the poor and participating in social movements as mutually exclusive, mutually negating, or, as in Poppendieck's formulation, subversive of social change.

Whereas The Salvation Army supported the state's welfare policy in its work to reform its clients, Loaves & Fishes protested the city's inadequate provision of housing and resources for the local poor. Loaves & Fishes thus provides a counterexample to conventional academic accounts of politics and charity that often consign charity to a position of appeasement and maintenance of the status quo.[9] As in Blau's formulation of social movement politics, Loaves & Fishes provided an organizational context for the mobilization of its adherents. The routine volunteers joined a larger conscience community to form a "collective identity" that "derive[d] from members' common interests, experiences, and solidarity" (Taylor and Whittier 1992: 105). Doug McAdam also noted this collective identity in his research on Freedom Summer volunteers:

> The image of the activist as a lone individual driven only by the
> force of his or her conscience applies to very few of the applicants.

Rather, the force of his or her involvement in the project seems to have been mediated through some combination of personal relationships and/or organizational ties. (1988: 50)

Loaves & Fishes established this organizational network by extending and channeling the idealism and energy of volunteers. It also provided a place for loners such as the sportscaster and retired accountant who chose to volunteer on particular days of the week and without being affiliated with a church group. For these loners, Loaves & Fishes created the personal relationships and organizational ties that mediated a commitment to helping the homeless with an established practice.

This framework enabled Loaves & Fishes to feed and care for its guests and to provide an advocacy coalition, or, in social movement terms, a conscience constituency, composed of both staff and volunteers, to keep political pressure on city government. Chris Delany told a volunteer that she would not want to run for the city council because she did not have faith that from their "perspective" the system could be changed. Yet she regularly petitioned city officials for more justice for the needy.

In Hoch and Slayton's (1989) terms, Loaves & Fishes staff advocated vigorously on behalf of the homeless in Sacramento, thereby wedding the politics of compassion with the politics of entitlement. In his work on volunteers and the Gay Men's Health Crisis, Kayal (1990, 1993) argued that volunteers' "carepartnering" work is political because it restructures ties among self, community, and society. While the staff at Loaves & Fishes shielded the volunteers from the "dirty work" of feeding the urban poor, the routine volunteers can be understood, as the AIDS volunteers Kayal studied, to be "bearing witness" to the suffering of others. That is, volunteer work at Loaves & Fishes challenged the volunteer to restructure ties to the Sacramento community so as to assume responsibility for the homeless members of the community.

For example, in the early 1990s LeRoy Chatfield proposed that the city build cottages to house some three thousand homeless people in single-family units in a community setting. Loaves & Fishes staff hoped to manage the cottages privately, and unlike the proposed cottages at The Salvation Army, they would not be affiliated with a drug and alcohol rehabilitation program. In the "Philosophy of Management" statement of the "1,000 Cottages" brochure the staff argued,

> A compassionate, affirming, and caring environment can be created for people when four rules are observed: no booze, no drugs, no violence, and no threats of violence. . . . [P]rivate sector, charitable organizations can be more flexible, firm and compassionate—and have more room to maneuver—in enforcing these four rules than do public sector government agencies. (November 1993)

Faced with the prospect of government funding and involvement, Loaves & Fishes established Sacramento Cottage Housing, Inc., to manage the project (*Sacramento News and Review* 1994: 5).[10] The Loaves & Fishes newsletter, however, encouraged readers to write to the city council, on letterhead if possible, to support the project. In spite of more than eight hundred letters of support, the city council deadlocked initially on Cottage Housing's application for a $136,000 loan to cover the start-up costs for sixty cottages (Gibson 1994). Two months later, after continued pressure from the Loaves & Fishes community, the city council voted approval for the project (Hicks 1994).[11]

When the city granted final approval for construction, Loaves & Fishes appealed for more housing for the poor the following day, Ash Wednesday. Dan Delany objected to the city's threat to halt construction of more units without assistance from the county. Chris Delany demanded, "We ask our city leaders to hear and heed the cry of the poor and homeless" (Lindelof 1995: B1). They vowed to ring a bell each Tuesday at noon during Lent outside City Hall.

To mobilize its conscience constituency, Loaves & Fishes blended the politics of compassion and entitlement. In their newsletter they held the city council responsible for providing low-income housing:

> We've said it before and we say it now, Sacramento will pay a grave moral price if we continue to permit elected officials to avoid their

responsibility of providing $200 a month rental housing for our brothers and sisters, and their children, who must live their lives at a level below that of subsistence. (June 1993)

The staff also spoke out about laws aimed at curtailing begging. Chatfield, then executive director of Loaves & Fishes, told a *Sacramento Bee* columnist that an "emergency measure" to limit soliciting alms was "another step toward criminalizing poverty" (McGrath 1993: A2). Loaves & Fishes also used its newsletter and the *Sacramento Bee* to mobilize public outrage over the treatment of the homeless by the police. Chatfield expressed his moral outrage at "Bronco Billy," a Sacramento officer accused by homeless people of harassing them, to a *Bee* reporter: "His level of police activity is petty, mean spirited, misguided, and does grave disservice to the image of the Sacramento Police Department as we have known it for 10 years" (Furillo 1994: B1). In further guidance of its conscience constituency, Loaves & Fishes provided forms for the volunteer attendees at the annual volunteer appreciation dinner to write to the Police Department and took sworn statements from their homeless guests to submit as citizen complaints to the department.

Volunteer work at Loaves & Fishes involved politically diverse community members in an organization critical of the city's provisions for the poor. The staff denounced the city for what they saw as abandonment of its poor. They worked to transform entitlement politics into moral priorities for the collective. For example, the lack of affordable housing for the poor became a Lenten vision of moral disgrace for Sacramento:

In 1994, Loaves & Fishes interviewed 2,173 guests who came to Loaves & Fishes searching for affordable housing. 75% of those we interviewed had lived in Sacramento for more than 2 years. Sadly, we could place only 17% into housing they could honestly afford. It's tragic. It unravels the quality of life for all Sacramentans. (Newsletter, Easter 1995)

Moral selving at Loaves & Fishes did not demand political involvement of the volunteers but, by implication, made political action con-

sistent with charitable action. In a study of the mobilization of homeless social movement organizations, Daniel M. Cress and David A.
Snow (1996: 1107) argue that the critical issue for social movements
of the poor "is not whether the poor should organize, but in what
ways and with whom?" Conscience constituencies may provide the
backbone of such a mobilization effort and yet leave the poor vulnerable should their moral sentiments stray. Loaves & Fishes staff
courted the local conscience constituency through mild direction: the
newsletters provided explicit directions on how to take political action. Weekly or monthly participation in the dining room dissolved
the isolation of their conscience constituents, thereby providing the
staff with more opportunities to underscore the moral component of
political action.

## FALL FROM GRACE: THE DEMISE OF THE POLITICS OF COMPASSION

> By 1994 Loaves & Fishes had become the darling char-
> ity of the Sacramento media, especially the *Sacramento
> Bee*. We could do no wrong: every program we under-
> took was prominently covered and praised. By 1996
> Loaves & Fishes had become the most controversial
> charity in the Sacramento media, especially the *Sacra-
> mento Bee*. We could do nothing right and every pro-
> gram that dealt with homeless men was especially criti-
> cized. We fell in the media from being "helpers" to
> becoming "enablers." The fact is we were no more
> praiseworthy in 1994 than we were blameworthy in
> 1996. Neither the "before" nor the "after" of Loaves &
> Fishes as portrayed in the media was real. Each was a
> creation of the media in response to its own perceptions
> about the worthiness of the issue of homelessness.
>
> *LeRoy Chatfield, letter*

Within the year after I ended my field research at Loaves & Fishes
and The Salvation Army in 1994, the *Sacramento Bee* and the Loaves &

Fishes newsletter began to chronicle what I came to think of as Loaves & Fishes' "fall from grace." As Chatfield so clearly articulated above, the media played a critical role in creating the fall from grace. I witnessed most of this crisis from afar, primarily through the lens of the *Bee* and the Loaves & Fishes newsletters but substantiated by a letter Chatfield (1999) wrote to me after reading a paper that I wrote on the politics of the fall from grace. But these sources tell us little about how volunteers experienced the changing political climate. Most significant in the latter regard, donor information provided by Chatfield on behalf of Loaves & Fishes and brief follow-up interviews with a few of the most committed routine volunteers hint at the strength of the support for Loaves & Fishes in the local community in the wake of the severe media chastisement.

Loaves & Fishes, once a beloved model of private initiative in the community, lost its favored status as it and the homeless population grew in the mid-1990s. As portrayed in the local media, Loaves & Fishes seemed to claim that the moral call to bring justice to homeless people superseded other rights, like those of local property owners to regulate the growing influx of poor people in their neighborhood. If, as the sociologist Donileen R. Loseke (1997: 438) so convincingly argues, "the power of the idea of private charity is that it *unites*," how did the collapse of the politics of compassion affect the ability of a community to coalesce around caring for its poor? What happens when the social service components of a social movement organization ignore (or judge as selfish) the claims of other residents with whom its shares geography?

A *Sacramento Bee* editorial attributed Loaves & Fishes' fall from grace to their failure to convince the local community to extend charitable love to all of the poor—especially those framed as the unworthy poor—in a moment of increasingly conservative welfare politics:

> Most troubling, by serving all who come no questions asked, Loaves
> & Fishes helps support the lifestyle of able-bodied men and women

who have chosen to live on the streets. Thus, the charity puts itself in conflict with city policy, which demands some level of effort and responsibility from the people it helps. An alcoholic must be in treatment. The unemployed must try to get a job. (1995: B6)

Just four days before Loaves & Fishes served its two millionth meal, the lead article of the September 24, 1995, *Sacramento Bee* proclaimed, "Bitter Expansion Dispute Clouds Ministry for Homeless" (Kollars 1995: A1). The article documented how a neighborhood activist, Walter Mueller, reported the Loaves & Fishes complex's expansion to City Hall and uncovered numerous alleged permit violations. The article spoke for many of the organization's frustrated neighbors. Claiming that he was a holiday toy organizer for children at Loaves & Fishes, Mueller advocated contained growth, not removal of the organization. Yet Chatfield (1999) countered in a letter to me that Loaves & Fishes had never sponsored a toy drive. He wrote, "The first we heard of Mr. Mueller was from reports we received about his weekly testimony before the City Council bashing/trashing homeless people and then much later began to add Loaves & Fishes to his diatribes before the Council."

Another community member cited in the article, Catherine Camacho, a mother of three and former volunteer at Loaves & Fishes, explained that she and other residents in the Loaves & Fishes neighborhood did not have the same conflict with The Salvation Army or the Union Gospel Mission. In her words, "We get tired of being accused of being heartless. We are working so hard to make downtown a safe place to live and work and raise our children. Loaves & Fishes has been unresponsive. The frustration against them is widespread" (Kollars 1995: A24). Of Camacho, Chatfield (1999) said that, although to his knowledge she never volunteered—or claimed to volunteer—at Loaves & Fishes, she had in 1989, as president of the local Alkali Flat Project Area, voted approval for seven special use permits sought by Loaves & Fishes. These differences highlight the complexity of community relations with Loaves & Fishes. Perhaps Heather Fargo, a longtime public supporter of Loaves & Fishes and a city council member, best characterized the resentment against Loaves & Fishes:

> It's not just frustration that we're feeling. It's almost a sense of betrayal. People are feeling abused. We have for so long been supportive and trying to do the right thing for the homeless. And I believe everyone out there is well-intentioned. But they have been blind to the impacts they are creating in the community. (Cited in Kollars 1995: A24)

City Manager Bill Edgar identified how he understood the crux of the antagonism when he asserted that feeding the poor was not enough: "You also have to manage the population" (Kollars 1995: A24).

The controversy only escalated in early 1996 when a San Francisco ad agency placed an advertisement on behalf of Loaves & Fishes decrying the presence of twenty-seven thousand homeless children in Sacramento in *Newsweek*, *Time*, *Sports Illustrated*, and *U.S. News and World Report*. The ad, drafted nearly three years earlier and allegedly run at that moment without Loaves & Fishes' knowledge, appeared only in regional distributions of these national magazines, although much of the community apparently assumed that it ran nationally (Bizjak 1996: B3). An editorial in the *Sacramento Bee* that week castigated Loaves & Fishes:

> The ad is not only false but worse a blatant attempt by a private agency dependent on local goodwill to advance its cause by denigrating the community on whose support it depends. . . . Promiscuous humility is no more attractive than flagrant arrogance. (1996: B6)

The media criticism of the ad overshadowed Loaves & Fishes reissuance of its "Good Neighbor Policy," with a commitment of an additional $20,000 in 1996 for neighborhood graffiti removal, portable toilets, street monitoring, and greater local garbage cleanup (newsletter, Loaves & Fishes 1996). In addition, by April Loaves & Fishes abandoned its efforts to expand Friendship Park, explaining, through its attorney, Tina Thomas, "We don't want to have a sour relationship with the city. We want to continue working and cooperating with the city" (Kollars 1996: B8).

By January 1997 the Sacramento City Council voted to sue Loaves & Fishes for failure to comply with zoning violations in its expansion and its refusal to halt its Sunday meal without a permit (Bizjak and Kollars 1997: A1, A10). Amid all this controversy, the Sunday meal dispute most profoundly ignited the moral passions of Loaves & Fishes. Chatfield said in an interview,

> I find it incredible that city politicians would vote to spend taxpayer money to sue a charity. . . . This may be a first in the nation where a city council sues a charity for feeding hungry people on the Christian day of Sunday. The irony is unsettling. (Cited in Bizjak and Kollars 1997: A1, A10)

Chatfield (1999) later reported that from the Loaves & Fishes perspective this was the "defining issue" of the organization's controversy with the City of Sacramento: "Feeding on Sunday became so central to the core of Loaves & Fishes that the Board of Directors and Staff voted to be arrested before they would stop the Sunday feeding."

Mayor Joe Serna, Jr., who had been friends with Chatfield in the twenty-five years following their participation in California's farm labor movement, voted against suing Loaves & Fishes but nonetheless voiced disagreement with Loaves & Fishes' treatment of all the poor and homeless as worthy guests: "You perpetuate homelessness by just accommodating it. . . . We need [Loaves & Fishes] to continue to serve poor folks. It's important. But the idea of them as guests just hanging out is absurd" (Bizjak 1997b: A20). Chatfield commanded much of the media attention in this heated debate. A *Sacramento News and Review* lead article captured the implicit moralism of the debate in its front-page caption, "Saint or Sinner? Has LeRoy Chatfield Taken Loaves & Fishes Beyond the Law?" (Pulley 1997). Similar coverage in the *Sacramento Bee* prompted Chris Delany and Dan Delany (1997) to write in a letter to the editor, "Don't single out Chatfield for blame; blame our board of directors."

In early March Loaves & Fishes countersued the City of Sacramento, claiming harassment and violation of its First Amendment right to practice religion. In its seventy-five-page countersuit, Loaves & Fishes drew on biblical sources and laid the groundwork for deposing city employees, including the mayor. Attorneys from Sacramento and the Bay Area joined together to provide free legal counsel for the charity (Kollars 1997b: A1, A9). Within a week, the mayor publicly declared the city council decision to sue Loaves & Fishes "a national embarrassment," asking what kind of city would challenge a charity's right to serve the poor a free meal on Sundays. Serna further implored that both sides agree to mediation (Delsohn and Bizjak 1997: A1). He criticized both sides of the dispute by revealing that not only had he refused the City Attorney's request for more staff to prosecute the case and would request reports itemizing moneys spent suing a Catholic charity, he had also chastised Chatfield: " '[He] gets his back up when he doesn't need to. . . . You have to be more flexible' " (Delsohn and Bizjak 1997: A9). By the end of the month both sides agreed to mediation, but Dan Delany expressed disappointment at a missed opportunity to testify in court about "the city's abandonment of the homeless" (Sanchez and Kollars 1997: B1, B5).

The city began searching for alternate sites for a Sunday meal under the auspices of a city council subcommittee, and Serna began the work of establishing a joint city-county commission to explore how government might meet the needs of the estimated forty thousand Sacramentans predicted to lose government aid under welfare reform (Bizjak 1997a: B1). As the city began searching for alternate programs for the poor, the Richards Boulevard Improvement Association took out a full-page ad in a Sunday Metro section of the *Sacramento Bee*, written as a "plea to Sacramento." It described the problem as a neighborhood overwhelmed with thousands of homeless people—some of whom defecate on the sidewalks and shoot up in the neighborhood—and closed with the compelling assertion:

We don't want to *close* Loaves & Fishes.

We *do want them to be good neighbors.*

And *take responsibility* for any harm they cause surrounding neighborhoods—however inadvertent. (1997: B5; emphasis in original)

The closing line proclaimed, "Please don't allow this to destroy our neighborhoods. It's not fair. It's not right. It's not Christian."

During this controversy, the *Sacramento Bee*'s coverage of Loaves & Fishes tipped from relatively unadulterated praise of its charitable services to the poor to castigation for enabling the unworthy poor. An editorial quoted earlier in this chapter chastised Loaves & Fishes for enabling "the lifestyle of able-bodied men and women who have chosen to live on the streets" (*Sacramento Bee* 1995: B6). The *Bee* further legitimated this perspective with its report that the mayor had characterized the Loaves & Fishes view of homeless people as "guests" as "absurd" (Bizjak 1997b: A20). A front-page lead article in March 1997, as the standoff heightened, proclaimed, "North-City Area a Magnet for Homeless . . . and Criticism" (Hubert and Griffith 1997: A1). In these reports, the *Bee*, which had previously focused on the poor as the beneficiaries of Sacramento's admirable charitable spirit, reconstructed them as the *unworthy* poor and the community as the repeated victim of Loaves & Fishes, the million-dollar charitable business.

Seven months after the city first sued Loaves & Fishes, the parties reached a mediated settlement. The agreement was reached just as depositions of council members were to be taken. Most significant, the agreement allowed for continuation of the Sunday meal. It followed within days of a U.S. Supreme Court ruling invalidating the 1993 Religious Freedom Restoration Act, which limited the ability of the state and the city to apply local zoning laws to religious organization. Chatfield said that, in spite of the ruling, "we do not believe that we need the permission of the City Council to feed the hungry and shelter the homeless" (Epstein 1997: A1, A20). Nonetheless, the ruling probably put additional pressure on the charity to settle. Serna pledged $15,000 for Loaves & Fishes' outstanding permit fees and $10,000 for future permit fees. The *Bee* reported, however, that the charity's financial losses were not so easily offset:

> [Loaves & Fishes] plans to suspend nearly all services—except the noon meal—in August because of money problems. The cash crunch is due to a drop in donations attributed to the controversial court battle, along with the about $200,000 in permit fees and building expenses that the charity has had to spend to correct numerous code violations. (Kollars and Bizjak 1997: A13)

Eight of the city council members voted in favor of the settlement (with one abstention), and Chatfield declared it "fair" (Kollars and Bizjak 1997: A1).

Although no longer lauded in the media for their works of mercy, Loaves & Fishes managed to grow every year from 1994 to 1997 in both donations and number of donors. In 1998 both declined. According to Chatfield (1999), by 1997 Loaves & Fishes received just over an additional $200,000 per year with an increase of 6,700 donors. In 1998 the organization received less money but still reported an increase of 900 donors.[12] Yet on two occasions during this time Loaves & Fishes reported a dramatic drop in donations. During the 1995 Christmas holiday, the organization reported that it had received nearly $50,000 less than in previous years (newsletter, Winter 1996). In June 1996, the newsletter reported that donations were down by 15 to 20 percent: "Though the economy is 'up,' we all seem to be suffering a stiff reduction in donations." The *Sacramento Bee*'s characterization of Loaves & Fishes as a "giant charity [that is] too big, too arrogant and too dismissive of the concerns of the surrounding community" (1995: B6) may have contributed to fluctuations in charitable giving of money. In spite of—or perhaps because of—Loaves & Fishes' beleaguered condition in the media, donations flowed in as never before.

Although Loaves & Fishes spurned government funding, its struggles ring a cautionary note about the vulnerability of charitable organizations to growth and increased bureaucratization. Dan Delany foreshadowed the institutional cost of growth almost a decade before this crisis: "[Loaves & Fishes] will probably end up being something capitalist, I'm afraid. So what? I have no illusions" (Delany and Delany 1987: 32). Chatfield asserted to a newspaper reporter in the middle of the crisis, " 'I'm not doing the real work of Loaves & Fishes. . . . I'm not the one out there working with the poor and feeding them. I used to do more of that, but I'm the bureaucracy now. I'm in the office most of the time' " (Delsohn 1997: B6). His words revealed how staff still valued personalist hospitality over bureaucratic growth even as Loaves & Fishes' institutionalization solidified.

In the midst of his public dispute with Chatfield, the mayor argued for Loaves & Fishes to relinquish services to the city: "LeRoy Chatfield is my friend. He's not my moral superior. We care passionately about the same people but government can go a long way toward achieving the same ends with a lot less animus" (Delsohn 1997: B6). But the May 1999 Loaves & Fishes newsletter reaffirmed in unequivocal terms the organization's commitment to maintain independence from government:

> The longstanding decision of our Board of Directors not to solicit
> or accept government funds for our work is both philosophical/spir-
> itual and practical. We believe that each one of us—and each one of
> you—has been called in a personal way to help the poor, the hungry
> and those who have been rejected by society.
>
> And the principle of not accepting government money is also
> practical. Loaves & Fishes would need to create its own substantial
> bureaucracy to interface with the government, not only to apply
> and re-apply over and over again for continuing funds, but to also
> account in great detail for these funds in accordance with elaborate
> contracts and time-consuming procedures. Frankly, we choose not

to spend the money and our valuable time on creating and sustaining such a bureaucracy. We doubt it is even cost effective in the long run.

And because there is no "how to" manuals given to us by government about how to go about our work of hospitality . . . we can be flexible, creative and experimental in trying to respond to the felt needs of the poor whom we have chosen to serve in a personal way.

Loaves & Fishes offered its adherents social services detached from the ethos of state welfare politics through the donations and work of community members. Its fall from grace may illustrate the illusory nature of the freedom achieved in distancing from the shadow state. While in years past a model for private initiative outside of the shadow state, the organization suffered censure as the politics of compassion faded and a "get tough on welfare" ethos gained new strength in public discourse. Yet, as evidenced in the May 1999 newsletter and donor statistics, the commitment to personalist hospitality remained steady among Loaves & Fishes staff and apparently among it supporters.

The close of 1997 witnessed Sacramento county supervisors backing away from a plan to begin immediate substitution of rehabilitation in favor of emergency housing. While they did decide not to reopen the ten-year-old emergency shelter at Cal Expo, they provided 126 additional beds at two downtown sites to compensate for the 286 lost beds at Cal-Expo. The county also funded an additional 36 beds at The Salvation Army Shelter Services Center. Transitional housing programs in Sacramento were expected to meet the needs of most homeless people: "The programs are part of the county's shift to a 'continuum of care' philosophy for the homeless rather than just providing beds and hot meals without asking clients to work toward self-sufficiency," said Cheryl Davis, director of the county's Department of Human Assistance. Yet the Roman Catholic Bishop William K. Weigand pleaded with the county supervisors to reopen the Cal Expo overflow shelter, citing the needs of those who slept on the steps of the downtown cathedral (Kollars 1997a: A27).

## CONCLUSION

The religious overtone in describing this story of crisis and resolution as Loaves & Fishes' fall from grace should not be left unexamined. In a country ostensibly committed to the separation of church and state, the voluntary sector provides an increasingly complicated interweaving of the sacred and secular. Almost all discussions of church and state open with reference to Thomas Jefferson's famous turn of phrase in a letter of 1802 charging that we should erect a "wall of separation" between church and state (Jefferson, cited in Demerath and Williams 1992: 4). As in these words from 1947, the U.S. Supreme Court has repeatedly invoked this powerful imagery to rule against the use of tax dollars to support religion: "That wall must be kept high and impregnable" (Monsma 1996: 1). The Salvation Army exemplifies the reality of the many nonprofit organizations that rely on government money to provide charity (Monsma 1996), while Loaves & Fishes illuminates the power and volatility of using religiously inspired moral rhetoric to mobilize local government in social service provision. In Wolfe's (1999: 29) words, "Two hundred years after the brilliant writings of Madison and Jefferson on the topic, Americans cannot make up their minds whether religion is primarily private, public, or some uneasy combination of the two."

In a community study of Springfield, Massachusetts, aptly titled *A Bridging of Faiths*, N. J. Demerath III and Rhys H. Williams document the power of religious clergy, particularly those affiliated with the ecumenical social movement branches of larger Catholic and Protestant churches, to make homelessness a pressing civic problem. These advocates used their "moral and material leverage" (1992: 146) to agitate for public support for government assistance for the poor. Like the Loaves & Fishes staff before their fall from grace, religious advocates in Springfield operated successfully from their strong ecumenical base because of what Demerath and Williams (1992: 161) characterize as their publicly "impeachable motives."

More conventional accounts of "civic skills" (Verba, Schlozman, and Brady 1995) neglect to credit the power of what Mary Pattillo-McCoy (1998) calls church culture in providing a powerful blueprint for social movement activism. As Pattillo-McCoy shows, Christian imagery and practice may be critical elements in a "tool kit" for social change in the black community. Loaves & Fishes activists made similar successful use of their religious imagery and practice. Nonetheless, their vulnerability seemed to lie in crossing what Demerath and Williams (1992: 142) identified as "the fine line between pride or piousness," or what I referred to in my analysis of Loaves & Fishes as the fine line between moral purity or righteousness.

As Loaves & Fishes and the City of Sacramento worked toward a tense resolution of their frayed relations, national legislation in the name of "welfare reform" aggressively encouraged what has come to be called faith-based charity. The "Charitable Choice" provision of the 1996 Personal Responsibility and Work Opportunity Act encouraged states to use "faith-based organizations in serving the poor and needy." The provision resolved to protect "the religious integrity and character of the faith-based organizations that are willing to accept government funds" (cited in Dionne and DiIulio 1999: 8). John D. DiIulio, Jr., a nonresident senior fellow of the Brookings Institution and a professor of politics, and James Q. Wilson, a prominent conservative African-American emeritus scholar of public policy, are advocates of Charitable Choice. They contributed to a special issue of the *Brookings Review* (1999) that amassed significant social scientific and moral support for the provision. Among the findings: one-third of the volunteers doing nonreligious activities still relate their work to a religious influence; African-American and liberal congregations are most likely to benefit from Charitable Choice; spiritually rigorous programs appear most beneficial to recipients (Dionne and DiIulio 1999); faith enables people to transform their lives as exemplified in Alcoholics Anonymous; faith-based prison programs are more transformative than secular programs (Wilson 1999); black church outreach programs and inner-city churches already help many of those most in trouble (Cnaan 1999; Di-Iulio 1999).[13]

The Charitable Choice provision legitimates government support for organizations such as The Salvation Army that already labor in the charitable social welfare branch of the shadow state.[14] If it legitimates the work of charitable organizations in the shadow state, it also places the state in the role of shadow church. As we have already considered, nonprofits funded by the government seem to be particularly likely to lose hold of social change politics as they come to resemble the states' often predominantly therapeutic welfare agencies. Refusal to accept government funding, however, clearly does not protect nonprofits from either a governmental or a public backlash, as witnessed by Loaves & Fishes' fall from grace.

Personal and social redemption are inextricably linked in the moral communities of charitable organizations. Citizens, politicians, and journalists hold these organizations accountable for the way in which their vision of charity affects the larger community. The radical underpinnings of moral selving at Loaves & Fishes became its downfall as the organization grew and the surrounding community came in increasingly close contact with the homeless. With the Charitable Choice provision more faith-based organizations may find themselves increasingly immersed in the bureaucracy of working with the state to help the poor. This is an unfinished story, yet it has meaning for other charitable organizations—either secular or faith-based—as they attempt to help poor people through hard times.

# Keeping the Faith at Loaves & Fishes

In fall 1998, curious about how some of the most committed of the routine volunteers responded to Loaves & Fishes' fall from grace, I called as many as possible to talk briefly with them about their commitment to volunteer work at Loaves & Fishes. I reached only seven volunteers, for in the intervening years telephone numbers had changed, but of this group only one had ceased to volunteer at Loaves & Fishes. My findings about their continued dedication to volunteerism, although not conclusive, are suggestive of the characteristics of constancy in volunteer work.

Of those still at Loaves & Fishes, two had been volunteering for five years, two for seven years, one for eight years, and another for almost eleven years. Miguel, the Mexican-American volunteer with the Metropolitan Community Church, told me that he had stopped volunteering after only a few years because he "just got busy with work." He did not think that the MCC, a group composed of unusually young volunteers, still participated in the work of feeding the poor at Loaves & Fishes.

Lori, a Unitarian crew leader, mother, and real estate agent, and Herb, a Jewish father of two who had been laid off from his job at Legal Services during a period of government cutbacks, continued to balance work, family, and volunteering at Loaves & Fishes. Lori had been volunteering for eight years with a six-month break in the last year because of a family illness, and Herb had been at Loaves & Fishes for seven years. Lori echoed her words of five years earlier when she explained, "I'm fortunate that at work I call the shots." This allowed her to serve as crew leader once a month and to stop in one other time a month. For her, the rewards of volunteering were "making a difference" and making people "feel welcomed . . . for at least part of the day"; the difficulties lay in "seeing people who will probably never get themselves in a different situation." Of Loaves & Fishes' fall from grace, Lori said, "Everybody worked hard. On *both* sides. We can't expect that there will not be fallout in the neighborhood." She saw no drop in the commitment to volunteering among her crew and seemed most focused on the work of volunteering and the lessons to learned from it. For example, she reiterated her appreciation that her son is "learning charity" from helping her, and in a similar vein fervently told me, "I hope that your work will encourage people to charity. *Action* as a lifestyle."

Herb reported that the Jewish Federation was "a little attenuated" as a group and that the "people coming [were] getting less support from the Federation." Nonetheless, the Federation still gave the financial support necessary for the meal and new retirees had augmented the group. As the father of a new baby and an import-export business owner trying to expand his business and doing "fill-in lawyering" as well, Herb explained that he was a "little bit more jealous" of his time than in the past. He found that he was "a little more reticent about political work" but still committed to volunteering at Loaves & Fishes. Of the battle with the city over zoning, Herb reported that both sides had made some accommodations and that the "city looked pretty silly" fighting Loaves & Fishes when it provided charity with no city funding. He expressed some frustration that most of the volunteers were retired: "Now, it seems like it's mostly older people, just sort of retired people. That's pretty discouraging."

The other four volunteers with whom I spoke were older people who had less difficulty balancing volunteering with other commitments.

Pete, seventy-seven and with nearly eleven years of volunteer work at Loaves & Fishes, left the kitchen after he "got sick of pots and pans" and began spending two days a week in the Loaves & Fishes library. Once a month he joined St. Joseph's of Elk Grove in the kitchen. Absent from Loaves & Fishes for almost six months during 1998 because of a bout with cancer, Pete seemed happy to be back volunteering in the library, where he described himself as "really trying to be a friend to everyone." He reiterated his commitment to homeless people, especially the mentally unstable, as originating in the difficulties his wife experienced with her own mental illness.

Catherine and Elizabeth, who both came to Loaves & Fishes after their mothers died, which freed them from caring for their elderly parents, had been volunteering for five and seven years respectively in 1998. Elizabeth continued to volunteer with the Unitarians and Cathedral Presentation. She still thought that Loaves & Fishes was well run and enjoyed going there, to "see a lot of good people." Echoing her praise of five years before, she assured me, "We still have very few fights. Only two in eight years." Of changes in herself, Elizabeth said, "I'm more empathetic to more people. I think that is probably the biggest change. I understand now that some of the people who look perfectly normal are *incapable* of working and being in the mainstream." Elizabeth seemed closer to accepting the poor, even if within a secular framework distanced from the Catholic Worker acceptance of them as Ambassadors of God.

Two years after I interviewed him, at age sixty-nine, Dan's struggle to understand the homeless' experiences in light of public criticism of Loaves & Fishes as too tolerant led him to spend two days on the streets. He slept one night in his station wagon and another at the Union Gospel Mission. He told a *Sacramento Bee* reporter, "What I learned is that these people are not on the street by choice. That this is not a good way to get freebies. There is no thrill to this lifestyle. And there are a lot of disturbed people on the street" (Sylva 1996: A2). Three years of volunteering at Loaves & Fishes enabled Dan, in his words, to "speak of the plight of the poor . . . with some credence." He continued, "I am not simply being theoretical" (Sylva 1996: A2).

Most striking, the routine volunteers spoke in terms astonishingly similar to those used in their interviews with me five years before. This continuity underscores how many moral careers at Loaves & Fishes take place over a much longer and less dramatic time frame than at The Salvation Army. As a caveat to this observation, it is important to note that younger volunteers appear to have more difficulty maintaining the commitment to volunteer, even those with some control over their work schedules. Yet many interesting questions remain: Were the less committed volunteers more alienated by Loaves & Fishes' fall from grace than these committed volunteers? Have these volunteers, and others like them, been politicized to take action on behalf of the poor precisely because of volunteering? Even more simply, do they vote differently as a result of their experiences at Loaves & Fishes? How has the experience of moral selving at Loaves & Fishes permeated other aspects of their lives?

# NOTES

## INTRODUCTION

1. Robert Putnam's work, although criticized for its method, sparked what Theda Skocpol and Morris Fiorina (1999) have called the "civic engagement debate," which raises critical questions about the vitality and form of civic participation in contemporary American democracy. As Skocpol and Fiorina remind us in their lucid review of this debate, our anxieties about civic engagement, while not necessarily empirically supported, indicate a significant sweeping anxiety among many Americans about alienation from voluntary and political organizations.

2. For example, ethnographers have explored how homeless women experience shelters (Golden 1992; Liebow 1993), how men experience what Jacqueline Wiseman ([1970] 1979) called the "institutional margins" of skid row, how culture structures very different experiences for homeless men and women (Passaro 1996), how homeless youth create street culture (Ruddick 1996), how soup kitchens provide cultures of sociability and hospitality (Glasser 1988; Murray 1990), how citywide networks of helping organizations shape the experience of homelessness (Dordick 1997; Rosenthal 1994; Snow and Anderson 1993; Wagner 1993), and how encounters between outreach workers and the homeless involve negotiations over resources both material and symbolic (Rowe 1999). See chapters 3 and 4 for further discussion of these works.

3. Daphne Holden's (1997) study of how volunteers struggle to sustain equality while serving as rule enforcers in a homeless shelter is a notable exception.

4. For example, Snow and Anderson (1987, 1993) use "identity work" to talk about street people's management of a stigmatized identity. J. William Spencer uses "self-work" in the context of role-playing exercises to explore an interactive presentational negotiation of role identity (1987) and role definition (1992). Arlie Russell Hochschild (1979) describes emotion work as often involving deep acting by an individual in an attempt to match emotional experience with cultural norms for feeling. In sociological terms, these types of self work do not necessarily involve a desire to change what is experienced as an underlying self but rather a situated identity or emotion.

5. For a detailed review of Gilligan's work, see Susan J. Heckman's *Moral Voices, Moral Selves* (1995). In addition, *Women and Moral Theory* (1987), edited by Eva Feder Kittay and Diana T. Meyers, not only provides an interpretation of Gilligan's work but also contributes additional empirical studies to the debate. *Justice and Care* (1995), edited by Virginia Held, introduces many of the central feminist writings on caring.

6. For example, Doug McAdam (1988) describes how gender shaped the experiences of Freedom Summer volunteers both during and after their participation in the civil rights movement. Arlene Kaplan Daniels (1988) explains how privileged women construct "invisible careers" in the world of civic voluntarism, and Philip M. Kayal (1933) opens up the world of predominantly gay male AIDS volunteerism as a spiritual and political act.

7. Qualitative studies of community service among high school students (Youniss and Yates 1997) and college students (Rhoads 1997) offer compelling evidence that community service structured to include meaningful work with pedagogical reflection may profoundly foster students' learning and civic virtue.

8. Initial pieces of the analysis offered in this book first appeared in an article (Allahyari 1996).

9. Margaret Anderson (1993) provides a useful reflection on how personal engagement by white, middle-class researchers can facilitate qualitative study across race and class differences.

10. Although some of these men spent time at both The Salvation Army and Loaves & Fishes, others shied away from Loaves & Fishes, as I discuss in chapters 2 and 4.

11. I chose volunteers to interview following the principles of theoretical sampling (Glaser and Strauss 1967). I interviewed volunteers representative of different categories of routine volunteers, volunteers whom others suggested might be of interest to my work, and volunteers who appeared in some way to

be unique or different to maximize what Barney Glaser and Anselm L. Strauss (1967: 65–69) refer to as "slices of data."

12. I interviewed the two white, formerly In-house staff members discussed in chapter 2. Both Dave and Kevin worked their way up the local hierarchy from In-house residents to kitchen staff to front office intake workers and counselors. Dave and Kevin personified idealized moral selving at The Salvation Army.

13. Although I attempted to follow the principles of theoretical sampling by reaching theoretical saturation (Glaser and Strauss 1967: 61–62) in my sampling of the drafted volunteers, I found it difficult to secure formal interviews. None of the routine volunteers at Loaves & Fishes denied me an interview or failed to make an appointment with me, but at The Salvation Army I met volunteers without telephones, volunteers who left town suddenly, and both In-house and ASP volunteers with uncertain schedules. I also struggled to maintain my presence as a woman unavailable for dating. To further complicate matters, aside from the kitchen staff and a few ASP volunteers, the drafted volunteers' attendance varied from day to day.

14. Although some routine volunteers came to Loaves & Fishes weekly, the volunteer groups were scheduled to come once a month. The infrequency of the group participation left less room for reflection in the setting than at The Salvation Army, where many drafted volunteers worked in the kitchen five days a week. Furthermore, as suggested by Nina Eliasoph's (1996) counterintuitive assertion that "civic practices" may relegate the most public-spirited of political talk to relatively private settings, volunteers may have felt sustained political conversation inappropriate among those gathered only occasionally in this seemingly public place.

15. While Howard S. Becker and Blanche Geer (1957: 28), in a comparison between participant-observation and interviews, argue that participant-observation is "the most complete form of the sociological datum," Martin Trow (1957) responds convincingly that sociologists should choose their methods according to the questions at hand. My research experience confirms Trow's stance.

16. Robin Leidner (1993) found in her research on interactive service workers that few McDonald's employees could articulate in interviews the subtle ways in which she observed them alter their tone and behavior to play the worker role.

17. Joel Blau (1992), Martha R. Burt (1989), and Christopher Jencks (1994)

provide useful descriptions of the difficulties of defining and measuring the homeless population as distinct from the poor. An exchange between James D. Wright (1988) and David A. Snow, Susan G. Baker, and Leon Anderson (1988) debates the prevalence of mental illness among the homeless population, and a piece by Snow, Anderson, and Paul Koegel (1994) spells out individualizing, medicalizing, and decontextualizing distorting tendencies in the increasingly vast literature on the homeless population.

18. John Stanfield II (1993) discusses the importance of racial categories to the construction of, and experience of, identity formation among ethnic peoples.

## CHAPTER 1. PERFORMING PERSONALIST HOSPITALITY

1. An understanding of Maurin's beliefs can be found in the essays in Patrick G. Coy's edited volume, *A Revolution of the Heart* (1988).

2. Harry Murray (1990) offers a thoughtful analysis of personalism in which he contrasts personalist hospitality's consideration for its guests with social service's treatment of its clients.

3. Dorothy Day (1963, 1978, [1952] 1981) provides insight into the early houses of hospitality. Marc Ellis (1978) published excerpts from a journal written while living at the New York City Catholic Worker house; this account provides a exceptionally vivid and moving story of personal transformation. Michael Harrington (1963; 1984) draws on his time at the same Catholic Worker house in his work on social and economic inequality. Murray (1990) gives us a rich sociological analysis of the practice of hospitality in three Catholic Worker houses. Robert Coles (1973, 1987, 1993) paints a heartfelt portrait of the Worker movement, its newspaper, and its New York house with an introduction to a collection of photographs of the Worker, in his biography of Dorothy Day, and in his reflections on meaningful service. And Rosalie Riegle Troester (1993) weaves together the voices of more than two hundred Catholic Workers to provide a richly detailed portrait of the people in the movement.

4. Day's (1963: 119) words explain this practice: "We never felt it necessary to ask permission to perform the works of mercy." In keeping with the emphasis on personal responsibility, decision making at these houses also does not follow any particular format. Murray's (1990) work provides a useful comparative

framework of houses of hospitality as he did fieldwork in three houses, one of which was formerly run by homeless people.

5. In a study of the New York Catholic Worker movement titled *Beyond Charismatic Leadership* (1987), Michele Teresa Aronica explores in greater detail how growth might challenge ideological commitment in Catholic Worker organizations.

6. In the first two months of 1991, daily guests in the dining room increased from 400 to 650 per day (newsletter, February 1991). By Easter 1991 the newsletter reported a 40 percent increase in guests since May 1990. By September 1991 Loaves & Fishes had spent $20,000 more on food than in the year ending September 1990 (newsletter, September 1991). The new dining room opened in March 1991 to accommodate the increase.

7. Loaves & Fishes did not receive contributions over $20,000 from any foundations, trusts, grants, corporations, or wills and estates. The organization does not report amounts of donations by private individuals or groups, except when announcing a group's decision to raise money for a specific project.

8. Students frequently attended the volunteer orientation session to learn about Loaves & Fishes so that they could write papers on homelessness and social services.

9. At the time I participated in the volunteer orientation session, the library had not yet opened.

## CHAPTER 2. ADMINISTERING SALVATIONISM

1. The historical section of this chapter, "The Roots of Salvationism at the Shelter Services Center," draws heavily on nonacademic, Salvationist histories that extol the glories of The Salvation Army. These views are useful for their unabashed celebration of Salvationist ideology. Most academic accounts provide a contrasting portrait of The Salvation Army. Although not yet published as I was writing this book, Diane Winston's *Red-Hot and Righteous* (1999) provides an excellent religious history of The Salvation Army that neither glorifies nor condemns the Salvationists' urban Social Campaign. As Commander Booth-Tucker wrote in 1890, "The mudpools of society possess a peculiar interest for the sociologist, be he humanitarian or statesman" (1972: 3). In chapter 4 I analyze how most non-Salvationist academics concerned about treatment

of alcoholics and the homeless in the 1900s present a critical view of The Salvation Army as an institution of social control.

2. For example, those employed at The Salvation Army sometimes received pamphlets with their paychecks (such as one titled "About Pornography") that I rarely saw.

3. Booth (1890) noted the captivation of the English with Henry Stanley's just published *In Darkest Africa* and asked, "As there is a darkest Africa is there not also a darkest England?" to which he answered in the affirmative that the parallel, although strained, merited thought.

4. The Salvation Army commissioned historian E. H. McKinley (1986: 11–12) records the importance of *In Darkest England* to the establishment of Salvationist social services in the United States, noting that the book was sold in bookstores as well as sent out free of charge to those subscribing to the *War Cry*. He argues that the book affected the workings of The Salvation Army in the United States far more than did General Booth himself.

5. McKinley's history of The Salvation Army reports that workingmen's hotels first appeared in Salvation Army registries in April 1887 (1986: 43).

6. Interviews with staff members, discussed later in this chapter, indicated that the Adult Rehabilitation Center in Sacramento was more explicitly evangelical.

7. With the writing of the Twelve Steps and the Twelve Traditions in the mid-1930s, Alcoholics Anonymous established itself as the first Twelve Step group. It functions as an informal, self-help group open to anyone concerned about his or her drinking behavior. A.A. describes itself as "a Fellowship of men and women who have lost the ability to control our drinking and have found ourselves in various kinds of trouble as a result of drinking. We attempt—most of us successfully—to create a satisfying way of life without alcohol. For this we find we need the help and support of other alcoholics in A.A." (Alcoholics Anonymous n.d.b).

8. Kevin's understanding of God is more attuned to that of A.A. principles than is the Major's stricter understanding. The Third Step of A.A. prescribes, "Make a decision to turn our will and our lives over to the care of God as we understood Him" (Alcoholics Anonymous 1970: 28).

9. In cities around the country, mall managers requested that The Salvation Army kettle collectors tone down their bells by substituting copper wires or paper clips for the standard bells, or eliminating the bells altogether (*Sacramento*

*Bee* 1992: A5). The pressures against this solicitation may have contributed to the decrease in the Sacramento Salvationist profits.

10. Loaves & Fishes relies on donated desserts.

11. The Ninth Tradition of A.A. begins, "A.A., as such, ought never be organized . . ." (Alcoholics Anonymous 1970: 29).

## CHAPTER 3. MORAL SELVING WITHIN PERSONALIST HOSPITALITY

1. Whereas this work attempts to understand the self work and moral politics of volunteering to feed the poor in two organizations with unique relations to the welfare state, Wuthnow's *Acts of Compassion* (1991) offers life stories that integrate learning compassion with different types of caring behaviors.

2. Numerous studies on volunteerism attempt to answer *why* individuals volunteer. Virginia A. Hodgkinson's (1989) comprehensive review estimated that seven hundred books and articles exploring motives for volunteerism and giving had been published in the decade preceding 1988 alone. Much of this work uses survey methods and statistical techniques to attempt to identify volunteers' motivations.

3. Rebecca J. Erickson (1995: 122) argues that "one is neither authentic nor inauthentic but more or less so."

4. One study of evangelical patterns of volunteering found that evangelicals do not give significantly more or less time to nonreligious organizations than nonevangelicals. Evangelicals do, however, in comparison to nonevangelicals, give significantly more time and money to religious organizations with spiritual concerns. The author of this study delineated tension in evangelical social work between those who desire spiritual ministry and social structure change and those who focus solely on "soul-winning" (Clydesdale 1990).

5. One study of Jewish giving found that Jews who gave money to the Jewish community tended also to give to non-Jewish philanthropies, although giving to Jewish philanthropies outranked giving to non-Jewish philanthropies. Although volunteer patterns followed the same general rules, the rate of volunteering lagged dramatically behind that of giving money (Rimor and Tobin 1990).

6. Those working within a faith-based vision of moral self-betterment can be understood as enacting what Wuthnow (1998a) has called a practice-oriented spirituality.

7. The accounts offered by the routine volunteers of the demands of volunteering suggest the limits to this type of action as a political solution, however. Many of the routine volunteers made this commitment to Loaves & Fishes after retirement or after family caretaking duties ended. Some volunteers worried about losing a day's income; a few volunteers worked ten hours days, four days a week, to get one day off work. And perhaps most significant, while these volunteers considered themselves and the guests they served part of the Sacramento community, most did not reside in the same neighborhood as Loaves & Fishes. Chapter 5 describes the struggle between neighborhood residents and businesspeople and Loaves & Fishes in the following years.

## CHAPTER 4. MORAL SELVING WITHIN SALVATIONISM

1. Social historical perspectives on self-esteem help us to understand what might be described as a cultural obsession with good self-esteem in the late twentieth century. In a social psychological study, John P. Hewitt (1998: xiii) characterizes self-esteem as "our latest panacea" for failures both social and individual. And in *The Therapeutic State* (1988), James L. Nolan, Jr., analyzes how welfare law evolved to assist the emotive self through treatment programs. Even efforts to "end welfare as we know it," Nolan argues persuasively, have not been antitherapeutic but rather evidence of a concern with self-esteem joined with a utilitarian concern for what works.

2. The drafted volunteers' concern with self-esteem in their moral selving suggested a complication of Gecas's (1991) model of three types of self-motivations with regard to the moral domain. Whereas Gecas argues that authenticity and self-efficacy underpin the moral domain, moral selving at The Salvation Army, as we shall see, revealed a context within which self-esteem and self-efficacy underpinned the construction of the moral self.

3. Although volunteers could write up staff members, this threat appeared to evoke little fear in the staff.

4. As these examples illustrate, the ASP volunteers often appeared to arrive at The Salvation Army with more employment opportunities available to them than did the In-house volunteers. Just as significantly, the ASP volunteers came with a more developed web of relationships outside The Salvation Army. I inferred that their work to improve self-esteem and self-efficacy relied less on this institutional web of relationships.

5. These instances of learning appropriate deference and demeanor reminded me of Jean L. Briggs's (1970) anthropological experience with the Utku Eskimos. Just as Briggs found herself studying emotional patternings after she experienced subtle ostracism for failure to manage her own anger, I found myself attuned to deference and demeanor after being corrected for failing to smile appropriately. In ethnomethodological terms (Garfinkel 1967), norms—including emotional norms—often become most obvious to us when they are violated.

6. Commissioner Kenneth L. Hodder, National Commander of The Salvation Army, declared 1994 the International Year of the Family. Not only did he hope to uphold the sanctity of the Christian family, he also affirmed "Christian family life as one of God's greatest gifts to His children" (1994a: 3).

7. Collins (1991) notes that this Afrocentric ethic of caring converges with feminist assertions that women's values privilege caring and connection. Collins points to the black church and social organization as supporting this ethic of caring for blacks.

8. See also Diane Winston's *Red-Hot and Righteous* (1999) for a history of the Army that purposively defies simplistic political categorization of Salvationist theology and charitable work.

9. For sympathetic accounts of A.A., see Baum and Burnes 1993; Denzin 1987a, 1987b, 1987c, 1993; Rudy 1986; Wagner 1993. By "sympathetic" I do not mean purely valuatory but rather that in these analyses recovery programs are understood to be critical to stability and well-being.

10. Jennifer Nedelsky (1989: 10), in a feminist legal analysis, argues that individuals can become more autonomous but that they can never be truly autonomous. Similarly, the drafted volunteers struggled to become more autonomous.

## CHAPTER 5. THE POLITICS OF CHARITY

1. I am indebted to Suad Joseph (1995) for her elucidation of this point.

2. For example, Joseph (1993) describes how "patriarchial connectivity" shaped the production of relationally oriented selves among working-class Arab families in Lebanon. In the aptly titled *Crafting Selves* (1990), Dorinne K. Kondo explores how Japanese workers in small industry engage in the complex, contradictory, and even ironic work of creating selves "in the plural" both following and struggling against the precepts of work, family, discipline, and gender ideologies. And finally, as discussed in chapter 2, Nippert-Eng (1995, 1996)

analyzes how workers sculpt selves—using objects such as keys and calendars—across boundaries between work and home.

3. Loaves & Fishes and The Salvation Army illustrate, however, that both impulsive and institutional selves, and dignity and honor, coexist in our world. Perhaps, as suggested by Berger (1973), the military serves as one of the last places where honor is valued.

4. Even with nonprofit status, organizations such as Loaves & Fishes remain within the purview of the state (McCarthy, Britt, and Wolfson 1991). For example, they must comply with tax and postage requirements and, perhaps most important, as we shall see later, they must also abide by local zoning laws and constraints on support of political candidates. In a study of pathways to nonprofit incorporation among homeless social movement organizations, Cress (1997) argues that political moderation is a function not of nonprofit status per se but rather of the pathway by which the organization came to adopt this form.

5. In keeping with Nicholas P. Lovrich, Jr., Brent S. Steel, and Mahdun Majed's (1986) testing of the street-level bureaucrat concept, the staff appeared to experience both greater autonomy and stress in this role.

6. In a study of the state, James L. Nolan, Jr. (1998), argues that a therapeutic ethos structures the justification of government not only in regard to welfare policy but also in regard to public education, criminal policy, and political rhetoric more generally.

7. In an insightful analysis of social work encounters between outreach workers and the homeless, Michael Rowe (1999: 49) notes specifically how The Salvation Army has moved to an environmental explanation of homelessness.

8. Most famously, Michael Harrington, in *The Other America* (1963), described the Catholic Workers' efforts to serve the destitute class. Harrington's treatment of the Catholic Workers as well as Murray's (1990), Aronica's (1987), and Troester's (1993) both accords with academic standards and addresses the movement with great respect. Furthermore, the writings of Dorothy Day, while not academic, are treated respectfully by scholars; see, for example, Coles 1973; Ellis 1978, 1988.

9. Kathleen D. McCarthy's collection, *Lady Bountiful Revisited* (1990), offers other counterexamples with its exploration of how women have historically wedded philanthropic work and political activism.

10. According to a *Sacramento Bee* story, the cottages would be financed with approximately 60 percent private money and 40 percent federal money (Gibson 1994: B4).

11. With the use of petitions, a Lenten vigil, and attendance at city council

meetings, Loaves & Fishes activists resemble the peace movement's "polite protesters" of the 1980s (Lofland 1993). The Loaves & Fishes political actors could also be characterized as exhibiting "a remarkable degree of genteel civility, restraint, and even affability" (Lofland 1993: 7).

12. Donations and number of donors as reported by the executive director, LeRoy Chatfield (1999), are as follows: 1994, $1,925,565 from 19,500 donors; 1995, $1,980,613 from 21,900 donors; 1996, $2,059,382 from 23,800 donors; 1997, $2,129,170 from 25,300 donors; and 1998, $1,955,296 from 26,200 donors.

13. In the 1980s government support for private initiatives to help fight poverty culminated in the Points of Light Foundation with state-sponsored promotion of volunteering (Adams 1987; Chambré 1989). There may be interesting historical comparisons to be made between volunteerism as a civil religion (Adams 1987) and the Charitable Choice provision.

14. The contentious ideological separation of church and state, although already contradictory and violated, will most likely result in legal challenges to Charitable Choice. Yet legal scholars and advocates of Charitable Choice have already begun to formulate a defense of the provision (Monsma 1996; Sider and Unruh 1999).

# REFERENCES

Acker, Joan. 1992. "Gendered Institutions: From Sex Roles to Gendered Institutions." *Contemporary Sociology* 21 (5): 565–69.

Adams, David S. 1987. "Ronald Reagan's 'Revival': Voluntarism as a Theme in Reagan's Civil Religion." *Sociological Analysis* 48 (1): 17–29.

Addelson, Kathryn Pyne. 1994. *Moral Passages: Toward a Collectivist Moral Theory*. New York: Routledge.

Adler, Patricia A., and Peter Adler. 1987. *Membership Roles in Field Research*. Newbury Park, Calif.: Sage.

Alcoholics Anonymous. 1965. *The A.A. Group . . . Where It All Begins*. New York: Alcoholics Anonymous World Services.

———. 1970. *A Member's Eye View of Alcoholics Anonymous*. New York: Alcoholics Anonymous.

———. n.d.a. *Information on Alcoholics Anonymous*. New York: Alcoholics Anonymous World Services.

———. n.d.b. *A Newcomer Asks. . . .* New York: Alcoholics Anonymous.

Allahyari, Rebecca Anne. 1995. "Visions of Charity: Constructing Moral Selves through Charitable Action." Ph.D. dissertation, University of California, Davis.

———. 1996. "'Ambassadors of God' and 'The Sinking Classes': Visions of Charity and Moral Selving." *International Journal of Sociology and Social Policy* 16 (1–2): 35–69.

Anderson, Elijah. [1976] 1981. *A Place on the Corner.* Chicago: University of Chicago Press.

Anderson, Margaret. 1993. "Studying across Difference: Race, Class, and Gender in Qualitative Research." Pp. 39–52 in *Race and Ethnicity in Research Methods*, edited by John H. Stanfield II and Rutledge M. Dennis. Newbury Park, Calif.: Sage.

Anderson, Nels. 1923. *The Hobo: The Sociology of the Homeless Man.* Chicago: University of Chicago Press.

Anderson, Ralph, and Kyra Jones Osmus. 1988. "Cold Nights and Long Days: A Comparison of Male and Female Volunteers in a Night Shelter." *Journal of Voluntary Action Research* 17 (1): 54–59.

Aronica, Michele Teresa, R.S.M. 1987. *Beyond Charismatic Leadership: The New York Catholic Worker Movement.* New Brunswick, N.J.: Transaction.

Baum, Alice S., and Donald W. Burnes. 1993. *A Nation in Denial: The Truth about Homelessness.* Boulder, Colo.: Westview Press.

Baumgartner, M. P. 1988. *The Moral Order of a Suburb.* New York: Oxford University Press.

Becker, Howard S. [1956] 1970. "Interviewing Medical Students." Pp. 103–6 in *Qualitative Methodology: Firsthand Involvement with the Social World*, edited by William J. Filstead. Chicago: Markham.

———. [1963] 1973. *Outsiders: Studies in the Sociology of Deviance.* New York: Free Press.

———. 1986. *Doing Things Together: Selected Papers.* Evanston: Northwestern University Press.

Becker, Howard S., and Blanche Geer. 1957. "Participant Observation and Interviewing: A Comparison." *Human Organization* 16 (3): 28–32.

Bederman, Gail. 1989. " 'The Women Have Had Charge of the Church Work Long Enough': The Men and Religion Forward Movement of 1911–1912 and the Masculinization of Middle-Class Fundamentalism." *American Quarterly* 41 (3): 432–65.

Belisle, Jennifer. 1994. "Maryhouse." *Catholic Worker*, March–April, p. 2.

Bellah, Robert N., Richard Madsen, William M. Sullivan, Ann Swidler, and Steven M. Tipton. [1985] 1996. *Habits of the Heart: Individualism and Commitment in American Life.* New York: Harper and Row.

———. 1991. *The Good Society.* New York: Alfred A. Knopf.

Bendroth, Margaret Lamberts. 1993. *Fundamentalism & Gender, 1975 to the Present.* New Haven: Yale University Press.

Berger, Peter L. 1967. *The Sacred Canopy: Elements of a Sociological Theory.* New York: Anchor Books.

———. 1973. "Excursus: On the Obsolescence of the Concept of Honor." Pp. 83–96 in Peter L. Berger, Brigitte Berger, and Hansfried Kellner, *The Homeless Mind: Modernization and Consciousness.* New York: Vintage Books.

Berger, Peter L., Brigitte Berger, and Hansfried Kellner. 1973. *The Homeless Mind: Modernization and Consciousness.* New York: Vintage Books.

Berger, Peter L., and Thomas Luckman. 1967. *The Social Construction of Reality: A Treatise in the Sociology of Knowledge.* New York: Anchor Books.

Bernard, Jessie. 1981. "The Good-Provider Role: Its Rise and Fall." *American Psychologist* 36 (1): 1–12.

Biggart, Nicole Woolsey. 1989. *Charismatic Capitalism: Direct Selling Organizations in America.* Chicago: University of Chicago Press.

Biskupic, Joan. 1996. "High Court Rejects Girls' Claim against School for Boys' Sexual Harassment." *Washington Post,* October 8, p. A3.

Bizjak, Tony. 1996. "Homeless Ad Takes Center by Surprise: Loaves & Fishes Says It Was Drafted 3 Years Ago." *Sacramento Bee,* February 1, p. B3.

———. 1997a. "City Panel to Search for Homeless Feeding Sites." *Sacramento Bee,* April 11, p. B1.

———. 1997b. "Tracing the Roots of City's Lawsuit: Loaves & Fishes Too Indulgent toward Needy, Officials Suggest." Sacramento Bee, January 9, pp. A1, A20.

Bizjak, Tony and Deb Kollars. 1997. "Frustrated Council Votes to Sue Loaves & Fishes." *Sacramento Bee,* January 8, pp. A1, A10.

Blau, Joel. 1992. *The Visible Poor: Homelessness in the United States.* New York: Oxford University Press.

Booth, William. 1890. *In Darkest England and the Way Out.* New York: Funk and Wagnalls.

Booth-Tucker, Frederick. 1972. *The Salvation Army in America: Selected Reports, 1988–1903.* Edited by Edwin S. Gaustad. New York: Arnon Press.

Bounds, Elizabeth M. 1997. *Coming Together/Coming Apart: Religion, Community, and Modernity.* New York: Routledge Press.

Briggs, Jean L. 1970. *Never in Anger: Portrait of an Eskimo Family.* Cambridge, Mass.: Harvard University Press.

Brinson, Dottie. 1993. "The Habit of Thanksgiving." *War Cry,* December 4, p. 6.

Bunis, William K., Angela Yancik, and David A. Snow. 1996. "The Cultural Patterning of Sympathy Toward the Homeless and Other Victims of Misfortune." *Social Problems* 43 (4): 387–402.

Burt, Martha R. 1989. *America's Homeless: Numbers, Characteristics, and Programs That Serve Them.* Washington, D.C.: Urban Institute Press.

Cahill, Spencer E., and Robin Eggleston. 1994. "Managing Emotions in Public: The Case of Wheelchair Users." *Social Psychology Quarterly* 57 (4): 300–12.

*Catholic Worker.* 1994. "The Aims and Means of the Catholic Worker Movement." May, p. 3.

Chambliss, Daniel. F. 1996. *Beyond Caring: Hospitals, Nurses, and the Social Organization of Caring.* Chicago: University of Chicago Press.

Chambré, Susan M. 1989. "Kindling Points of Light: Volunteering as Public Policy." *Nonprofit and Voluntary Sector Quarterly* 18 (3): 249–68.

Charmaz, Kathy. 1991. *Good Days, Bad Days: The Self in Chronic Illness and Time.* New Brunswick, N.J.: Rutgers University Press.

Chatfield, LeRoy. 1999. Letter to the author, April 28.

Clark, Candace. 1990. "Emotions and Micropolitics in Everyday Life: Some Patterns and Paradoxes of 'Place.' " Pp. 305–33 in *Research Agendas in the Sociology of Emotions,* edited by Theodore D. Kemper. Albany: State University of New York Press.

———. 1997. *Misery and Company: Sympathy in Everyday Life.* Chicago: University of Chicago Press.

Clydesdale, Timothy T. 1990. "Soul-winning and Social Work: Giving and Caring in the Evangelical Tradition." Pp. 187–210 in *Faith and Philanthropy in America: Exploring the Role of Religion in America's Voluntary Sector,* edited by Robert Wuthnow and Virginia A. Hodgkinson and Associates. San Francisco: Jossey-Bass.

Cnaan, Ram. 1999. "Our Hidden Safety Net: Social and Community Work by Urban American Religious Congregations." *Brookings Review* 17 (2): 50–53.

Coles, Robert. 1973. *A Spectacle Unto the World: The Catholic Worker Movement.* New York: Viking Press.

———. 1987. *Dorothy Day: A Radical Devotion.* Reading, Mass.: Addison-Wesley.

———. 1993. *The Call of Service: A Witness to Idealism.* Boston: Houghton Mifflin.

Collier, Richard. 1965. *The General Next to God: The Story of William Booth and The Salvation Army.* St. James Place, U.K.: Collins.

Collins, Patricia Hill. 1991. *Black Feminist Thought: Knowledge, Consciousness, and the Politics of Empowerment.* New York: Routledge.

Collins, Randall. 1981. "On the Microfoundations of Macrosociology." *American Journal of Sociology* 86 (5): 984–1014.

———. 1990. "Stratification, Emotional Energy, and the Transient Emotions." Pp. 27–57 in *Research Agendas in the Sociology of Emotions*, edited by Theodore D. Kemper. New York: State University of New York Press.

Cooley, Charles Horton. 1909. *Social Organization: A Study of the Larger Mind*. New York: Charles Scribner's Sons.

Coy, Patrick G., ed. 1988. *A Revolution of the Heart: Essays on the Catholic Worker*. Philadelphia: Temple University Press.

Cress, Daniel M. 1997. "Nonprofit Incorporation among Movements of the Poor: Pathways and Consequences for Homeless Social Movement Organizations." *Sociological Quarterly* 38 (2): 343–60.

———. n.d. "A Deficiency of Method or Purpose? Ethnographic Shortcomings, the Interactionist Stranglehold, and Comparative Ethnography." Unpublished manuscript.

Cress, Daniel M., and David A. Snow. 1996. "Mobilization at the Margins: Resources, Benefactors, and the Viability of Homeless Social Movement Organizations." *American Sociological Review* 61: 1089–1109.

Czarniawska, Barbara. 1997. *Narrating the Organization: Dramas of Institutional Identity*. Chicago: University of Chicago Press.

Daniels, Arlene Kaplan. 1985. "Good Times and Good Works: The Place of Sociability in the Work of Women Volunteers." *Social Problems* 32 (4): 363–74.

———. 1988. *Invisible Careers: Women Civic Leaders from the Volunteer World*. Chicago: University of Chicago Press.

Dávila, Robert D. 1993. "Fortunate Break Bread with Needy in Capital." *Sacramento Bee*, November 26, p. B1.

Day, Dorothy. 1963. *Loaves and Fishes*. New York: Harper and Row.

———. 1978. *From Union Square to Rome*. Silver Spring, Md.: Preservation of the Faith Press.

———. [1952] 1981. *The Long Loneliness: An Autobiography*. San Francisco: Harper and Row.

———. 1983. *By Little and By Little: The Selected Writings of Dorothy Day*. Edited by Robert Ellsberg. New York: Alfred A. Knopf.

Delany, Chris, and Dan Delany. 1987. Interview by Rosalie Riegle Troester. Marquette University Archives, November 13.

———. 1997. Letter to the Editor. *Sacramento Bee*, January 22.

Delsohn, Gary. 1997. "Loaves Chief a 'Lightning Rod' in Homeless Feud." *Sacramento Bee*, April 13, pp. B1, B6.

Delsohn, Gary, and Tony Bizjak. 1997. "Serna Rips into City's Suit against Loaves & Fishes." *Sacramento Bee*, March 19, pp. A1, A9.

Demerath, N. J., III, and Rhys H. Williams. 1992. *A Bridging of Faiths: Religion and Politics in a New England City*. Princeton: Princeton University Press.

Denzin, Norman. 1987a. *The Alcoholic Self*. Newbury Park, Calif.: Sage.

———. 1987b. *The Recovering Alcoholic*. Newbury Park, Calif.: Sage.

———. 1987c. *Treating Alcoholism: An Alcoholics Anonymous Approach*. Newbury Park, Calif.: Sage.

———. 1993. *The Alcoholic Society: Addiction and Recovery of the Self*. New Brunswick, N.J.: Transaction.

Dewey, John. [1908] 1960. *Theory of the Moral Life*. New York: Holt, Rinehart and Winston.

DiIulio, John J., Jr. 1999. "Supporting Black Churches: Faith, Outreach, and the Inner-City Poor." *Brookings Review* 17 (2): 42–45.

Dionne, E. J., Jr., and John J. DiIulio, Jr. 1999. "What's God Got to Do with the American Experiment?" *Brookings Review* 17 (2): 4–9.

Dordick, Gwendolyn A. 1997. *Something Left to Lose: Personal Relations and Survival among New York's Homeless*. Philadelphia: Temple University Press.

Douglas, Mary. 1990. Foreword to *The Gift: The Form and Reason for Exchange in Archaic Societies*, by Marcel Mauss. New York: W. W. Norton.

Duneier, Mitchell. 1992. *Slim's Table: Race, Respectability, and Masculinity*. Chicago: University of Chicago Press.

Durkheim, Emile. [1912] 1995. *The Elementary Forms of the Religious Life*. Translated by Karen E. Fields. New York: Free Press.

Eliasoph, Nina. 1996. "Making a Fragile Public: A Talk-centered Study of Citizenship and Power." *Sociological Theory* 14 (3): 262–89.

Elie, Paul. 1998. "The Patron Saint of Paradox." *New York Times Magazine*, November 8, pp. 44–47.

Ellis, Carolyn. 1991. "Sociological Introspection and Emotional Experience." *Symbolic Interaction* 14 (1): 23–50.

Ellis, Marc H. 1978. *A Year at the Catholic Worker*. New York: Paulist Press.

———. 1988. "Peter Maurin: To Bring the Social Order to Christ." Pp. 15–46 in *A Revolution of the Heart: Essays on the Catholic Worker*, edited by Patrick G. Coy. Philadelphia: Temple University Press.

Epstein, Aaron. 1997. "Top Court Strengthens Law's Hand on Religion." *Sacramento Bee*, June 26, pp. A1, A20.

Erickson, Rebecca J. 1995. "The Importance of Authenticity for Self and Society." *Symbolic Interaction* 18 (2): 121–44.

Fellows, Lawrence. 1979. *A Gentle War: The Story of the Salvation Army*. New York: Macmillan.

Fine, Gary Alan. 1987. *With the Boys: Little League Baseball and Preadolescent Culture*. Chicago: University of Chicago Press.

———. 1991. "On the Macrofoundations of Microsociology: Constraint and the Exterior Reality of Structure." *Sociological Quarterly* 32 (2): 161–77.

———. 1992. "Agency, Structure, and Comparative Contexts: Toward a Synthetic Interactionism." *Symbolic Interaction* 15 (1): 87–107.

Fine, Gary Alan, and Kent Sandstrom. 1993. "Ideology in Action: A Pragmatic Approach to a Contested Concept." *Sociological Theory* 11 (1): 21–38.

Foucault, Michel. 1979. *Discipline and Punish: The Birth of the Prison*. Translated by Alan Sheridan. New York: Vintage Books.

Franklin, Clyde W., II. 1992. " 'Hey, Home—Yo, Bro': Friendship among Black Men." Pp. 201–14 in *Men's Friendships*, edited by Peter M. Nardi. Newbury Park, Calif.: Sage.

Furillo, Andy. 1994. "Cop Draws Wrath of Homeless, Praise of Business People." *Sacramento Bee*, January 2, pp. B1, B3.

Garfinkel, Harold. 1967. *Studies in Ethnomethodology*. Cambridge: Polity Press.

Gariepy, Colonel Henry. 1990. *Christianity in Action: The Salvation Army in the USA Today*. Wheaton, Ill.: Victor Books.

Gecas, Viktor. 1982. "The Self-Concept." *Annual Review of Sociology* 8: 1–33.

———. 1991. "The Self-Concept as a Basis for a Theory of Motivation." Pp. 171–87 in *The Self-Society Dynamic: Cognition, Emotion, and Action*, edited by Judith A. Howard and Peter L. Callero. New York: Cambridge University Press.

Gibson, Steve. 1994. "Homeless Cottages Rejected by City Council." *Sacramento Bee*, July 20, pp. B1, B4.

Gilligan, Carol. 1982. *In a Different Voice: Psychological Theory and Women's Development*. Cambridge, Mass.: Harvard University Press.

Glaser, Barney, and Anselm L. Strauss. 1967. *The Discovery of Grounded Theory: Strategies for Qualitative Research*. Chicago: Aldine.

Glasser, Irene. 1988. *More Than Bread: Ethnography of a Soup Kitchen*. Tuscaloosa: University of Alabama Press.

Goffman, Erving. 1961. *Asylums: Essays on the Social Situation of Mental Patients and Other Inmates*. New York: Anchor Books.

————. 1963. *Stigma: Notes on the Management of Spoiled Identity.* New York: Simon and Schuster.

————. [1956] 1967. *Interaction Ritual.* New York: Pantheon Books.

Golden, Stephanie. 1992. *The Women Outside: Meanings and Myths of Homelessness.* Berkeley: University of California Press.

Goldner, Fred H., R. Richard Ritti, and Thomas P. Ference. 1977. "The Production of Cynical Knowledge in Organizations." *American Sociological Review* 42 (4): 539–51.

Gordon, Steven L. 1989. "Institutional and Impulsive Orientations in Selectively Appropriating Emotions to the Self." Pp. 115–35 in *The Sociology of Emotions: Original Essays and Research Papers,* edited by David D. Franks and E. Doyle McCarthy. Greenwich, Conn.: JAI Press.

Guyette, Curt. 1994. "Hotel Salvation." *Sacramento News and Review,* March 3, pp. 12–15.

Hall, Edward T. 1983. *The Dance of Life: The Other Dimension of Time.* Garden City, N.Y.: Doubleday/Anchor.

Halle, David. 1993. *Inside Culture: Art and Class in the American Home.* Chicago: University of Chicago Press.

Harrington, Michael. 1963. *The Other America: Poverty in the United States.* New York: Macmillan.

————. 1984. *The New American Poverty.* New York: Penguin Books.

Hays, Kim. 1994. *Practicing Virtues: Moral Traditions at Quaker and Military Boarding Schools.* Berkeley: University of California Press.

Hayward, Brad. 1993. "Fewer Donations Coming In for Groups That Help Needy." *Sacramento Bee,* December 23, p. B1.

Heckman, Susan J. 1995. *Moral Voices, Moral Selves: Carol Gilligan and Feminist Moral Theory.* University Park: Pennsylvania State University Press.

Held, Virginia, ed. 1995. *Justice and Care: Essential Readings in Feminist Ethics.* Boulder, Colo.: Westview Press.

Hewitt, John P. 1989. *Dilemmas of the American Self.* Philadelphia: Temple University Press.

————. 1998. *The Myth of Self-Esteem: Finding Happiness and Solving Problems in America.* New York: St. Martin's Press.

Hicks, Larry. 1994. "Planned Cottages for Homeless Win Backing of City." *Sacramento Bee,* September 21, pp. A1, A17.

Himmelfarb, Gertrude. 1991. *Poverty and Compassion: The Moral Imagination of the Late Victorians.* New York: Vintage Books.

Hoch, Charles, and Robert A. Slayton. 1989. *New Homeless and Old: Community and Skid Row.* Philadelphia: Temple University Press.

Hochschild, Arlie Russell. 1975. "The Sociology of Feeling and Emotion: Selected Possibilities." Pp. 280–307 in *Another Voice: Feminist Perspectives on Social Life and Social Science,* edited by Marcia Millman and Rosabeth Moss Kanter. New York: Doubleday/Anchor.

———. 1979. "Emotion Work, Feeling Rules, and Social Structure." *American Journal of Sociology* 85 (3): 551–75.

———. 1983. *The Managed Heart: Commercialization of Human Feeling.* Berkeley: University of California Press.

———. 1989. "The Economy of Gratitude." Pp. 95–113 in *The Sociology of Emotions: Original Essays and Research Papers,* edited by David Franks and E. Doyle McCarthy. Greenwich, Conn.: JAI Press.

Hochschild, Jennifer L. 1995. *Facing Up to the American Dream: Race, Class, and the Soul of the Nation.* Princeton: Princeton University Press.

Hodder, Commissioner Kenneth L. 1994a. "1994 International Year of the Family." *War Cry,* January 1, p. 3.

———. 1994b. "The Wall of Separation." *War Cry,* July 2, pp. 4–5.

Hodgkinson, Virginia A. 1989. *Motivations for Giving and Volunteering: A Selected Review of the Literature.* Washington, D.C.: Independent Sector.

Holden, Daphne. 1997. " 'On Equal Ground': Sustaining Virtue among Volunteers in a Homeless Shelter." *Journal of Contemporary Ethnography* 26 (2): 117–45.

Horowitz, Ruth. 1986. "Remaining an Outsider: Membership as a Threat to Research Rapport." *Urban Life* 14 (4): 409–30.

———. 1989. "Getting In." Pp. 45–54 in *In the Field: Readings on the Field Research Experience,* edited by Carolyn D. Smith and William Kornblum. New York: Praeger.

———. 1995. *Teen Mothers: Citizens or Dependents?* Chicago: University of Chicago Press.

Hubert, Cynthia, and Dorsey Griffith. 1997. "North-City Area a Magnet for Homeless . . . and Criticism." *Sacramento Bee,* March 23, pp. A1, A14–15.

Hughes, Everett Cherrington. 1958. *Men and Their Work.* London: Free Press of Glencoe.

Hughes, Michael, and David H. Demo. 1989. "Self-Perceptions of Black Americans: Self-Esteem and Personal Efficacy." *American Journal of Sociology* 95 (1): 132–57.

Israel, Major Mrs. Betty. 1993. "Our Thanksgiving Angel." *War Cry*, November 20, p. 21.

Jasper, James M. 1997. *The Art of Moral Protest: Culture, Biography, and Creativity in Social Movements*. Chicago: University of Chicago Press.

Jencks, Christopher. 1994. *The Homeless*. Cambridge, Mass.: Harvard University Press.

Jensen, Lene Arnett. 1995. "Habits of the Heart Revisited: Autonomy, Community, and Divinity in Adults' Moral Language." *Qualitative Sociology* 18 (1): 71–86.

Joseph, Suad. 1993. "Gender and Relationality among Arab Families in Lebanon." *Feminist Studies* 19 (3): 465–86.

———. 1995. Letter to the author, June 15.

Kanter, Rosabeth Moss. 1972. *Commitment and Community: Communes and Utopias in Sociological Perspective*. Cambridge, Mass.: Harvard University Press.

Katz, Michael B. 1986. *In the Shadow of the Poorhouse: A Social History of Welfare in America*. New York: Basic Books.

Kayal, Philip M. 1990. "Healing Brokenness: Gay Volunteerism in AIDS." *Humanity and Society* 14 (3): 280–96.

———. 1993. *Bearing Witness: Gay Men's Health Crisis and the Politics of AIDS*. Boulder, Colo.: Westview.

Kittay, Eva Feder, and Diana T. Meyers, eds. 1987. *Women and Moral Theory*. Totowa, N.J.: Rowman and Littlefield.

Kleinman, Sherryl. 1984. *Equals before God: Seminarians as Humanistic Professionals*. Chicago: University of Chicago Press.

———. 1996. *Opposing Ambitions: Gender and Identity in an Alternative Organization*. Chicago: University of Chicago Press.

Kleinman, Sherryl, and Martha A. Copp. 1993. *Emotions and Fieldwork*. Newbury Park, Calif.: Sage.

Kleinman, Sherryl, and Gary Alan Fine. 1979. "Rhetorics and Action in Moral Organizations: Social Control of Little Leaguers and Ministry Students." *Urban Life* 8 (3): 275–94.

Kleinman, Sherryl, Barbara Stenross, and Martha McMahon. 1994. "Privileging Fieldwork over Interviews: Consequences for Identity and Practice." *Symbolic Interaction* 17 (1): 37–50.

Kollars, Deb. 1995. "Bitter Expansion Dispute Clouds Ministry for Homeless." *Sacramento Bee*, September 24, pp. A1, A24.

———. 1996. "Charity Drops Attempt to Keep Park." *Sacramento Bee*, April 6, pp. B1, B8.

———. 1997a. "Cold Facts Prompt County to Modify Homeless Strategy." *Sacramento Bee*, December 7, pp. A1, A27.

———. 1997b. "Loaves & Fishes Fires Back with Lawsuit against City." *Sacramento Bee*, March 11, pp. A1, A9.

Kollars, Deb, and Tony Bizjak. 1997. "City, Loaves & Fishes Settle Dispute." *Sacramento Bee*, July 2, pp. A1, A13.

Kondo, Dorinne K. 1990. *Crafting Selves: Power, Gender, and Discourses of Identity in a Japanese Workplace*. Chicago: University of Chicago Press.

Lamont, Michèle. 1992. *Money, Morals, and Manners: The Culture of the French and the American Upper-Middle Class*. Chicago: University of Chicago Press.

———. 1995. "Colliding Moralities: Boundaries and Identity among Black and White Workers." Paper presented at the conference Interpreting Historical Change at the End of the Twentieth Century: The Challenges of the Present Age to Historical Thought and Social Theory, University of California, Davis, February 25.

Lamont, Michèle, and Marcel Fournier, eds. 1992. *Cultivating Differences: Symbolic Boundaries and the Making of Inequality*. Chicago: University of Chicago Press.

Lasch, Christopher. 1978. *The Culture of Narcissism: American Life in an Age of Diminishing Expectations*. New York: W. W. Norton.

Leidner, Robin. 1993. *Fast Food, Fast Talk: Service Work and the Routinization of Everyday Life*. Berkeley: University of California Press.

Liebow, Elliot. 1993. *Tell Them Who I Am: The Lives of Homeless Women*. New York: Free Press.

Lindelof, Bill. 1995. "A Lenten Call to Aid City's Homeless." *Sacramento Bee*, March 2, p. B1.

Lipsky, Michael. 1980. *Street-Level Bureaucracy: Dilemmas of the Individual in Public Services*. New York: Russell Sage Foundation.

Loaves & Fishes. 1983–99. Newsletters and pamphlets. Loaves & Fishes Archives. Sacramento, Calif.

———. 1990–94. Internal Revenue Service Form 990. Registry of Charitable Trusts. Sacramento, Calif.

Lofland, John. 1993. *Polite Protesters: The American Peace Movement of the 1980s*. Syracuse: Syracuse University Press.

Lofland, John, and Norman Skonovd. 1981. "Conversion Motifs." *Journal for the Scientific Study of Religion* 20 (4): 373–85.

Lofland, Lyn H. 1994. "Structural Environment: Hierarchical Location." Lecture in course Self and Society, University of California, Davis, March 3.

Loseke, Donileen R. 1993. "Constructing Conditions, People, Morality, and Emotion: Expanding the Agenda of Constructionism." Pp. 207–16 in *Constructionist Controversies: Issues in Social Problems Theory*, edited by Gale Miller and James A. Holstein. New York: Aldine de Gruyter.

———. 1997. "'The Whole Spirit of Modern Philanthropy': The Construction of the Idea of Charity, 1912–1992." *Social Problems* 44 (4): 425–44.

Lovrich, Nicholas P., Jr., Brent S. Steel, and Mahdun Majed. 1986. "The Street-Level Bureaucrat—A Useful Category or a Distinction without a Difference? Research Note on Construct Validation." *Review of Public-Personnel Administration* 6 (2): 14–27.

Lutz, Catherine A. 1988. *Unnatural Emotions: Everyday Sentiments on a Micronesian Atoll and Their Challenge to Western Theory*. Chicago: University of Chicago Press.

MacIntyre, Alasdair. 1984. *After Virtue: A Study in Moral Virtue*. Notre Dame: Notre Dame University Press.

Mack, Phyllis. 1987. "Feminine Symbolism and Feminine Behavior in Radical Religious Movements: Franciscans, Quakers and the Followers of Gandhi." Pp. 115–30 in *Disciplines of Faith: Studies in Religion, Politics and Patriarchy*, edited by Jim Obelkevich, Lyndal Roper, and Raphael Samuel. New York: Routledge & Keegan Paul.

Magnuson, Norris. 1977. *Salvation in the Slums: Evangelical Social Work, 1865–1920*. Metuchen, N.J.: Scarecrow Press.

Martineau, Harriet. [1838] 1989. *How to Observe Morals and Manners*. New Brunswick, N.J.: Transaction.

Matthews, Nancy A. 1994. *Confronting Rape: The Feminist Anti-Rape Movement and the State*. New York: Routledge.

McAdam, Doug. 1988. *Freedom Summer*. New York: Oxford University Press.

McCarthy, Cameron. 1990. *Race and Curriculum: Social Inequality and the Theories and Politics of Difference in Contemporary Research on Schooling*. New York: Falmer Press.

McCarthy, John D., David W. Britt, and Mark Wolfson. 1991. "The Institutional Channeling of Social Movements by the State in the United States." *Research in Social Movements, Conflicts and Change* 14: 45–76.

McCarthy, John, and Mayer Zald. 1977. "Resource Mobilization and Social Movements: A Partial Theory." *American Journal of Sociology* 82 (6): 1212–41.

McCarthy, Kathleen D., ed. 1990. *Lady Bountiful Revisited: Women, Philanthropy, and Power.* New Brunswick, N.J.: Rutgers University Press.

McGrath, Dan. 1993. "Law Keeps Beggars, Not Poverty, at Bay." *Sacramento Bee,* December 12, p. A2.

——. 1994. "Salvation Army Soldier Funded the Good Fight." *Sacramento Bee,* March 27, p. A2.

McKinley, Edward H. 1980. *Marching to Glory: The History of The Salvation Army in the United States of America, 1880–1980.* San Francisco: Harper and Row.

——. 1986. *Somebody's Brother: A History of the Salvation Army Men's Social Service Department.* Vol. 21. Lewiston, N.Y.: Edwin Mellen Press.

Mead, George Herbert. [1934] 1962. *Mind, Self, and Society: From the Standpoint of a Social Behaviorist.* Chicago: University of Chicago Press.

Miller, George A., Eugene Galanter, and Karl H. Pribram. 1960. *Plans and the Structure of Behavior.* New York: Henry Holt.

Mills, C. Wright. 1963. *Power, Politics and People.* New York: Oxford University Press.

Monsma, Stephen V. 1996. *When Sacred and Secular Mix: Religious Non-profit Organizations and Public Money.* Lanham, Md.: Rowman and Littlefield.

Mukerji, Chandra. 1994. "Toward a Sociology of Material Culture: Science Studies, Cultural Studies and the Meanings of Things." Pp. 143–62 in *The Sociology of Culture,* edited by Diana Crane. Cambridge: Blackwell.

Murray, Harry. 1990. *Do Not Neglect Hospitality: The Catholic Workers and the Homeless.* Philadelphia: Temple University Press.

Nedelsky, Jennifer. 1989. "Reconceiving Autonomy: Sources, Thoughts and Possibilities." *Yale Journal of Law and Feminism* 1 (7): 7–36.

New York State Catholic Bishops. 1995. "Death Is Not the Answer." *Catholic Worker,* January–February, p. 1.

Nippert-Eng, Christena. 1995. *Home and Work: Negotiating Boundaries through Everyday Life.* Chicago: University of Chicago Press.

——. 1996. "Calendars and Keys: The Classification of 'Home' and 'Work.'" *Sociological Forum* 11 (3): 563–82.

Nolan, James L., Jr. 1998. *The Therapeutic State: Justifying Government at Century's End.* New York: New York University Press.

Norman, James R. 1994. "'They Care about You.'" *Forbes,* January 3, pp. 40–41.

Olesen, Virginia. 1994. "Selves and a Changing Social Form: Notes on Three Types of Hospitality." *Symbolic Interaction* 17 (2): 187–202.

Ono, Brian. 1993. "Local Evening News." CBS. KOVR, Sacramento, Calif. December 20.

Passaro, Joanne. 1996. *The Unequal Homeless: Men on the Streets, Women in Their Place.* New York: Routledge.

Pattillo-McCoy, Mary. 1998. "Church Culture as a Strategy of Action in the Black Community." *American Sociological Review* 63 (4): 767–84.

Poppendieck, Janet. 1998. *Sweet Charity? Emergency Food and the End of Entitlement.* New York: Viking.

Pulley, Michael. 1997. "Saints and Sinners: My Search for the Truth about Loaves & Fishes." *Sacramento News and Review*, January 16, pp. 14–17.

Putnam, Robert D. 1995a. "Bowling Alone: America's Declining Social Capital." *Journal of Democracy* 6 (1): 65–78.

———. 1995b. "Tuning In, Tuning Out: The Strange Disappearance of Social Capital in America." *PS: Political Science and Politics* 28 (4): 664–83.

———. 1996. "The Strange Disappearance of Civic America." Pp. 263–85 in *Ticking Time Bombs: The New Conservative Assaults on Democracy*, edited by Robert Kuttner. New York: Free Press.

Rhoads, Robert A. 1997. *Community Service and Higher Learning: Explorations of the Caring Self.* Albany: State University of the New York Press.

Richards Boulevard Improvement Association. 1997. Paid advertisement. *Sacramento Bee*, April 13, p. B5.

Riesman, David, with Nathan Glazer and Reuel Denney. [1950] 1961. *The Lonely Crowd: A Study of the Changing American Character.* New Haven: Yale University Press.

Rimor, Mordechai, and Gary A. Tobin. 1990. "Jewish Giving Patterns to Jewish and Non-Jewish Philanthropy." Pp. 134–64 in *Faith and Philanthropy in America: Exploring the Role of Religion in America's Voluntary Sector*, edited by Robert Wuthnow and Virginia A. Hodgkinson and Associates. San Francisco: Jossey-Bass.

Robertson, Michael. 1996. "Piety and Poverty: The Religious Response to the Homeless in Albuquerque, New Mexico." Pp. 105–19 in *There's No Place Like Home: Anthropological Perspectives on Housing and Homelessness in the United States*, edited by Anna Lou Dehavenon. Westport, Conn.: Bergin & Garvey.

Rosenthal, Rob. 1994. *Homeless in Paradise: A Map of the Terrain.* Philadelphia: Temple University Press.

Rowe, Michael. 1999. *Crossing the Border: Encounters between Homeless People and Outreach Workers.* Berkeley: University of California Press.

Ruddick, Susan M. 1996. *Young and Homeless in Hollywood: Mapping Social Identities.* New York: Routledge.

Rudy, David R. 1986. *Becoming Alcoholic: Alcoholics Anonymous and the Reality of Alcoholism.* Carbondale: Southern Illinois University Press.

Ryan, William. [1971] 1976. *Blaming the Victim.* New York: Vintage Books.

*Sacramento Bee.* 1992. "Malls Silence Salvation Army Bells." December 21, p. A5.

———. 1993. "Loaves & Fishes at 10." Editorial, December 5, p. B4.

———. 1994. "Salvation Army Tops in Donations." October 31, p. A18.

———. 1995. "Trouble over Loaves & Fishes." Editorial, October 4, p. B6.

———. 1996. "Loaves and Fishes and Falsehood." Editorial, January 28, p. B6.

*Sacramento News and Review.* 1994. "Cottage Squeeze." Editorial, August 11, p. 5.

Salamon, Lester M. 1987. "Of Market Failure, Voluntary Failure, and Third-Party Government: Toward a Theory of Government-Nonprofit Relations in the Modern Welfare State." *Journal of Voluntary Action Research* 16 (1–2): 29–49.

The Salvation Army. 1994. *The Salvation Army Year Book, 1994.* London: International Headquarters of The Salvation Army.

———. n.d. *This Is the Salvation Army.* Pamphlet.

Sanchez, Edgar, and Deb Kollars. 1997. "In City Hall and on the Street, Loaves & Fishes Furor Rolls On." *Sacramento Bee*, March 29, pp. B1, B5.

Sapiro, Virginia. 1990. "The Gender Bias of American Social Policy." Pp. 36–64 in *Women, the State, and Welfare*, edited by Linda Gordon. Madison: University of Wisconsin Press.

Schwalbe, Michael L. 1991. "Social Structure and the Moral Self." Pp. 281–303 in *The Self-Society Dynamic: Cognition, Emotion, and Action*, edited by Judith A. Howard and Peter L. Callero. New York: Cambridge University Press.

———. 1992. "Male Supremacy and the Narrowing of the Moral Self." *Berkeley Journal of Sociology* 37: 29–54.

Sennett, Richard, and Jonathan Cobb. 1973. *The Hidden Injuries of Class.* New York: Vintage Books.

Shibutani, Tamotsu. 1955. "Reference Groups as Perspective." *American Journal of Sociology* 60 (6): 562–69.

Sider, Ronald J., and Heidi Rolland Unruh. 1999. "No Aid to Religion? Charitable Choice and the First Amendment." *Brookings Review* 17 (2): 46–49.

Silver, Ira. 1996. "Role Transitions, Objects, and Identity." *Symbolic Interaction* 19 (1): 1–12.

Simmel, Georg. [1917] 1950. *The Sociology of Georg Simmel.* Translated by Kurt H. Wolff. New York: Free Press.

Skocpol, Theda. 1996. "Unraveling from Above." Pp. 292–301 in *Ticking Time Bombs: The New Conservative Assaults on Democracy*, edited by Robert Kuttner. New York: Free Press.

Skocpol, Theda, and Morris P. Fiorina. 1999. "Making Sense of the Civic Engagement Debate." Pp. 1–23 in *Civic Engagement in American Democracy*, edited by Theda Skocpol and Morris P. Fiorina. Washington, D.C.: Brookings Institution Press/New York: Russell Sage Foundation.

Smith, Sidonie, and Julie Watson, eds. 1996. *Getting a Life: Everyday Uses of Autobiography.* Minneapolis: University of Minnesota Press.

Smith, Steven Rathgeb, and Michael Lipsky. 1993. *Nonprofits for Hire: The Welfare State in the Age of Contracting.* Cambridge, Mass.: Harvard University Press.

Smolowe, Jill. 1993. "Giving the Cold Shoulder." *Time*, December 6, pp. 28–31.

Snow, David A., and Leon Anderson. 1987. "Identity Work among the Homeless: The Verbal Construction and Avowal of Personal Identities." *American Journal of Sociology* 92 (6): 1336–71.

———. 1993. *Down on Their Luck: A Study of Homeless Street People.* Berkeley: University of California Press.

Snow, David. A., Leon Anderson, and Paul Koegel. 1994. "Distorting Tendencies in Research on the Homeless." *American Behavioral Scientist* 37 (4): 461–75.

Snow, David A., Susan G. Baker, and Leon Anderson. 1988. "On the Precariousness of Measuring Insanity in Insane Contexts." *Social Problems* 35 (2): 192–96.

Snow, David A., and Robert D. Benford. 1992. "Master Frames and Cycles of Protest." Pp. 133–55 in *Frontiers in Social Movement Theory*, edited by Aldon D. Morris and Carol McClurg Mueller. New Haven: Yale University Press.

Snow, David A., Louis A. Zurcher, and Gideon Sjoberg. 1982. "Interviewing by Comment: An Adjunct to the Direct Question." *Qualitative Sociology* 5 (2): 285–311.

Spencer, William J. 1987. "Self-Work in Social Interaction: Negotiating Role-Identities." *Social Psychology Quarterly* 50 (2): 131–42.

———. 1992. "Negotiating Role Definitions and the Working Consensus in Self-Work." *Sociological Inquiry* 62 (3): 291–307.

Spradley, James P. 1970. *You Owe Yourself a Drunk: An Ethnography of Urban Nomads*. Boston: Little, Brown.

Stack, Carol B. 1994. "Different Voices, Different Visions: Gender, Culture, and Moral Reasoning." Pp. 291–301 in *Women of Color in U.S. Society*, edited by Maxine Baca Zinn and Bonnie Thornton Dill. Philadelphia: Temple University Press.

Stanfield, John, II. 1993. "Epistemological Considerations." Pp. 16–36 in *Race and Ethnicity in Research Methods*, edited by John H. Stanfield II and Rutledge M. Dennis. Newbury Park, Calif.: Sage.

Stein, Michael. 1989. "Gratitude and Attitude: A Note on Emotional Welfare." *Social Psychology Quarterly* 52 (3): 242–48.

Steinberg, Ronnie J., and Jerry A. Jacobs. 1994. "Pay Equity in Nonprofit Organizations: Making Women's Work Visible." Pp. 79–120 in *Women and Power in the Nonprofit Sector*, edited by Teresa Odendah and Michael O'Neill. San Francisco: Jossey-Bass.

Stinchcombe, Arthur L. 1965. "Social Structure and Organizations." Pp. 142–93 in *Handbook of Organizations*, edited by James G. March. Chicago: Rand McNally.

Stivers, Richard. 1994. *The Culture of Cynicism: American Morality in Decline*. Cambridge, Mass.: Blackwell.

Sylva, Bob. 1993. "A Clean Break." *Sacramento Bee*, June 2, pp. C1, C5.

———. 1996. "2-Day Odyssey on Streets for a Look at the Homeless." *Sacramento Bee*, January 20, p. A2.

Taylor, Verta, and Nancy E. Whittier. 1992. "Collective Identity in Social Movement Communities." Pp. 104–29 in *Frontiers in Social Movement Theory*, edited by Aldon D. Morris and Carol McClurg Mueller. New Haven: Yale University Press.

Timmer, Doug A., D. Stanley Eitzen, and Kathryn D. Talley. 1994. *Paths to Homelessness: Extreme Poverty and the Urban Housing Crisis*. Boulder, Colo.: Westview.

Tocqueville, Alexis de. [1838] 1899. *Democracy in America*. Translated by Henry Reeve. New York: Colonial Press.

Tracy, Elizabeth, and Randy Stoecker. 1993. "Homelessness: The Service Providers' Perspective on Blaming the Victim." *Journal of Sociology and Social Welfare* 20 (3): 43–59.

Trattner, Walter I. 1989. *From Poor Law to Welfare State: A History of Social Welfare in America*, 4th ed. New York: Free Press.

Troester, Rosalie Riegle, ed. 1993. *Voices from the Catholic Worker*. Philadelphia: Temple University Press.

Tronto, Joan C. 1993. *Moral Boundaries: A Political Argument for a Theory of Care.* New York: Routledge.

Trow, Martin. 1957. "Comment on 'Participant Observation and Interviewing: A Comparison.' " *Human Organization* 16 (3): 33–35.

Turner, Ralph H. 1976. "The Real Self: From Institution to Impulse." *American Journal of Sociology* 81 (5): 989–1016.

———. 1978. "The Role and the Person." *American Journal of Sociology* 84 (1): 1–23.

Turner, Ralph H., and Steven Gordon. 1981. "The Boundaries of the Self: The Relationship of Authenticity in the Self-Conception." Pp. 39–57 in *Self-Concept: Advances in Theory and Research,* edited by Mervin D. Lynch, Ardyth A. Normen-Hebeisen, and Kenneth J. Gergen. Cambridge, Mass.: Ballinger.

Turner, Victor. [1974] 1982. "Liminal to Liminoid, in Play, Flow, Ritual: An Essay in Comparative Symbology." Pp. 20–60 in *From Ritual to Theatre: The Human Seriousness of Play.* New York: Performing Arts Journal Publications.

Verba, Sidney, Kay Lehman Schlozman, and Henry E. Brady. 1995. *Voice and Equality: Civic Voluntarism in American Politics.* Cambridge, Mass.: Harvard University Press.

Wagner, David. 1993. *Checkerboard Square: Culture and Resistance in a Homeless Community.* Boulder, Colo.: Westview.

Wallace, Samuel E. 1965. *Skid Row as a Way of Life.* Totowa, N.J.: Bedminister Press.

Warren, Carol A. B. 1988. *Gender Issues in Field Research.* Newbury Park, Calif.: Sage.

Weinberg, Darin. 1996. "The Enactment and Appraisal of Authenticity in a Skid Row Therapeutic Community." *Symbolic Interaction* 19 (2): 137–62.

Wilson, James Q. 1999. "Moving Private Funds to Faith-based Social Service Providers." *Brookings Review* 17 (2): 36–41.

Winston, Diane. 1999. *Red-Hot and Righteous: The Urban Religion of The Salvation Army.* Cambridge, Mass.: Harvard University Press.

Wiseman, Jacqueline P. [1970] 1979. *Stations of the Lost: The Treatment of Skid Row Alcoholics.* Chicago: University of Chicago Press.

Wolch, Jennifer R. 1990. *The Shadow State: Government and Voluntary Sector in Transition.* New York: Foundation Center.

———. 1994. "Who Are the Homeless? (And Why Are They Still Here?) A Commentary on Elliot Liebow's *Tell Them Who I Am.*" Paper presented at the annual meeting of the American Sociological Association, Los Angeles.

Wolfe, Alan. 1989. *Whose Keeper? Social Science and Moral Obligation*. Berkeley: University of California Press.

———. 1999. "Judging the President: The Perplexing Role of Religion in Public Life." *Brookings Review* 17 (2): 28–31.

Wood, Denis, and Robert J. Beck, with Ingrid Wood, Randall Wood, and Chandler Wood. 1994. *Home Rules*. Baltimore: Johns Hopkins University Press.

Worden, Steven. 1998. Review of *Out of Place: Homeless Mobilizations, Subcities, and Contested Landscapes*, by Talmadge Wright, and *Something Left to Lose: Personal Relations and Survival among New York's Homeless*, by Gwendolyn A. Dordick. *American Journal of Sociology* 104 (1): 248–50.

Wright, James D. 1988. "The Mentally Ill Homeless: What Is Myth and What Is Fact?" *Social Problems* 35 (2): 182–91.

Wright, James D., and Peter H. Rossi. 1994. Review of *A Nation in Denial: The Truth about Homelessness*, by Alice S. Baum and Donald W. Burnes. *Contemporary Sociology* 23 (1): 41–42.

Wuthnow, Robert. 1991. *Acts of Compassion: Caring for Others and Helping Ourselves*. Princeton: Princeton University Press.

———. 1992. *Rediscovering the Sacred: Perspectives on Religion in Contemporary Society*. Grand Rapids, Mich.: W. B. Eerdmans.

———. 1995. *Learning to Care: Elementary Kindness in an Age of Indifference*. New York: Oxford University Press.

———. 1998a. *After Heaven: Spirituality in America Since the 1950s*. Berkeley: University of California Press.

———. 1998b. *Loose Connections: Joining Together in America's Fragmented Communities*. Cambridge, Mass.: Harvard University Press.

Youniss, James, and Miranda Yates. 1997. *Community Service and Social Responsibility in Youth*. Chicago: University of Chicago Press.

Zaldívar, R. A. 1995. "Minimum-Wage Hike Plan Brings Hope, Debate." *Sacramento Bee*, January 27, pp. A1, A28.

# INDEX

Acker, Joan, on gendered institutions, 212

Adult Children of Alcoholics (ACA). *See* Alcoholics Anonymous

Afrocentric ethic of caring, 185, 249n. 7

Alcoholics Anonymous (A.A.): Fifth Tradition, 157, 158; First Tradition, 157; founding principles of, 246n. 7; Fourth Step, 159; Ninth Tradition, 247n. 11; sympathetic scholarly accounts of, 249n. 9; Third Step, 246n. 8; Twelfth Step, 88, 194; Twelfth Tradition, 158. *See also* drafted volunteers, A.A.-inspired self-work and

Alcoholic Self, 159

alternation, volunteer resocialization and, 113, 134

Alternative Sentencing Program (ASP) volunteers. *See under* Salvation Army Shelter Services Center

altruism, impulsive and institutional selves and, 208

Ambassadors of God. *See under* Catholic Workers

American character, pessimistic accounts of, 1–2, 4

American Dream, 176

Anderson, Elijah, *A Place on the Corner*, 190

Anderson, Nels, *The Hobo*, 194–95

Anderson, Ralph, and Kyra Jones Osmus, on male and female volunteers, 207

authenticity. *See under* self-concept

Baum, Alice S., and Donald W. Burnes, *A Nation in Denial*, 198, 249n. 9

Baumgartner, M. P., on moral minimalism, 149

Becker, Howard S.: on doing culture, 31–32; on privileging cynicism in interviewing, 198

Becker, Howard S., and Blanche Geer, on comparing participant-observation and interviewing, 243n. 15

Bellah, Robert N. et. al., on civil society, 2, 149

Berger, Peter L.: on honor, 209, 210, 250n. 3; on religion, 33–34

Berger, Peter L., and Thomas Luckman, on alternation, 113, 125

Berger, Peter L., et. al., on pluralization of social lifeworlds, 210

Timmer, Doug A., et. al., on shelter morality, 144–45

Tocqueville, Alexis de, on voluntary associations, 1, 213

total institution. *See under* Salvation Army Shelter Services Center

Troester, Rosalie Riegle, on voices from Catholic Worker, 38, 244n. 3, 250n. 8

Tronto, Joan C., on ethic of care, 8, 212–13

Trow, Martin, on comparing participant-observation and interviewing, 243n. 15

Turner, Ralph H., on institutional and impulsive selves, 206

Turner, Ralph H., and Steven Gordon, on authenticity and self, 208

Turner, Victor, on ritual, 134

utopian communities, 119–20

victim blaming, 138, 198, 218

voluntary sector, social service provision by, 215. *See also* nonprofit organizations

volunteerism: meaning of in civil society, 1–3, 107–8, 213, 241n. 1, 251n. 13; motivations and, 3, 34, 213, 235, 245n. 8, 247n. 2, 248n. 7; role of in caring for the poor, x, 1, 107–8, 250n. 9; social inequality and, 3, 19, 250n. 9; social movement politics and, 197, 203, 235–36, 248n. 7; as social virtue, 1, 23; welfare state and, 23–24, 149–50, 203. *See also* civic engagement debate; volunteers

volunteers: AIDS and, 7, 221, 242n. 6; compassion as a role of, 3; community service requirements for, 13, 242n. 7; Freedom Summer and, 220–21, 242n. 6; gender differences of, 8, 242n. 6, 250n. 9; as invisible labor, 129, 242n. 6; routinization of

work by, 59, 129–30; self-betterment of, 4; sociability work and, 129. *See also* committed volunteers; drafted volunteers; holiday volunteers; routine volunteers; shelters, rule enforcement by; volunteerism

Wagner, David: on citywide networks helping homeless, 241n. 2; on homeless and self-help politics, 197, 249n. 9

Wallace, Samuel, *Skid Row as a Way of Life*, 194–95

*War Cry*, 31, 74

Washington, Trevor, on Salvation Army Shelter Services, 191

Weigand, Bishop William K., and Loaves & Fishes, 233

Weinberg, Darin, on treatment communities, 159

welfare and state policy: Charitable Choice provision and, 24, 235–36, 251nn. 13, 14; creating independent workers and, 217, 225–26; regulation of charities and, 214–15, 225–26, 228; resources for poor and, 214–15, 229; social control of poor and, ix, 223; and welfare reform of 1996, 235–36, 248n. 1, 251n. 13. *See also* charity, within shadow state; charity, welfare reform; welfare ideologies

welfare ideologies: and built environment at Loaves & Fishes, 9–10, 32–33, 45, 221–22, 226–33; and built environment at Salvation Army Shelter Services Center, 10–11, 86, 233; implicit morality in, ix–x, 4, 19, 98–101, 103–4, 138, 228, 248n. 1, 250n. 6. *See also* moral selving, within welfare ideologies

Wilson, James Q., on Charitable Choice provision, 235

Winston, Diane, on history The Salvation Army, 245n. 1

Text:    10/15 Janson
Display:    Janson
Composition:    Binghamton Valley Composition
Printing and binding:    The Maple-Vail Book Manufacturing Group